YAD VASHEM STUDIES
49 (1)

The publication of this volume was made possible
through the generous support of
Mrs. Johanna (Hannie) Catherina Kiprono Biwott
in memory of the members of her community in Amsterdam
who did not survive the Holocaust

YAD VASHEM STUDIES

49 (1)

Edited by
SHARON KANGISSER COHEN

THE INTERNATIONAL INSTITUTE
FOR HOLOCAUST RESEARCH

JERUSALEM 2021

Editor
Sharon Kangisser Cohen

Associate Editor
Nathan Cohen

Managing Editor
James McIntosh

Assistant Editor
Adina Drechsler

Language Editor
Leah Aharonov

Editorial Board

Yitzhak Arad	Havi Dreifuss	David Silberklang
Omer Bartov	Mary Fulbrook	Yfaat Weiss
Yehuda Bauer	Alexandra Garbarini	Michael Wildt
Christopher R. Browning	Dan Michman	Arkadi Zeltser
Christoph Dieckmann	Robert Rozett	

ISSN 0084-3296

Typesetting: Judith Sternberg
Printed in Israel by Old City Press Ltd., Jerusalem

CONTENTS

❧ ❧

REVIEWS

Introduction

❧ ❧

The current volume (49:1) of *Yad Vashem Studies* opens with two memorial pieces. The first was written by Beth B. Cohen in remembrance of the life and work of Dr. William B. Helmreich, whose groundbreaking *Against All Odds: Holocaust Survivors and the Successful Lives They Made in America* considers how Holocaust survivors managed to begin their lives anew in the United States. This work propelled research into the general experience of survivors in rebuilding their lives, a field that has grown significantly in the last few decades. The second memorial piece, written by Christopher Browning and Omer Bartov, reflects on the significant contribution that Theodore Zev Weiss made to the field of Holocaust studies, research, and education. The biographies of both men—Theodore as a Holocaust survivor and William as a member of the second generation—clearly show how their personal histories affected their lives' work and their professional endeavors.

Unfortunately, as this volume was being prepared for publication, we learned of the passing of one of our former longstanding members of the Editorial Board, Prof. Otto Dov Kulka. Prof. Kulka, a child survivor of the Holocaust, devoted his life to historical research and documentation of the period. He researched and taught in wide and varied fields at the Hebrew University of Jerusalem, including early modern Jewish history, sixteenth-century Jewish thought, the history of antisemitism, Christian-Jewish relations from the sixteenth to twentieth centuries, and Jewish history under National Socialist rule. In 2013, he published a penetrating memoir of his experiences during the Holocaust titled *Landscapes of the Metropolis of Death: Reflections on Memory and Imagination*. His memoir, written nearly seventy years after his liberation, was awarded the Jewish Quarterly Wingate Prize. Over the years he was a devoted member of the Editorial Board of *Yad Vashem Studies*, generous with his time and insightful in his reviews. He will be sorely missed. We also mourn the recent passing of Prof. Rachel Feldhay Brenner, whose research focused on Jewish Diaspora literature, Israeli literature, and on representations of the Holocaust in literature and autobiographical writings. She was Professor of Hebrew and Semitic Studies at the University of Wisconsin, Madison and active in the Association of Israel Studies and served as its president from 2007-2009.

This volume includes a range of disciplinary approaches to research on the Holocaust and its aftermath. Three of the articles explore the experiences of individuals hailing from various European countries whose lives were irrevocably affected by the war. Edel Sheridan-Quantz's article provides us with an example of a painstaking search for the fate of one individual victim of the Holocaust, Hilde Koch (1896-1942). Her work furnishes us with a rare look into the creative process of the recovery of an individual's "footprints" and the valuable work of historians in their ability to reassemble the lives and fate of the victims. Sheridan-Quantz also demonstrates how Koch continued to use her art during the war in order to communicate her difficult circumstances as a victim of Nazi persecution. James Diamond's article presents us with a challenging exploration of six of the sermons given by Rabbi Kalonymus Kalman Shapira in the Warsaw ghetto. This penetrating piece affords us an insight into how this prominent rabbi reacted to the relentless and escalating persecution of the Jewish community in the ghetto. Based on a meticulous reading and interpretation of the sermons, Diamond makes us aware of the evolving state of mind and theological struggle of an important religious figure during the period of ghettoization. Zohar Segev's biographical essay centers on the life and activities of Jacob Robinson (1889-1977), a lawyer, diplomat, Holocaust researcher, and public figure who emigrated to the United States from Lithuania in 1940. Robinson devoted much of his professional acumen to Holocaust research and commemoration, and Segev's article outlines his involvement in the construction of Holocaust memory, which he saw as an important tool in shaping the Jewish people and the world after World War II. The last article in the volume can be seen as an extension of the work of Jacob Robinson as it explores issues connected to the politics of memory and commemoration of individual victim groups. In their interdisciplinary work, Amit Kama and Sharon Livne draw our attention to an incident that took place at Yad Vashem in 1994, when a group of Jewish gay men and lesbians from around the world held a ceremony to commemorate members of the LGBT community murdered by the Nazis. This article not only reconstructs the events but in particular focuses on its representation in the Israeli media; it attempts to highlight the ongoing discussion regarding the boundaries of Holocaust memory and commemoration in Israeli society.

The book reviews published in this volume are diverse, providing a critical view of recent scholarship that examines wartime and postwar events. Avinoam Patt has contributed an important appraisal of Dina Porat's meticulous work, *Li Nakam Veshilem: HaYishuv, Hashoah, Vekvutzat Hanokmim Shel Abba Kovner*. In his review Patt explains how Porat, by means of thorough archival research, gives a detailed outline of the revenge plan, as well as examines the "significance of the plot from the broader perspective of the history of the Holocaust and the State of Israel." Marta Marzańska-Mishani does an impressive job of summarizing the complex, detailed and chilling book by Joanna Tokarska-Bakir, *Pod klątwą. Społeczny portret pogromu kieleckiegowhich*, regarding the 1946 pogrom in Kielce, which was a watershed event for the surviving Jews in Poland. The review gives researchers who are not fluent in Polish an apt summary and description of this work, which hopefully will be translated into English. In Jan Láníček's review of Wolf Gruner's *The Holocaust in Bohemia and Moravia: Czech Initiatives, German Policies, Jewish Responses*, he praises Gruner for the exploration of this largely understudied area, especially since very little exists about it in English. The main themes of the book relate to the involvement of the "so-called Czech authorities in the persecution and the role of the Jewish community structures." Láníček points out that the book has led to a "critical backlash among Czech historians, sensitive to any criticism of the Czech population during the war from their colleagues." Lastly, Jan Burzlaff assesses the "visual turn" in Holocaust studies, which looks to explore visual representation beyond its traditional use as illustration. He compares three recent books (Tal Bruttmann, Stefan Hördler, and Christoph Kreutzmüller, *Die Fotografische Inszenierung des Verbrechens. Ein Album aus Auschwitz*; Christophe Cognet, *Éclats: Prises de vue clandestines des camps nazis*; Martin Cüppers, Annett Gerhardt, Karin Graf, Steffen Hänschen, Andreas Kahrs, Anne Lepper, and Florian Ross, *Fotos aus Sobibor: Die Niemann-Sammlung zu Holocaust und Nationalsozialismus*) that reproduce more than 330 photographs from Auschwitz-Birkenau, Sobibor, and several concentration camps in order to understand the role and use of photographs in the Nazi period. In his review, he demonstrates how collections can shed light on the provenance and meaning of other photographic collections.

During the course of 2020, two of our long-serving editorial board members and esteemed scholars, Prof. Michael Marrus and the late Prof. Otto Dov Kulka, retired from the board. Their work over the years was invaluable to the success of *Yad Vashem Studies*, and, on behalf of the board, I would like to voice our deep appreciation for their time and efforts. We also would like to welcome Prof. Mary Fulbrook as a new member of the Editorial Board. Prof. Fulbrook's expertise in German history, Europe after the Holocaust, and historiography will undoubtedly contribute to our work in ensuring that *Yad Vashem Studies* maintains its position as a leading academic journal on the Holocaust.

Lastly, I would like to welcome James McIntosh, who has joined the staff of *Yad Vashem Studies*, replacing Daniella Zaidman-Mauer after twenty-three years of devoted work. We would like to thank Daniella for the commitment and dedication to the journal that she showed over such a significant period of time. We also welcome Avigail Tsirkin-Sadan to our Hebrew editing staff.

Unfortunately, the COVID-19 pandemic is still with us, and, as noted by Beth B. Cohen, William B. Helmreich was one of its victims. As many students and researchers find it difficult to access articles and scholarship due to the pandemic, we will continue to make all issues of *Yad Vashem Studies* freely available to the public. I close with the hope for healthier times for us all.

Sharon Kangisser Cohen

William B. Helmreich (1945–2020)—In Memoriam

Beth B. Cohen

American sociologist William B. Helmreich's life was unexpectedly cut short when he passed away from complications due to COVID-19 on March 28, 2020.[1] Helmreich was among the first victims of the coronavirus when it devastated New York City and the environs in the early months of the pandemic. At the time of his death, Helmreich was Distinguished Professor of Sociology at the Colin Powell School of Civic & Global Leadership at City College of New York, professor of sociology at City University Graduate Center, and Permanent Senior Fellow at Yale University. A prolific scholar with wide-ranging interests, he left a legacy of eighteen books on diverse topics, which included race and ethnic relations, urban sociology, immigration, consumer behavior, the sociology of New York City, and religion. Although one of his most notable works, *Against All Odds: Holocaust Survivors and the Successful Lives They Made in America*, was his sole monograph in the field of Holocaust studies, it was a significant and lasting contribution to the discipline.[2] In 1993, *Against All Odds* received the National Jewish Book Award in the category of Contemporary Jewish Life.

Helmreich's roots profoundly shaped both the course and substance of his life. His father, Leo Helmreich, was born in Poland into a Hasidic family of the Chortkiver sect. Leo's father operated a small smoke shop in Łańcut, where he also sold paint and other household supplies. By the time Leo was a young man, an older brother, Herman, had moved to Cologne, Germany, seeking a religious but more modern Jewish lifestyle. Leo followed his brother both geographically and spiritually.

---

1   I wish to thank the people who readily agreed to comment via email. I am especially grateful to William Helmreich's widow, Helaine, and his son, Jeffrey Helmreich, who generously spoke to me via telephone and provided many details that are included here.
2   *Against All Odds: Holocaust Survivors and the Successful Lives They Made in America* (New York: Simon and Schuster, 1992).

He relocated to Germany, where he joined the family flatware business that Herman had established in Cologne.

Sometime after Hitler came to power, Leo and his brother received a tip from a non-Jewish friend that they were about to be arrested, and so they decided to escape. Leo chose Antwerp, Belgium, where there was a vibrant Orthodox community. There, with the help of a matchmaker, Leo met his future wife, Sally, whose family worked in the diamond industry and, like Leo's, had origins in Poland. Once Belgium was occupied, the married couple and their young son, Mark, who was born in 1939, spent the early years as a family on the run, first on farms and in forests in Belgium, and then on to France, where they eluded capture in Paris and Marseilles. Eventually they joined forces with a small group of refugees and managed to cross into Switzerland from France. Unlike thousands who tried unsuccessfully to enter Switzerland, they were admitted but placed in a labor camp. On August 25, 1945, shortly after the war ended, William was born in Zurich.

The Helmreich family had hoped to settle in Palestine. Like many survivors, however, leaving Europe was uppermost in their minds. Perhaps because U.S. President Harry Truman had issued a directive, in December 1945, with a quota that favored German refugees, visas to the United States came through quickly. The family arrived in the United States in 1946, in one of the first groups of survivors to do so, when William was ten months old. As a result of his wife's family connections, Leo was initially able to secure factory work in the diamond business. The family settled into a modest apartment on 106th Street on the Upper West Side of Manhattan, a milieu that included many Holocaust survivors and their children. William's first language was German, his second Yiddish, and only when he entered primary school did he begin learning English.

William spent most of his life near or in New York, the city he dearly loved. As a boy he attended the Manhattan Day School, a modern-Orthodox elementary school. After a brief period in high school during which he studied at the Ner Yisrael Yeshiva in Baltimore, he returned to Manhattan and completed his high school education at Manhattan Talmudic Academy (MTA), a prep school for Yeshiva University (YU). His insider's view of Orthodox education in America would later inform at least one of his studies. Michael Berenbaum, director of the Sigi Ziering Institute: Exploring the Ethical and Religious Implications of the Holocaust at the American Jewish University, and a professor of

Jewish Studies at that university, has remarked, "His writings on the world of the Yeshiva were probing, accepting, and real scholarship—not just hagiography."[3]

Midway through his undergraduate degree at YU, Helmreich enrolled in a sociology class, and his future course was set. After he received his B.A., Helmreich headed to Washington University in St. Louis to study with some of the luminaries in sociology, such as Irving Louis Horowitz and Alan Ward Gouldner, who served on the faculty there. During his graduate studies William returned to New York for a friend's wedding and there met his future wife, Helaine. They were married in 1970, and Helaine told me, "We would have celebrated our fiftieth wedding anniversary in June."[4]

At Washington University, Helmreich wrote his PhD dissertation on the Black Power movement. In 1973, this analysis became his first book: *The Black Crusaders: A Case Study of a Black Militant Organization.*[5] Following graduation he taught at several institutions until, in the late 1970s, upon Elie Wiesel's recommendation, Helmreich found his academic home. His long career at the Graduate Center of the City University of New York and at its City College spanned decades, and only ended with his death. During that time he wrote or edited another seventeen books.

A common thread mentioned by colleagues and friends was Helmreich's vast and eclectic scholarly interests. Hasia Diner, Paul and Sylvia Steinberg professor of American Jewish History at New York University, has commented,

> There is much to say about William Helmreich as a scholar and writer. Besides his joyous embrace of New York City, its streets, its people, and the range of their stories, he opened up two important subjects. Not that these are the only intellectual legacies of William Helmreich, but they stand out for me. His study of Newark Jewry is one. This large, institutionally rich, complicated center of Jewish life, Helmreich told us, deserves to be placed into the national narrative. Its long history alone makes *The Enduring Community:*

---

3   Via email, August 21, 2020.
4   Telephone conversation with Helaine Helmreich, August 13, 2020.
5   William B. Helmreich, *The Black Crusaders: A Case Study of a Black Militant Organization* (New York: Harper and Row, 1973).

The Jews of Newark and MetroWest a model of Jewish urban biography.[6] The other is his study of Holocaust survivors.[7]

Jerome Chanes, Senior Fellow at the Center for Jewish Studies, CUNY Graduate Center, remembered,

> Willie was always generous with sharing his expertise in Jewish and general sociology, which was extensive, indeed. Willie Helmreich was a genuine sociological polymath; there was little in the arenas of the sociology of ethnicity and in Jewish sociology—to say nothing of the history and sociology of the generation of Holocaust survivors—that Willie did not know. Most of all, I cherish those all-too-few encounters with Willie, from which I learned much.[8]

Jeffrey Gurock, Libby M. Klaperman Professor of Jewish History, Yeshiva University, agreed, noting, "Willie Helmreich was a most creative scholar with an uncommon range of interests born of his background as a child of refugees, his experiences in a changing neighborhood, his early education in a yeshiva, and his love of New York City." While many knew him for his prolific scholarship, Gurock recalled,

> What is less known about Willy [*sic*] was his activist stance as fighter against antisemitism at City College of New York (CCNY) when he courageously took on Professor Leonard Jeffries who, among his many canards against Jews, accused them of financing the African Slave Trade. Willie's favorite story about our collegial and friendly relationship was the time he brought me to CCNY—over Jeffries' objection—to a symposium on the history of Harlem to remind everyone of its Jewish history.[9]

Helmreich was already an established sociologist when he began his study of Holocaust survivors in the 1980s. The seed was planted after conversations with a number of people, including Elie Wiesel and Joseph Berger, *The New York Times* journalist and author, son of survivors and a childhood friend.[10] He met, too, with a group of children of survivors who also urged him to embark on this project. *Against All Odds* appeared

6   *The Enduring Community: The Jews of Newark and MetroWest* (New York: Transaction Press, 1999).
7   Via email, August 10, 2020.
8   Via email, September 7, 2020.
9   Via email, August 7, 2020.
10 Berger's memoir chronicles his experiences in a survivor family in New York;

during a time when much of the research on Holocaust survivors was situated in the field of psychology and largely focused on the pathology of survivors and the lasting effect of trauma. Motivated by the example of his parents and others he knew who had built stable families and careers after the Holocaust, Helmreich's study challenged the notion that survivors were irrevocably damaged. As the title suggests, *Against All Odds: Holocaust Survivors and the Successful Lives They Made in America* is a portrait of survivors that highlights how survivors were able to move forward in the United States despite the ordeals they had endured. In his review in *Contemporary Jewry*, Morton Weinfeld, professor of sociology at McGill University, observed, "Helmreich's book provides a welcome corrective to that of the predominant and dysfunctional 'survivor syndrome' which emerged out of earlier work using clinical or self-selected samples."[11]

Unique for the time, Helmreich's study is absorbed with questions about what happened to the general population of survivors after— and not during—the war. His starting point is the fact that the group experienced horrific events, albeit in different ways, and that their memories of these events continued to persist throughout their lives. He emphasizes the role that sheer luck played in one's wartime fate but, by contrast, scrutinizes survivors' agency in their postwar survival—how they "learned to live and hope again."[12]

In order to explore this question, Helmreich synthesizes an array of archival documents ranging from the Hebrew Immigrant Aid Society (HIAS) to the National Council of Jewish Women to the United Service for New Americans, seamlessly weaving survivors' stories into his lively analysis. He concludes that those individuals who successfully adapted to life in the United States shared specific traits. In fact he found ten characteristics common to survivors who were able to live positive and useful postwar lives—and he argues that they were the majority. Comparing his random sample to a group of American-born Jews, he found that among survivors there were fewer divorces, and they sought psychiatric treatment less frequently than their American peers, but they enjoyed similar economic standing. They were not supermen, he

---

Displaced Persons: Growing Up American After the Holocaust (New York: Scribner, 2001).

11   Morton Weinfeld, *Contemporary Jewry*, 14 (1993), pp. 176–178.

12   Helmreich, *Against All Odds*, p. 14.

reminds us; it was "not a story of remarkable people. It is a story of just how remarkable people can be."[13]

Praise for the work came from scholars across several disciplines. Hasia Diner stated,

> *Against All Odds* remains the first serious study of Holocaust survivors in the United States. Helmreich cracked open the door behind which lay the histories of tens of thousands of individuals who came to America, worked, raised families, participated in organizational and community life, and in a variety of ways grappled with the traumatic experiences they had endured. Helmreich importantly emphasized that they did not do all these the same way, but as they did them, they emerged as historical actors who need to be studied.[14]

But his son Jeffrey, professor of philosophy and law and co-director of the Center for Legal Philosophy, University of California, Irvine, remembers that he also had the ability "to make them feel that they were unique and not just reducible to this one category of 'survivors.'"[15]

Jerome Chanes wrote, "his groundbreaking work, *Against All Odds*, taught a whole generation of scholars how to articulate the vocabulary of the study of Holocaust survivors."[16] Michael Berenbaum concurred: "Bill was one of the first academics to write seriously about the strength of survivors and their major successes in the United States. He covered many of the themes that the Israeli film *The Phoenixes*[17] covered but in a systematic academic way and also as a good storyteller."[18]

Helmreich's analysis also resonated with professionals who worked with survivors and other traumatized populations. Psychologist Eva Fogelman recalled,

> In 1992, when William Helmreich's book *Against All Odds: Holocaust Survivors and the Successful Lives They Made in America* was published, I invited him to speak to my students at a program I was directing for clinicians, "Psychotherapy with Generations of the Holocaust and Related Traumas," at the Training Institute for

---

13 Ibid., p. 276.
14 Diner, email, August 10, 2020.
15 Telephone conversation with Jeffrey Helmreich, August 12, 2020.
16 Chanes, email, September 7, 2020.
17 Micha Shagrir, *The Phoenixes* (Hebrew title: *Ufot Hahol*), 2008.
18 Berenbaum, email, August 21, 2020.

Mental Health in New York. Helmreich was going against the tide that stereotyped Holocaust survivors as an emotionally challenged group who had limited capacities to cope with everyday life. His sociological research gave voice to the majority of Holocaust survivors who were able to get married, build families, and were successful professionally despite not having formal education, which was curtailed because of the German invasion of their country during World War II.

In addition, the book had an impact on changing the larger Jewish community's attitude toward Holocaust survivors. Fogelman recollected, "The Jewish community in particular began to perceive the Holocaust survivors in their midst through a more life-affirming lens."[19]

In a departure from Holocaust scholarship of the 1980s, Helmreich based *Against All Odds* on approximately 170 survivors he interviewed throughout the United States. He also spent two years in Israel (1986–1987; 1990–1991), during which he was affiliated with Yad Vashem, Hebrew University, and Bar-Ilan University. While there he recorded experiences of survivors who had made *aliya* to Israel from the United States. Helaine Helmreich recalled his painstaking research and his desire to tell survivors' authentic stories as both a scholarly endeavor as well as "a labor of love." Jeffrey Helmreich described the way his father steeped himself in his chosen subject as a "world immerser." Still, Helmreich retained his objectivity. As Stephen J. Whitfield, Max Richter Professor of American Civilization, Brandeis University, considered in *The New Leader,* "Altogether the author spent nearly six years on this project, and amassed over 15,000 pages of raw data in the course of his interviews. His prose is fluent and assured, and he obeys the first rule of Holocaust writing: Record the horrific actualities matter-of-factly, without rhetorical inflation."[20]

In her 1993 review, Deborah E. Lipstadt, Dorot Professor of Modern Jewish and Holocaust Studies, Emory University, asserted that Helmreich's "comprehensive analysis of the survivors who came to the United States and the lives they built is a welcome addition to

19 Eva Fogelman's pioneering therapeutic work includes a focus on child survivors of the Holocaust and their descendants; she was a Pulitzer Prize nominee for *Conscience and Courage: Rescuers of Jews During the Holocaust* (New York: Doubleday, 1994). The comments were made via email, September 6, 2020.
20 Stephen J. Whitfield, "A Death Somehow Survived," *The New Leader,* 75:16 (December 1992).

the field." Still, she observed that, at times, the author, "glosses over the more problematic areas such as relationships between survivors and their children or those who did not become professional or economic successes."[21] Although interesting as a point of Holocaust historiography, Lipstadt suggested that while this is a fertile ground for future research, it would be unlikely since survivors were aging and the opportunity for conducting primary research was thus waning. In fact, Helmreich's study did provoke scholarly interest in survivors' postwar experiences and encouraged a new direction and body of research, of which my own work is a beneficiary. In direct response to his study, my dissertation research focused on the reception of Holocaust survivors by the American Jewish community. Although I had the pleasure of meeting him only once, at NYC's Tenement Museum, to discuss developing an exhibit of a survivor family's postwar apartment, Helmreich's work significantly influenced my own.[22]

Helmreich's encounters with people—whether friends, colleagues, interviewees, or strangers—were legendary. His wonderful ability to forge a personal connection with others was never as vividly demonstrated as in his last body of work on the five New York boroughs. Inspired by a game, "The Last Stop," that he had played with his father while growing up, in which they would ride a subway line and explore the neighborhood where it stopped (a tradition he continued with his own children), Helmreich began a four-year mission to walk every street in New York City's five boroughs. This led to the publication, in 2013, of *The New York Nobody Knows: Walking 6,000 Miles in the City,*[23] in which he chronicled his strolls and conversations with individuals he encountered along the way. Michael Berenbaum stated,

> He walked every street on every block in New York City, a herculean accomplishment and spoke with someone—and often many—on each block. No one has done that before and he made it into a marvelous study of New York with its mosaic of people and because Bill was Bill he made friends—unlikely friends on each and every block...He was that way with all people and always, always

---

21 Deborah E. Lipstadt [no title], *American Historical Review*, 98:5 (December 1993), pp. 1701–1702.

22 Beth B. Cohen, *Case Closed: Holocaust Survivors in Postwar America* (New Brunswick: Rutgers University Press, 2007).

23 William B. Helmreich, *The New York Nobody Knows: Walking 6,000 Miles in the City* (Princeton: Princeton University Press, 2013).

fascinated by the human story. He may have met a stranger in his life but when they left his presence, they were never strangers.[24]

Helmreich had nearly completed his five-borough book contract with Princeton University when the pandemic struck. His family is committed to seeing the completion and publication of the last volume on Staten Island.

Jeffrey Helmreich asserted that his father's identity as the son of Holocaust survivors was key to everything he did, even if the connection may have seemed remote. It deeply shaped his approach to his academic work, as well as his engagement with life around him, and was a driving force in his identity, his relationship to Israel, and his sense of self. This included establishing the Center for Conflict Resolution at City University and his incessant quest for peaceful coexistence between different ethnic groups, as well as the way he consistently related to and treated whomever he encountered. Helmreich never forgot that his parents' survival and his birth were nothing short of a miracle, and that the openness of the United States to immigrants, to survivors of genocide, was a gift and a responsibility that he took seriously, informing every aspect of how he lived.

In the closing of the new introduction to the second printing of *Against All Odds*, Helmreich asks: "Will those who are exposed [to Holocaust studies] learn its deeper lesson, lessons about man's capacity for evil, about the collective responsibility of all who inhabit the earth to act humanely towards each other?" He goes on to conclude,

> In my view, knowledge about the Holocaust will only become meaningful if it moves people to act, to translate their awareness into genuine commitment. The connections must be made by pedagogues and it is they who must inspire those who study with them to act. If this does not happen our efforts will, in the larger sense, have been in vain.[25]

Twenty-five years later his words still resonate—perhaps more urgently than ever.

---

24 Berenbaum, via email, August 21, 2020.
25 Helmreich, *Against All Odds*, p. 7.

Theodore Z. Weiss (1931–2020)—In Memoriam

Omer Bartov and Christopher R. Browning

D r. Theodore Z. Weiss, known by friends and colleagues as Zev, was the founder and longtime director of the Holocaust Educational Foundation (HEF). Beginning in the late 1970s, the initial project of this institution was to record survivor testimonies from the Chicago area, which were then stored in the Fortunoff Archive collection on the Yale University campus. In the mid-1980s, at a time when academic courses and scholarly meetings on the Holocaust were not common in the United States, Dr. Weiss reached the insightful conclusion that the path to raising Holocaust consciousness in North America ran through higher education. Thus he endeavored with unremitting determination to persuade colleges and universities in the United States and Canada to introduce Holocaust courses into their curricula. Despite initial resistance from history departments and university leaders, the first HEF-sponsored course on the history of the Holocaust (taught by Peter Hayes) was launched at Northwestern University in 1988, followed since by numerous such courses around the country.

Dr. Weiss was just as dedicated to training instructors in teaching about the Holocaust. To that end the HEF offered funding and resources for course development and teaching staff. Just as importantly, in 1989, Dr. Weiss inaugurated a biennial conference, "Lessons and Legacies," which convenes an international community of Holocaust scholars in order to share their research with one another, as well as to discuss pedagogical approaches to teaching the history of the Holocaust. "Lessons and Legacies" has become the preeminent academic conference on the Holocaust in North America and has now expanded to Europe in alternate years. In addition, the HEF established the Summer Institute on the Holocaust and Jewish Civilization, an annual teaching institute at Northwestern University, where scholars planning new courses, as well as graduate students in Holocaust studies, are offered lectures and workshops on Jewish history, culture, and religion, and discuss new methods and approaches to Holocaust studies.

Dr. Weiss was born in Demecser, Hungary, and was raised in a traditional Jewish family. In June 1944, at the age of twelve, he was deported with his family to Auschwitz-Birkenau, where his parents and siblings were quickly murdered. Having survived Auschwitz and Gleiwitz and a death march to the Sachsenhausen concentration camp, Dr. Weiss was liberated by the U.S. Army at Gunskirchen, near Mauthausen, on May 8, 1945. He arrived in Canada in 1947, where he attended McGill University and the Hebrew Teachers Seminary. As of 1956, Dr. Weiss taught at synagogue schools, beginning in Rochester, New York, and eventually in Wilmette, Illinois, where he served as the Education Director at the Beth Hillel Academy for many years. In 1962, Zev married Alice, an assistant professor at the State University of New York in Albany.

A firm believer in the value of bringing the history of the Holocaust to higher educational institutions and to the public at large, Dr. Weiss insisted that "learning remains the best antidote to humanity's most inhuman impulses."[1] In his role as president of the Holocaust Educational Foundation, over time he actively promoted launching courses on the Holocaust at over 400 colleges and universities throughout the United States and Canada, as well as persuading hundreds of faculty members to teach the Holocaust in the context of their fields, including history, political science, religion, philosophy, psychology, and literature. Thus, over the decades, Dr. Weiss created a thick network of scholars and teachers who dedicated themselves to ensuring that the traumatic events which he, along with millions of others, had experienced as a teenager, would not be forgotten. He leaves behind a crucial legacy whose effects will be felt for decades to come.

---

1   Quoted in Anita Weiner, *Expanding Historical Consciousness: The Development of the Holocaust Educational Foundation* (Skokie: Holocaust Educational Foundation, 2002), p. xi.

"...I have no illusions"[1]
Hilde Koch Neuberger: A Life Story in Fragments

Edel Sheridan-Quantz

"Which, of the many stories each of these objects could tell, is the one to be told?"[2]

The physical objects—both lost and preserved—that speak of past lives, do not lead us to an "ultimate biographical truth."[3] In the case of Hilde Koch, these objects—the official documents, the family photographs, the personal library appropriated by the German state, the artworks preserved through long internment, and the final hurried letters—tell or suggest multiple stories. Sometimes these are overlapping, and sometimes they are apparently contradictory: of a beloved daughter and sister; of a young woman hoping to make a mark as an artist and eagerly processing a wealth of artistic influences in her own work; of the wife and stepmother with a love of Nordic legends and German Expressionism; of the deportee defiantly asserting her professional identity as an artist (*dessinatrice*) in a French camp and able to transcend the desolation of internment in Gurs to create a luminous gift for the niece she never saw; of the sister thanking her sibling for her love and wishing her the good future she herself would not have; of the wife about to be deported for a second time, taking care that her husband be told of her fate, and even wildly hoping to be able to rejoin him in their home city; or of the artist who, in days of chaos and peril, ensured the preservation of "my pictures." She would

1 Translated by the author; written by Hilde Neuberger nee Koch, on August 29, 1942; from postcards and letters written by Hilde Neuberger and sent from the detention camp in Vénissieux, France, to her sister Leonie Ehrmann in Bellac and Villard de Lans, France, in 1942; Yad Vashem Archives (YVA), O.75/2804.
2 Leora Auslander and Tara Zahra, "Afterlives: From Things to Memories", in Auslander and Zahra, eds., *Objects of War: The Material Culture of Conflict and Displacement* (Ithaca: Cornell University Press, 2019), pp. 221–222, cited on p. 222.
3 Levke Harders, "Legitimizing Biography: Critical Approaches to Biographical Research," *Bulletin of the GHI*, 55 (2014), pp. 49–56, cited on p. 56.

surely have concurred with Primo Levi's reflection, in the context of being stripped of his belongings in Auschwitz, on how intimately some objects are intertwined with the human sense of self: "these things are part of us, almost like limbs of our body."[4]

Individual life stories help to make big issues comprehensible and to communicate the human reality of history. These are among the reasons why biographies are a central element in Holocaust memorials worldwide.[5] But what makes Hilde Koch's life relevant to broader scholarly enquiry?

Hilde Koch is of interest as a Jewish Expressionist illustrator whose work was printed by a formerly successful but now forgotten (and also Jewish) publisher of children's books during the Weimar Republic. Her biography could be expected to potentially throw some light on aspects of women's participation in professional training and careers in early twentieth-century Germany. And it could answer questions about specifically "Jewish" elements of her art or experience.

Hilde Koch represents a "problematic" category of biographical subject, an apparently almost untraceable life.[6] At the outset of this study, all that was known about her was her name and her three published works. Thus she was simultaneously in the public sphere and yet "unknown." Without a date or place of birth, the reconstruction of her life story was, on the face of it, almost impossible. In a pre-digital era, her identity might never have been discovered.

The realist approach to biography "holds that there is some objective knowledge of reality," while constructionists argue that "both the...'story' and its interpretation by the researcher are shaped by narrative conventions."[7] In the context of a constructionist approach as favored in this study, gaps in sources can be welcomed "as a means to create plurality and multiple perspectives instead of claiming that we are conveying ultimate biographical truth."[8] Microhistorians have developed research methods for biographical subjects whose lives are

---

4 Primo Levi, *If This is a Man: The Truce* (London: Abacus, 2013), p. 29.
5 Katja Köhr, *Die vielen Gesichter des Holocaust* (Göttingen: V & R unipress, 2012).
6 For an example of the reconstruction of such a life, see Götz Aly, *Im Tunnel. Das kurze Leben der Marion Samuel 1931–1943* (Frankfurt am Main: Fischer-Taschenbuch-Verlag, 2005).
7 Brian Roberts, *Biographical Research* (Buckingham and Philadelphia: Open University Press, 2002), p. 7.
8 Levke Harders, "Legitimizing Biography," p. 56.

less visible in conventional sources. This study of Hilde Koch's life applies such methods, which involve the exhaustive examination of every detail discovered and the gathering of as much source material as possible that is directly related to the biographical subject and her immediate environment.[9]

The "fragments" that make up the structure chosen to represent Hilde Koch's life are centered around specific sources or categories of sources. With the exception of the first two fragments, they are presented not in the order of their discovery, but in accordance with the chronology of Hilde's life.

First Fragment—The Published Illustrations of an Elusive Artist

In 1920, three children's books illustrated by a previously unpublished artist, Hilde Koch, appeared under the imprint of the international printer-publisher Adolf Molling in Hannover.[10] In spite of Molling's prominent connection with the Dadaist artist Kurt Schwitters, the Jewish publisher was forgotten after the enforced sale of the business and the emigration of its owners as a consequence of the Nazi persecution. And apart from brief entries in a few specialized bibliographies,[11] Hilde Koch remained unmentioned in the literature on German book illustration.

The three books published by Molling with illustrations by Hilde Koch include an edition of Ernst Moritz Arndt's *Märchen* ("Fairy Tales"), edited by Hans Sturm-Gundal; *Kinderbuch* ("Children's Book") by Josefa

---

9   Sigurður Glyfi Magnússon, "The Life Is Never Over: Biography as a Microhistorical Approach," in Hans Renders, Binne de Haan, and Jonne Harmsma, eds., *The Biographical Turn: Lives in History* (London and New York: Routledge, 2017), pp. 42–52.

10 Edel Sheridan-Quantz, "'Bilderbücher in allen Sprachen': Die internationale Verlagstätigkeit von A. Molling & Comp, 1887–1939," *Deutsche Chronik* (2015), pp. 123–148.

11 Regina Freyberger, *Märchenbilder - Bildermärchen: Illustrationen zu Grimms Märchen 1819–1945. Über einen vergessenen Bereich deutscher Kunst* (Oberhausen: Athena, 2009), p. 622; Aiga Klotz, *Kinder- und Jugendliteratur in Deutschland 1840–1950: Gesamtverzeichnis der Veröffentlichungen in deutscher Sprache* (Stuttgart: J.B. Metzlersche Verlagsbuchhandlung, 1990–2013), vols. 1 and 3; Karl Heinz Schäfer and Josef Schawe, eds., *Ernst Moritz Arndt: Ein bibliographisches Handbuch* (Bonn: Röhrscheid, 1971), p. 207; Michael Vogt, ed., *'Dichterin der Kinderseele': Josefa Metz Lesebuch* (Bielefeld: Aisthesis, 2004), p. 165.

Metz; and Grimm's *Schneeweißchen und Rosenrot* ("Snow-White and Rose-Red"). The books have paper-covered boards with illustrations by Hilde Koch, and brown or black cloth spines (Fig. 1). They are printed on poor quality post-World War I paper that has darkened considerably in the hundred years since they came off the press in Hannover. All three books have stylized endpapers, almost certainly designed by Hilde Koch.

Arndt's *Märchen* contains four full-page color illustrations in a striking and expressive style, with lively silhouette vignettes interspersed in the text (Figs. 2, 3). *Kinderbuch* is a miscellany of original poems, little plays, and short tales by the Jewish writer Josefa Metz.[12] It has four full-page color illustrations as well as black-and-white illustrations on every second or third page. The color plates are vivid; the black-and-white ones dramatic (Fig. 3). The originals for the color illustrations in these two books were probably watercolors with black ink outlines. The monochrome illustrations in *Kinderbuch* appear to be printed from chalk drawings. *Schneeweißchen und Rosenrot* is a large octavo picture book with eight vibrantly colored full-page illustrations and smaller two-tone (brown and yellow) illustrations beside the text on the facing pages. The originals for the color illustrations were probably watercolors or gouaches, with ink outlines. The two-tone images appear to be ink wash or watercolor, with ink outlines.[13] The book is part of a series of ten picture-book editions of well-known fairy tales, begun by Molling shortly before World War I and completed in 1926.[14] The other nine books in the series are illustrated by four well-known artists—Hanns Anker, Hellmut Eichrodt, Heinrich-Eduard Linde-Walther, and Eugen Osswald. Hilde Koch is the only "unknown" artist to be included in the series, and the only woman.

These three books were rediscovered when the author began to research the history of Adolf Molling & Comp. in 2009. In spite of the poor quality of the postwar paper, the colors of the illustrations appeared to be as vibrant as when they were first printed. Their magentas, blues, and yellows seemed almost to leap off the page, propelled by the fluid and mobile composition of the pictures. Surely their creator must have

---

12 Josefa Metz wrote more than a dozen children's books for Molling.

13 Hans Ries, Munich, shared his expertise in the appraisal of the techniques used in the illustrations.

14 See Edel Sheridan-Quantz, "Aschenbrödel reist um die Welt—Mollings Märchenbücher," *Imprimatur: Jahrbuch für Bücherfreunde*, 22 (2011), pp. 63–102.

Fig. 1. *Schneeweißchen und Rosenrot*, illustrated by Hilde Koch and published by Molling in 1920.

Fig. 2. Color illustration from Arndt's *Märchen*.

Fig. 3. Black-and-white illustrations from Arndt's *Märchen*
and Josefa Metz's *Kinderbuch*.

been a personality about whom it was worth knowing more, but with such a common name, and lacking a date or place of birth, the odds appeared to be stacked against identifying her.

Second Fragment—A Professional Affiliation

The reconstruction of Hilde Koch's life story was made possible by a serendipitous discovery. The seller of a booklet published in 1921, by the Frankfurt am Main and Offenbach branch of a new professional association, the *Bund der Deutschen Gebrauchsgraphiker* (BDG, Association of German Commercial Artists),[15] included a list of the branch's members in the online description of the publication, probably because of the numerous famous names it contained. Among illustrious figures such as Johann Vincenz Cissarz and Franz Karl Delavilla, or the typographer Rudolf Koch, one of only four women among the

15 *Bund Deutscher Gebrauchsgraphiker: Ortsgruppe Frankfurt a.M. Offenbach* (Frankfurt am Main: R. Th. Hauser & Co., 1921), no page numbers.

thirty-two members listed stood out: Hilde Koch, with an address at Wolfsgangstraße 130, in Frankfurt am Main. In 1921, this was only 500 meters from the office of the BDG at Unterlindau 51.

Examples of the group's output are reproduced in the booklet and include an emblem by Hilde Koch (Fig. 4). The booklet also provides a clue to a possible connection with Molling in Hannover: among the members listed is the Hannoverian artist Ferdy Horrmeyer (1890–1978), many of whose political and commercial posters were printed by Molling. He could have introduced Hilde Koch to his printers. A copy of *Schneeweißchen und Rosenrot* sold in Munich in 2002,[16] originally belonged to Franz Karl Delavilla, so it seemed reasonable to assume that the book's illustrator could indeed be identical with the Hilde Koch who was a member of the Frankfurt/Offenbach branch of the BDG.

Many of the artists in the Frankfurt/Offenbach branch of the BDG had distinguished careers. Several had illustrated picture books: Fritz Franke's illustrations for *Die Biene Maja* are still in print today; Karl Großmann and Aenne Müller-Knatz both had picture books published

Fig. 4. Emblem by Hilde Koch, Bund Deutscher Gebrauchsgraphiker, 1921. By kind permission of the BDG (Berufsverband Deutscher Kommunikationsdesigner).

16 Auction14, May 10, 2003; http://www.von-zezschwitz.de/detail.php?id=14&chapter =0&objectid=4716&PHPSESSID=4535657d5acbb7f2cd04dd05764c912b (accessed December 12, 2009, and June 1, 2011).

by Stalling in Oldenburg. The BDG booklet also suggests a possible context for Hilde Koch's training as an artist: several of the group's members taught at one or both of Frankfurt's art colleges. Johann Vincenz Cissarz was a professor at the *Städelschule*; Franz Karl Delavilla and Albert Windisch taught at the *Kunstgewerbeschule*, or School of Applied Arts, and at the *Städelschule* after the former was integrated into it.

In early twentieth-century Germany, higher education was becoming accessible for women. In Frankfurt, the founder of the *Städelschule* had specified, as early as 1817, that no student was to be turned away because of gender. However, this principle was not implemented until the early 1870s, when a separate class for women was established. By 1913, women had full access to art classes at the school. Most *Kunstgewerbeschulen* (Schools of Applied Art) permitted women to attend classes from around 1900.[17]

Hilde Koch could therefore have attended either of the two art colleges in Frankfurt. However, it was not unusual for parents to require a chaperone for any activity that took their daughters out of the family home, or to object to the "immorality" of an artistic education involving drawing from the nude.[18] No archival evidence could be found for Hilde Koch's attendance at either the *Städelschule* or the *Kunstgewerbeschule*. She may have taken private classes, a path chosen by many upper-middle-class women, or attended a private school.[19] The Frankfurt *Adressbuch* (city directory) for 1916 lists twenty private drawing teachers and two private art schools.

After 1921, the Frankfurt/Offenbach regional branch of the BDG was subsumed in a larger association for the Rhine-Main area. Three membership lists for the Rhine-Main BDG are available, for 1923, 1924, and 1929, and a nationwide BDG directory for 1926/27. The 1923 list names fifty-two members, with only two women—Hilde Koch and Aenne Müller-Knatz.[20] They are also the only two women members among the total of sixty-seven listed for 1924.[21] Two line illustrations by

17 Ingrid von der Dollen, *Malerinnen im 20. Jahrhundert. Bildkunst der "Verschollenen Generation": Geburtsjahrgänge 1890–1910* (Munich: Hirmer, 2000), pp. 28, 32.
18 Ibid., p. 27.
19 Ibid., pp. 32–37.
20 *Marken und Zeichen* (Frankfurt am Main: R. Th. Hauser & Co., 1923), no page numbers.
21 Bund Deutscher Gebrauchsgraphiker, *Buchkunst Ausstellung: Veranstaltet von der*

Hilde Koch are reproduced in the 1924 publication (Fig. 5). Hilde Koch is not listed in the BDG directory for 1926/27.[22] In 1929, the Rhine-Main branch of the BDG had seventy-seven members, all men.[23]

Fig. 5. Illustrations by Hilde Koch in Buchkunst Ausstellung, 1924. By kind permission of the BDG (Berufsverband Deutscher Kommunikationsdesigner).

Third Fragment—Public Records

The Frankfurt *Adressbuch* for 1921 lists a Julius Koch as the owner-occupier of the building at Wolfsgangstraße 130, the address given for Hilde Koch in the BDG list. As historic city directories only list heads of households, Julius Koch could possibly have been Hilde Koch's father, brother, or husband. An examination of the Frankfurt city directories

Landesgruppe Rhein-Main des Bundes Deutscher Gebrauchsgraphiker (Frankfurt am Main: R. Th. Hauser & Co., 1924), no page numbers.

22 *BDG Adressbuch: Mitgliederverzeichnis des Bundes Deutscher Gebrauchsgraphiker 1926/27* (Berlin: Gebr. Mann, 1927).

23 Bund Deutscher Gebrauchsgraphiker, *Graphische Werbekunst aus dem Rhein-Main-Gebiet* (Frankfurt: Ludwig und Mayer, 1929).

between 1860 and 1940, revealed that Julius Koch was first recorded as a resident of the city in the 1894 directory. Over four decades he is listed variously as a banker, factory owner, merchant, private secretary, and bank employee. From 1932, he is listed as being of independent means.

The registration of residents' addresses with local authorities was first introduced in Berlin in 1812, and spread through Germany in the nineteenth century. Where they survive, *Einwohnermeldekarten*, or residents' registration cards, are a valuable source for social history and genealogy, as they include all family members. But no registration cards for Julius or Hilde Koch are preserved in Frankfurt's city archives. The owners of Adolf Molling & Comp. in Hannover were Jewish, but

Fig. 6. Hilde Neuberger nee Koch (YVA, 14071289), Otto Neuberger (YVA, 14228973), and Julius Koch (YVA, 14071543).

the firm did not specialize in Jewish themes or authors/illustrators. So it could not be automatically assumed that Hilde Koch was Jewish. A Jewish Hilde Koch designed a *Verpflichtungsschein*, or commitment note, for B'nai B'rith around 1925,[24] but it is not clear if she was the illustrator of Arndt's *Märchen, Schneeweißchen und Rosenrot*, and *Kinderbuch*. However, a search of the Yad Vashem database of Holocaust victims using the two names Julius and Hilde Koch, and the location Frankfurt am Main produced a match with the few facts as known. The database contains pages of testimony for Julius Koch from Frankfurt, for his daughter Hilde, and her husband Otto Neuberger, with photographs

---

24 Leo Baeck et al., *Zum 50 jährigen Bestehen des Ordens Bne Briss in Deutschland* (Frankfurt am Main: J. Kauffmann Verlag, 1933), p. 85.

(Fig. 6). The testimonies were submitted in 1999, by Gabriel (Gabi) Neuberger, Otto Neuberger's son from his first marriage. They indicate that Hilde Koch was born in Frankfurt on July 17, 1896, to the banker Julius Koch (born in Offenbach on November 15, 1863) and Clementine nee Metz. An online search with this information led to a digitized copy of Clementine's death certificate, which in turn made it possible to narrow the search for her birth record in Cologne's historic registry books. She was born in Cologne on March 24, 1873, and died in Frankfurt on August 28, 1924.[25] Birth records for two daughters born to Julius Koch and Clementine Metz were also found: Clara Hilda[26] Koch, born on July 17, 1896, and Leonie Hermine, born on September 14, 1899.[27]

The information given in Clementine Metz's birth register made it possible to trace her family tree. It emerged that she was a first cousin of Josefa Metz, the author of the three books illustrated by Hilde Koch, providing a second potential link with Molling in Hannover.

The testimonies also show that Hilde's husband, Otto Neuberger, was born in Korb near Stuttgart on November 17, 1886, and had been married before. His profession is given simply as "businessman"; no profession is given for Hilde. An enquiry to Mannheim's *Stadtarchiv*[28] produced copies of three registration cards for Otto Neuberger and one for Julius Koch. Otto Neuberger's first card shows that he came to Mannheim as an apprentice on April 15, 1901, at the age of fourteen. His second card starts with his return to Mannheim from military service in World War I on December 11, 1918, and lists his profession as sales representative. The third registration card for Otto Neuberger shows that he and his first wife, Ida nee Spieß, had two children— Lore Sophie, born on December 27, 1921, and Walter Gerd,[29] born on

---

25 (Incomplete) scan of Frankfurt registry of deaths, www.ancestry.de; *Zivilstandsregister, Landgerichtsbezirk Köln, Standesamt Köln, Geburten*, 1873, vol. 4, http://historischesarchivkoeln.de/lav/index.php (accessed January 8, 2020).

26 Hilde's name is variously given as Clara Hilda, Klara Hilde, and Hilde Klara in the sources consulted.

27 (Incomplete) scan of Frankfurt registry of births at www.ancestry.de; *Institut für Stadtgeschichte*, Frankfurt.

28 Re-named MARCHIVUM in 2018.

29 Walter Gerd later changed his name to Walter Gabriel and was known as Gabriel or Gabi.

August 17, 1926. Ida Neuberger died in Leysin, Switzerland, on February 24, 1933.[30]

Otto Neuberger and Hilde Koch married in 1934; Hilde is recorded on Otto's registration card as moving to Mannheim on August 16, 1934. She was now, at thirty-eight, stepmother to twelve-year-old Lore and eight-year-old Walter (Gabi). The newly-constituted family moved from the Neubergers' old apartment at C7, 7,[31] in the center of Mannheim to Akademiestraße 7, just west of the city center on September 16, 1934.

Fourth Fragment—The Inherited Memories of Leonie Ehrmann nee Koch

All attempts to contact Hilde Koch's stepson, Gabi Neuberger, failed.[32] In 2018, a connection was made with Hilde Koch Neuberger's niece, Myriam Nachsatz nee Ehrmann, the daughter of Hilde's sister, Leonie, through the genealogical website Geni/MyHeritage. Myriam Nachsatz was unaware that Hilde had ever published her work, but she had carefully preserved numerous original artworks inherited from her mother, as well as family photographs and some letters. Among the artworks was an unpublished illustration for Arndt's *Märchen*, confirming that the Hilde Koch who was a member of the BDG in Frankfurt and married Otto Neuberger in Mannheim was indeed the same person as the illustrator published by Molling. Myriam Nachsatz had also kept alive her late mother's memories of her lost sister.[33] She told the story as she knew it in a telephone interview, in a mixture of German and English with a little French.[34]

Julius Koch lived a prosperous life. The Frankfurt city directories show that when he first came to the city he lived for about a year at Palmstraße 16 (Nordend). From 1896 on the directories record him at

---

30 Account by Walter Gabriel Neuberger of his life, *Weil Family Collection*, Leo Baeck Archives, AR 11718, p. 94.

31 Mannheim's address system is unique in Germany. The city was laid out on a grid system when it was founded in 1606. Each block in the historic city center has a code—for example, C7—and each building has a number.

32 He died in 2014.

33 Leonie's memories, as mediated by her daughter Myriam, can be described as *postmemory*; see Marianne Hirsch, *The Generation of Postmemory. Writing and Visual Culture after the Holocaust* (New York: Columbia University Press, 2012), p. 5.

34 Telephone interview with Myriam Nachsatz, October 27, 2018; emails and phone calls from October 2018 to May 2020.

a number of addresses in Frankfurt's salubrious Westend. Hilde Koch was born at Parkstraße 10; Leonie at Trutz 40. In April 1911, when Hilde was fourteen and Leonie eleven, the family moved to Wolfsgangstraße 130, to a house that Julius Koch had just bought.

Leonie told her daughter that the sisters had a close relationship but were very different personalities. Hilde was a "true daughter of high society" and loved to sing, dance, and paint; in other words, she had learned (and enjoyed) the traditional "accomplishments" of an upper-middle-class woman. Leonie in contrast was athletic and loved sports; she was "the diving champion of Frankfurt." She liked to hike, camp, and ski, and owned a canoe and a sailing boat that she took out on the rivers Main and Rhine. In her claim for reparations, Leonie gave an account of her education.[35] She had attended the *Edithaschule*,[36] an interdenominational private school for girls aged six to sixteen on Bleichstraße in the center of Frankfurt. It seems likely that Hilde also attended this school. A contemporary advertisement for the *Edithaschule* shows what type of education the Kochs chose for their daughters: "First Class Finishing School. Solid education in the attached 10-grade girls' school, Edithaschule, or in music, science, housekeeping.—Electric light, central heating. A1 recommendations. For prospectus, apply to the principal M. Stockmann."[37]

After Leonie left the *Edithaschule*, she trained at the *Frauen-Bildungsverein* (Women's Education Association) and at Julius Gans's *Handelsfachschule für Mädchen* (Commercial School for Girls). She worked as a secretary and clerk for various businesses and banks from 1918 to 1934, dealing with correspondence in English and French, as well as German. According to Myriam, "she was the revolutionary in the family. She earned her own money and bought what she wanted."[38]

The portfolio of Hilde's artwork inherited by Myriam contains prints in different techniques (engraving on paper and chalk lithography), pencil drawings, an acrylic and tempera painting, and a watercolor with ink outlines. Several of the engravings on paper are portraits; there is one

35 Reparation file for Leonie Ehrmann, Hessisches Landesarchiv Wiesbaden (HLA), Abt. Fonds 518, No. 10631, pp. 6, 9–11.
36 The school was founded in 1841; Maria Rudolph and Otto Schlander, *Die Frauenbildung in Frankfurt am Main* (Frankfurt am Main: Lang, 1978), p. 94.
37 *Moderne Kunst: Illustrierte Zeitschrift* 27.1912/1913; https://digi.ub.uni-heidelberg. de/diglit/moderne_kunst1912_1913/0024.
38 Telephone interview with Myriam Nachsatz.

female nude, some streetscapes and landscapes, and numerous dramatic figural scenes. One print of two horses seems to have been influenced by Franz Marc. Of the portraits, two can be tentatively identified as showing her mother Clementine and her sister Leonie (Fig. 7). All of these works are expressionistic in character. The figural scenes and streetscapes are laden with symbolism and are highly emotional; they were possibly influenced by World War I etchings of Otto Dix and George Grosz (cover image). Many show scenes of suffering and one is a pietà, showing the Virgin Mary with the crucified Jesus.

The elegant chalk lithographs are typical of the 1920s (Fig. 8). The pencil drawings are somber in atmosphere, many with gaunt, suffering figures (Fig. 9). They bring to mind Hugo Steiner-Prag's "Golem" prints, or the work of Alfred Kubin. Two show a Catholic priest wearing a cassock and Roman hat, offering comfort to an ill or dying person. The acrylic and tempera painting is framed and represents the Christian Saint Francis of Assisi (Fig. 10). The watercolor was evidently created for Molling's edition of Arndt's *Märchen* but was not published in the book. Most of these artworks are now in the Yad Vashem art collection.

The recurring use of Christian imagery in Hilde's surviving work is striking. As well as the incidences cited here, *Schneeweißchen und Rosenrot* features an image of the Madonna and Child visible on the wall of the sisters' home in one illustration.

Fig. 7. Hilde Neuberger Koch (1896–1943), *Portrait of a woman*, 1920s.
Engraving on paper. 17.9 x 15.1 cm (left) and 19.3 x 13.6 cm (right).
Photo © Collection of the Yad Vashem Art Museum, Jerusalem (#19240B on the left, #19242B on the right). Gift of Myriam Nachsatz, Holon.

◀ Fig. 8. Hilde Neuberger Koch (1896–1943), *Tree in a storm*, 1920s. Chalk on paper, 16.1 x 10.5 cm.
Photo © Collection of the Yad Vashem Art Museum, Jerusalem (#19253). Gift of Myriam Nachsatz, Holon.

Fig. 9. Hilde Neuberger Koch (1896–1943), *Social meeting*, 1920s. Pencil on paper, 15.9 x 12.7 cm.
Photo © Collection of the Yad Vashem Art Museum, Jerusalem (#19261). Gift of Myriam Nachsatz, Holon.

Fig. 10. Hilde Neuberger Koch (1896–1943), *St. Francis*, 1920s. Acrylic and tempera on cardboard, 36 x 29.2 cm.
Photo © Collection of the Yad Vashem Art Museum, Jerusalem (#19263). Gift of Myriam Nachsatz, Holon.

Also among the artworks preserved by Leonie is a small hardbound blank book with watercolor and ink illustrations of frolicking cherubs for a calendar for 1918. These paintings are signed with a distinctive "FF" monogram and dated 1917. The artist is Fritz Franke, illustrator of *Die Biene Maja*, a fellow member of the BDG and a year older than Hilde.[39]

Hilde Koch's art demonstrates openness to a broad range of influences from innovative contemporary practitioners. It is not the work of an artistically isolated woman. Taken together with the evidence of her association with personalities such as Franke and Delavilla and the other members of the Frankfurt/Offenbach branch of the BDG, the influences apparent in Hilde Koch's work suggest that her artistic education was received in these circles.

Fifth Fragment—Robbery and "Reparation"

When Leonie Koch wanted to marry in 1934, the fact that her older sister was still unmarried presented a problem: "Her father said, 'your sister is older, she has to marry first.'"[40] Julius Koch's old-fashioned conviction was the reason for Hilde's (arranged) marriage to Otto Neuberger, whom Julius Koch knew through business connections. On July 24, 1934, Leonie married Francis Jesse Ehrmann, who had left Frankfurt to work in the French capital in 1932. Francis had grown up in Frankfurt, and he and Leonie had known each other for many years.[41]

Most of what could be discovered about Hilde's married life in Mannheim comes from files relating to the compensation claims[42] made by Hilde's sister Leonie Ehrmann and stepson Gabi Neuberger. The files relate to property belonging to Hilde (and Otto) that was confiscated, destroyed, or robbed during the Nazi period. Otto Neuberger worked as a representative for numerous firms that supplied woolen knitted fabrics and hosiery to wholesalers, department stores, and other large stores in Baden and the Palatinate.[43] He was evidently successful, as he owned

39 Prof. Friedrich Heller, Linz, helped identify the monogram.
40 Interview with Myriam Nachsatz, October 27, 2018.
41 Phone call with Myriam Nachsatz, April 1, 2020.
42 The *Bundesentschädigungsgesetz* (Federal Compensation Law) of June 29, 1956, regulated the payment of compensation to victims of the Nazi regime in West Germany.
43 Reparation file for Otto Neuberger, Generallandesarchiv Karlsruhe (GLAK), 480, No. 24472, p. 130.

two properties in Mannheim and lived in comfort. The Neubergers' apartment, on the third floor of the building at Akademiestraße 7, had five well-furnished rooms, a kitchen and bathroom, and a room for a maid in the attic.[44] Oil paintings, etchings, and Japanese woodcuts hung on the walls. The Neubergers had a radio, a gramophone, and a piano.[45] Hilde's personal belongings included a library of about 500 books and a collection of original prints by the Expressionists Heckel, Kirchner, Nolde, and others.[46] Among her books were classics, art books, modern bibliophile editions, works by Strindberg, Dostoevsky, and Tolstoy, as well as the "Thule Collection" of Icelandic and Nordic sagas published by Diederichs in Munich between 1911 and 1930.[47]

The Nuremberg laws of September 15, 1935, turned German Jews into second-class citizens in their own country. They were now increasingly driven out of their businesses and employment. On Yom Kippur (which fell on October 5, 1938) all Jews in Mannheim had to surrender their radios, and the Neubergers' radio was taken from their apartment.[48] On the same day a new law invalidated Jews' passports. An edict of August 17, 1938, required all Jews whose first names were not sufficiently "Jewish" to adopt obligatory additional names of "Sara" or "Israel." But when Julius Koch visited Leonie in Paris in 1938, and the Ehrmanns urged him to stay in Paris, which they felt was safer than Germany, he replied, "I am German, things can't get that bad."[49]

In the early hours of November 10, 1938, SA men and members of the NSDAP demolished the synagogue in the Mannheim city center and attacked almost every Jewish home and business in the city.[50] Hilde's stepson Gabi later recalled:

> At the time of *Kristallnacht* I was still in Germany, and they sent us home from school. Around midday, a group of 4–6 SA men appeared and at first they wanted to arrest my father; however, this did not come about thanks to my father's remonstrations. Then

44 Restitution file for Otto Neuberger, GLAK, 508 Zugang 2004-60, No. 3044.
45 Reparation file for Otto Neuberger, GLAK, 480, No. 24472, p. 20.
46 Restitution file for Otto Neuberger, GLAK, 508 Zugang 2004-60, No. 3044.
47 Reparation file for Klara Hilde Neuberger, GLAK, 480, No. 8601, p. 7.
48 Restitution file for Otto Neuberger, GLAK, 508 Zugang 2004-60, No. 3044.
49 Interview with Myriam Nachsatz, October 27, 2018.
50 Christiane Fritsche, *Ausgeplündert, zurückerstattet und entschädigt. Arisierung und Wiedergutmachung in Mannheim* (Ubstadt-Weiher: verlag regionalkultur, 2013), pp. 282–284.

they went into the dining room and the living room and smashed almost all the china. They knocked over the china cupboard so that everything broke, they threw the books onto the street, etchings hanging on the walls were torn to pieces, the oil paintings in the living and dining room were cut up because they could not be torn...When these people left the apartment it looked wrecked.[51]

In February 1939, all Jews in Germany were required to give up their jewelry and precious metals to the municipal pawnbroking office. Only one setting of silver cutlery for each member of a household could be retained. Otto and Hilde received a "ludicrous" sum for their valuables and were only permitted to keep their wedding rings.[52] Julius Koch was forced to sell the house on Wolfsgangstraße in Frankfurt and "sought refuge"[53] with his daughter and son-in-law in Mannheim on May 22, 1939.[54] The Neubergers planned to emigrate to Palestine, and Julius may have hoped that he could accompany them. However, Otto suffered a stroke, and the British refused him a permit to enter the country.[55] On October 22, 1939, Lore and Walter (Gabi) Neuberger, now aged seventeen and thirteen, sailed unaccompanied from Trieste to Haifa.[56]

Hilde, Otto, and Julius had to share the apartment at Akademiestraße 7, with strangers following the enactment of the *Gesetz über Mietverhältnisse mit Juden* (Law Concerning Jewish Tenants) on April 30, 1939, which paved the way for the ghettoization of Jews in Germany. Two Jewish men were billeted with the Neubergers, who gave them their two largest rooms to the front of the apartment. Julius Koch, Hilde, and Otto lived in the three smaller rooms at the back of the apartment.[57]

Hilde wrote to Leonie in Paris on December 10, 1939, reporting that the children "...have already settled in well and write very cheerful

51 Translated by the author; restitution file for Otto Neuberger, GLAK, 508 Zugang 2004-60, No. 3044.
52 Ibid.
53 Reparation file for Julius Koch, HLA, Abt. 518, No. 20685.
54 Registration card for Julius Koch, MARCHIVUM.
55 Interview with Myriam Nachsatz, October 27, 2018.
56 Account by Walter Gabriel Neuberger of his life, Leo Baeck Archives, AR 11718, p. 95.
57 Restitution file for Otto Neuberger, GLAK, 508 Zugang 2004-60, No. 3044.

letters. Otto's condition is, sadly, unchanged..."[58] Just over a fortnight later, a surprising piece of good news came from Paris—Leonie, who was now forty, was expecting a baby. Julius wrote a joyful reply: "I have no dearer wish than that it may be granted me to see the [child] once..." Hilde was equally pleased: "We were absolutely delighted about your letter, especially as you were able to give us such great news. I wish you all the best, and that your wish for a girl will be fulfilled...I hope you will have much joy in the child, be it a boy or a girl."[59]

Leonie's daughter Myriam was born in Paris on March 18, 1940. Two months later the Germans invaded France, and on June 15, 1940, the Wehrmacht occupied Paris. The French government departed to Vichy, and the country was divided into an occupied zone and a free zone (Vichy Zone). This had implications both for Leonie in Paris and Hilde in Mannheim.

Leonie's husband, Francis Ehrmann, worked at the Luxour tannerie de cuir moderne, a tannery owned by Samuel Wolf (Shlomo Zeev) Goldberg. Samuel Goldberg was Jewish; he and his wife Esther (nee Rottenburg) were originally from Poland.[60] When the Germans occupied Paris in June 1940, Leonie and Myriam fled the city in Samuel Goldberg's "very small car"; he also brought his wife, Esther, and their two children, Jacques and Michel, on the same journey. It was a bitter reflection for Leonie that if Julius had remained in Paris in 1938, as she had begged him to do, her own small family might not have survived. Julius would not have fit into the tiny car with them, which would have made their escape impossible.[61]

Francis was away working as a *prestataire* when Leonie fled from Paris. *Prestation*, or compulsory labor for foreign refugees in France, was introduced by a decree of January 13, 1940.[62] Leonie and Myriam found shelter near Limoges, first in Millac, and later in Bellac.

58 Translated by the author from a letter in the possession of Myriam Nachsatz.
59 Ibid.
60 See http://phep2.technion.ac.il/goldberg/ghtout/gp20.htm#head0; http://phep2.technion.ac.il/goldberg/ghtout/gp5.htm#head0 (accessed January 19, 2020).
61 Interview with Myriam Nachsatz, October 27, 2018; reparation file for Leonie Ehrmann, HLA, Abt. 518, No. 10631, p. 6; Michel E. Goldberg, "Jacques Monod, Protein Folding, and Me," in Giorgio Semenza and Vladimir P. Skulachev, eds., *Stories of success—personal recollections. XI* (Amsterdam: Elsevier, 2008), pp. 115–231, cited on p. 116.
62 Christian Eggers, *Unerwünschte Ausländer. Juden aus Deutschland und Mitteleuropa*

On October 22, 1940 (the last day of *Sukkot*), more than 6,500 Jews from southwestern Germany were deported to France;[63] nearly 2,000 were from Mannheim.[64] The aim of the so-called *Wagner-Bürckel-Aktion* was to make the first two districts in Germany *Judenrein* by November 9, 1940, the anniversary of the 1923 Munich Putsch.[65] The deportation was planned in secret and carried out ruthlessly at very short notice, taking the victims completely by surprise. Only Jews in so-called "mixed marriages" (with non-Jews) and the bedridden were spared. The suddenness of the deportation and the uncertainty as to its destination caused great distress; in Mannheim alone, eight people committed suicide on the morning of October 22, rather than present themselves for the transport.[66]

Hilde Neuberger and Julius Koch, together with twelve other residents from the house at Akademiestraße 7, were deported on October 22, 1940.[67] Since Otto had not recovered from his stroke, he was not included in the transport. Hilde and Julius had to pack quickly and leave him behind in the apartment. A neighbor later recalled: "On the day of the deportation, Herr Neuberger was not transportable, because he was paralyzed…I was ordered by a SS man to stay with Herr Neuberger… Herr Neuberger was sitting in an armchair in his living room."[68]

The day after Hilde and Julius were deported, Otto was admitted to the Jewish Hospital at Collinistraße 53 (now Bassermannstraße).[69] The Neubergers' apartment was sealed. Shortly afterward their belongings were auctioned in the apartment. The properties of the other Jewish residents of the building were subject to the same procedure.[70]

---

in französischen Internierungslagern 1940–1942 (Berlin: Metropol-Verlag, 2002), pp. 53–57.

63 Ibid., pp. 255–270.

64 See https://deportation.yadvashem.org/index.html?language=en&itemId=1129024 6&ind=5 (accessed January 2, 2020).

65 Eggers, *Unerwünschte Ausländer*, pp. 258–259.

66 Erhard Roy Wiehn, ed., *Oktoberdeportation 1940. Die sogenannte 'Abschiebung' der badischen und saarpfälzischen Juden in das französische Internierungslager Gurs als Vorstation von Auschwitz. 50 Jahre danach zum Gedenken* (Konstanz: Hartung-Gorre, 1990), p. 622.

67 *Verzeichnis der am 22 Oktober 1940 aus Baden ausgewiesenen Juden* (Karlsruhe: Der Generalbevollmächtigte für das Jüdische Vermögen in Baden, 1941).

68 Translated by the author; restitution file for Otto Neuberger, GLAK, 508 Zugang 2004-60, No. 3044.

69 *Dokumentation 44*, MARCHIVUM.

70 Restitution file for Otto Neuberger, GLAK, 508 Zugang 2004-60, No. 3044.

Sixth Fragment—A Chanukah Gift for Myriam

The deportees were put on sealed passenger trains with no notion of their destination. The French authorities were under the impression that the transports consisted of expelled French citizens. When they realized that they were actually German Jews, they requested that they be returned to Germany. The Germans ignored these requests, so a place had to be found to accommodate the thousands of deportees. The Vichy government directed the trains toward Camp Gurs at the foot of the Pyrenees, halfway between the resort town of Biarritz and Lourdes, a Catholic place of pilgrimage. The trains reached the small town of Oloron-Sainte-Marie, 15 kilometers from Gurs, on the evening of October 24, 1940. Here the passengers were transferred to trucks, which took hours.

The exiles arrived tired, cold, and wet to a sodden camp awash in mud. The camp at Gurs had been created to receive refugees from Spain after the fall of Catalonia in the spring of 1939, and was only intended to be used for a few months.[71] It was officially designated as a *centre d'acceuil*, or reception camp, but the physical conditions belied this mild description. The camp was organized in *îlots* (islands) of twenty-five to twenty-seven barracks; each island or group was enclosed by barbed wire. Hilde's camp registration card records that she was assigned to *îlot* I, barrack 8. By a poignant irony, this is the first surviving record since her membership in the BDG in which she could reassert her status as an artist. In Gurs, robbed of her rights, her home, and most of her belongings, she nevertheless reclaimed her professional identity: in the space for occupation, the word *sans* (without) is crossed out and replaced with *dessinatrice*, or artist.[72]

Men and women were separated on arrival in Gurs, and visits between the men's and women's sections were not permitted until December 1940.[73] Julius Koch was sent to *îlot* D in the men's section.[74] It is unlikely that Hilde had any opportunity to see her father again after they arrived in Gurs: Julius Koch died there on November 7, 1940, a

---

71 Eggers, *Unerwünschte Ausländer*, p. 111.
72 Registration card for Hilda [*sic*] Neuberger nee Koch, *Archives Départmentales Pyrenées Atlantiques*, 72 W 66.
73 Eggers, *Unerwünschte Ausländer*, pp. 262–264.
74 Registration card for Julius Koch, *Archives Départmentales Pyrenées Atlantiques*, 72 W 63.

week before his seventy-seventh birthday. The death certificate issued in Gurs records that he died of *sénilité* (old age).[75] This was probably not the sole cause, as a form of dysentery swept through the camp in the winter of 1940/41. More than 600 men and women died in the three months between November 1940 and January 1941; the older people were the worst affected.[76]

The barracks at Gurs had wooden hatches instead of windows, and so it was extremely dark. The roofs were leaky, and there was no furniture.[77] Food was in short supply and of very poor quality. Had food rations and basic necessities not been augmented by aid organizations, such as the Quakers, Secours Suisse, and Oeuvre de Secours aux Enfants (OSE), many internees would have starved.[78] There was also a lively black market in food and other essentials.[79] Mail could be sent and received.[80]

In spite of the difficult conditions, many internees used their time in creative ways. There was no forced labor, and the inmates were able to choose their own activities. The aid organizations also supplied books, musical instruments, paper, paints, and brushes to the camp inmates. Artists could improve their purchasing power on the camp's black market, as portraits and greeting cards, for example, were much in demand.[81] The inmates organized cultural activities, and there was a *Kulturbaracke* in each *îlot*. Readings, plays, and concerts were arranged, and the daily life in the camp was recorded in drawings, paintings, handmade booklets, and even comics.[82] The images created by Leo

75 Death certificate for Julius Koch, *Archives Départmentales Pyrenées Atlantiques*, 72 W 37.

76 Eggers, *Unerwünschte Ausländer*, p. 267.

77 For a first-hand account, see "Bericht des Mannheimer Kinderarztes Dr. Eugen Neter (29.10.1876–8.10.1966) über Camp des Gurs, verfaßt 1946," in Hans-Joachim Fliedner, *Die Judenverfolgung in Mannheim 1933–1945: Darstellung und Dokumente* (Stuttgart, Berlin, Cologne: Kohlhammer, 1991), pp. 310–327.

78 "Bericht Dr. Eugen Neter," p. 321.

79 Volkhard Knigge and Detlef Hoffmann, "Die südfranzösischen Lager," in Detlef Hoffmann, ed., *Das Gedächtnis der Dinge. KZ-Relikte und KZ-Denkmäler 1945–1995* (Frankfurt am Main: Campus-Verlag, 1998), pp. 206–223, cited on p. 213.

80 Paul Sauer, ed., *Dokumente über die Verfolgung der jüdischen Bürger in Baden-Württemberg durch das nationalsozialistische Regime 1933–1945* (Stuttgart: Kohlhammer, 1966), p. 260; Knigge and Hoffmann, "Die südfranzösischen Lager," p. 213; "Auszüge aus Briefen der Quäker," in Fliedner, *Die Judenverfolgung in Mannheim*, pp. 327–333.

81 Jörn Wendland, *Das Lager von Bild zu Bild: Narrative Bildserien von Häftlingen aus NS-Zwangslagern* (Cologne: Böhlau Verlag, 2017), p. 36.

82 Thomas Bullinger, ed., *Gurs: ein Internierungslager in Südfrankreich 1939–1943.*

Breuer, Julius C. Turner, and Löw & Bodek of daily life in the camp are iconic;[83] one of the most extraordinary artistic productions from Gurs is Horst Rosenthal's satirical *Mickey au Camp de Gurs* featuring Walt Disney's Mickey Mouse.[84]

Among the artworks preserved by Myriam Nachsatz is a much-handled booklet inscribed on the front cover in black ink highlighted with white paint: *Les Animaux. Un livre d'images pour la petite Mirjam dessiné par sa tante Hilde Neuberger au Camp de Gurs Chanoukkah 5702*[85]

Fig. 11. Left: Hilde Neuberger Koch (1896–1943), *The Animals: Picture Book for Little Mirjam*, Gurs Camp, 1941. Ink and watercolor on paper, 22 × 26.7 cm.
Photo © Collection of the Yad Vashem Art Museum, Jerusalem (#19238). Gift of Myriam Nachsatz, Holon.
Right: Hilde Neuberger Koch (1896–1943), *Stork and chicks*, Gurs Camp, 1941. Watercolor and ink on paper, 22 × 26.7 cm.
Photo © Collection of the Yad Vashem Art Museum, Jerusalem (#19238/11). Gift of Myriam Nachsatz, Holon.

Zeichnungen, Aquarelle, Fotografien. Sammlung Elsbeth Kasser (Hamburg: Hamburger Stiftung zur Förderung von Wissenschaft und Kultur, 1993); Gabriele Mittag, *"Es gibt Verdammte nur in Gurs": Literatur, Kultur und Alltag in einem südfranzösischen Internierungslager 1940–1942* (Tübingen: Attempto, 1996).

83 See Bullinger, *Gurs: ein Internierungslager in Südfrankreich.*

84 The entire comic can be viewed online at https://imgur.com/gallery/Um6mSN0 (accessed January 2, 2020).

85 December 14–22, 1941.

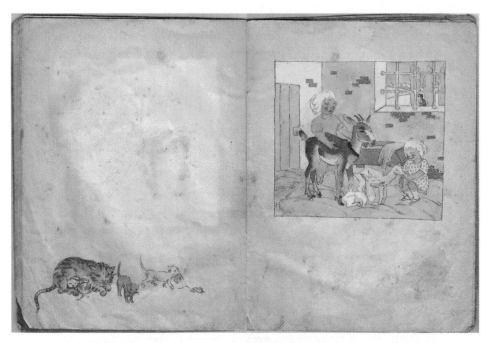

Fig. 12. Hilde Neuberger Koch (1896–1943), *Girls playing with goats*, Gurs
Camp, 1941. Watercolor and ink on paper, 22 × 26.7 cm.
Photo © Collection of the Yad Vashem Art Museum, Jerusalem (#19238/08). Gift of
Myriam Nachsatz, Holon.

("Animals. A picture book for little Myriam drawn by her aunt Hilde
Neuberger in Camp Gurs, Chanukah 5702"; see Figs. 11, 12, and 14).

The booklet is composed of five sheets of plain off-white paper
hand-sewn into a blue-gray laid paper cover. It has no text, and contains
ten full-page watercolor illustrations with ink outlines, including the
title page, and nine vignettes facing the full-page illustrations, with a
tenth on the last page of the booklet. The Pyrenees feature in eight of the
full-page illustrations. The dramatic mountain scenery both delighted
and tormented the inmates of Gurs:

> The Pyrenees! When we saw these steeply towering, snow-
> covered mountains on the first morning, the sight was a profound
> experience, but at the same time a surprise, because we did not
> know where fate had led us. So now we saw the Pyrenees for
> long months, years; the morning sun falls on the snowy slopes in
> incomparable colors and shades, and the mountain peaks glow in
> blazing fire in the evenings. A painful sight for many of those living

behind the barbed wire. You can understand the refrain frequently heard in the camp: "I cannot bear the sight of you, you Pyrenees."[86]

There is nothing distressing or disturbing about the mountains in Hilde Koch's last surviving work. They provide a picturesque background for gentle illustrations of happy children in harmony with pets, farm animals, and wild creatures.

Seventh Fragment—In Hilde's Own Words

During the summer of 1942, the Germans began systematic deportations of Jews from France to the death camps. In August/September 1942, the Vichy police sent a total of 9,872 Jews from the Vichy Zone to Drancy to be put on transports to the East.[87] But when the razzias and transports began, Hilde was no longer in Gurs. According to her Gurs registration card, she was transferred to Montmélian in Savoie in the French Alps on July 9, 1942.

From 1940, Montmélian was a *centre d'accueil* for foreigners and Jews. From May or June 1942, it was used as a triage center for *inaptes*, foreigners who were deemed unfit to work as *prestataires*.[88] The camp was located in an unused military barracks, and conditions were somewhat better than in the internment camps. It was administered by the Service Social des Étrangers (SSE). The SSE was answerable to the ministry of labor and mediated between the various authorities dealing with foreigners.[89] The head of the SSE, the Quaker Gilbert Lesage (1910–1989), used the organization to work secretly to rescue many Jews from deportation.[90]

Two letters and three postcards to Leonie record what were probably the last days of Hilde's life. They were written in Montmélian, and in the Vénissieux camp near Lyon. The first two communications are a letter on plain paper, dated August 23, 1942, and a postcard showing

86 Translated by the author, "Bericht Dr. Eugen Neter," pp. 315–316.
87 Serge Klarsfeld, *Vichy—Auschwitz: Die „Endlösung der Judenfrage" in Frankreich* (Darmstadt: WBG, 2007), p. 185.
88 Geoffrey P. Megargee, ed., *The United States Holocaust Memorial Museum Encyclopedia of Camps and Ghettoes 1933-1945* (Bloomington: Indiana University Press, 2018), vol. III, pp. 184–185.
89 Ibid., pp. 148–151, 145.
90 See https://www.yadvashem.org/righteous/stories/lesage.html (accessed June 1, 2020).

the village of Montmélian, stamped the same day. Both are written in ink. The letter, in German, is full of concern for the possible fate of Leonie, Myriam, and Francis. Hilde refers to the plan to round up the Jewish forced laborers with their families:

> … the local *prestataires'* wives have almost all had news from their husbands to hold themselves in readiness for evacuation, as these have had instructions from their commandants to hold themselves ready, and those who were detached have been sent back to their companies, and their wives' whereabouts have been noted. I am understandably very worried about you and expect, if possible, a reply from you as quickly as possible. On the other hand I also hear…that women with children under 5 (some even say under 8) may stay where they are, as may their husbands; that would be good for you.[91]

Hilde writes that the internees in Montmélian had no official information about what was planned for them: "Here we know nothing at all, those in charge wrap themselves, as always, in mysterious silence and will not be asked…As to what will happen to the rest of us, we still know absolutely nothing…"

Hilde was in touch with Otto through people in Switzerland:

> I have heard indirectly from Otto via St. Gallen, for some reason his acquaintances there didn't dare to send us his letter. So he was still in M[annheim] on 27.7, I don't know any more, apparently he didn't get my recent letters and is very worried. But he did hear from the children in January.[92]

The postcard is in French and looks to have been written in haste; it sounds like a final farewell:

> Dear Leonie, I hope you and yours are well, now and forever. That's how it is with me today—I kiss you and say farewell, to Francis and Tati [Myriam] too. Always, your sister Hilde.[93]

Hilde addressed the postcard to Leonie in Bellac, but it was redirected to Villard-de-lans near Grenoble. Hilde's aunt, Anna Koch, and her cousin,

---

91 Translated by the author, YVA, O.75/2804.
92 Ibid.
93 Ibid.

Juliette Azoulay (Anna's daughter),[94] were in hiding in Villard-de-lans. Myriam was able to confirm that Leonie took her to Villard-de-lans in 1942, to visit Anna and Juliette.[95] Perhaps Leonie had even hoped to be able to visit or meet Hilde: Villard-de-lans is 38 kilometers southwest of Grenoble; Montmélian is 50 kilometers north of the city.

Four days later Hilde wrote again to Leonie, this time in German, using a pencil on a blank postcard dated August 27, 1942. Together with thirty-four other Jewish internees at Montmélian, she had been arrested on August 26, and brought to Vénissieux,[96] a camp created by the French at the town's goods station. The camp was used in the transfer to Drancy of non-French Jews rounded up in southern and southeastern France; approximately 1,200 foreign Jews were arrested in the region of Lyon between August 20 and 26, 1942, and interned in Vénissieux. Hilde was not willing to give up all hope:

> Dear Léonie, if you were sent my farewell card please don't get upset yet, we were brought here *par erreur*, as has just become apparent. At any rate I still have a very small chance of staying in the country, the Service Social will do what it can for us. So we are staying here for the time being, it is not exactly pleasant but the food is good and the treatment also. It is near Lyon. But I will never forget yesterday! Anyway, I am not terribly hopeful but at least we can take a breather after the fright. If the long journey is in the cards, I will do my utmost to get to M[annheim] to Otto. Because that is not entirely impossible. So it is not yet a parting forever. Kisses, your Hilde.[97]

While Hilde's hope of being able to escape to Otto in Mannheim on the "long journey" was probably illusory, her belief that it might be possible to be spared from deportation to Drancy was not entirely unfounded. The camp at Vénissieux was in chaos, with orders and counter-orders coming in rapid succession. On the morning of August 29, members of several aid organizations managed by a mixture of daring and subterfuge

94 Anna Koch nee Katz (1869–after 1950) married Julius Koch's brother Heinrich (1867–?) in 1893; the couple lived in Paris; phone call with Myriam Nachsatz, April 1, 2020.
95 Phone call with Myriam Nachsatz, March 28, 2020.
96 Liste Nominative des Étrangers Israelites Partis le 26 Août 1942, *Archives Départementales de la Savoie*, 1362 W4.
97 Translated by the author, YVA, O.75/2804.

to negotiate with the Vichy authorities to have all the children but one, and some adults who they claimed were French citizens, removed from the lists for transport to Drancy. The 544 remaining Jews were taken at 5:00 A.M. to the nearby Saint-Priest railway station and put on a train to Drancy.[98]

Hilde was not among those removed from the list, and her last two surviving communications date from August 29, 1942. One, in pencil on a blank postcard (Fig. 13), is written in the knowledge that it may be her last:

> Dear Leonie, as I don't know if you will get the card I have just written, I am writing to you again; the time has come, let Frau M. Zucker, Basel, 18 Rufacherstrasse know, they are to see that Otto is informed by and by. I am calm, as you should be, you still have many responsibilities. All the best to your loved ones! And a thousand thanks to you for your love and goodness. There will probably be no news. Farewell, stay healthy and be happy! A thousand kisses, my thoughts will always be with you. Always, your Hilde. Please tell Jannchen, I cannot.[99]

Like her first card to Leonie from Montmélian, this was also redirected to Villard-de-lans.

The other message from the same day is a hastily scribbled letter on squared paper, also in pencil and written in *Baraque 9* at Vénissieux:

> Dear Leonie, I am writing down two addresses for you, by means of which we may be able to stay in touch in the future. 1. Mme M. Zucker, <u>Basel</u> Rufacherstrasse 18 and 2. Mme Marie B[*illegible*] <u>St. Gallen</u>, Zwinglistrasse 25. They did a good job of looking after my correspondence with Otto. I still don't know anything, but I have no illusions. When you write to the two addresses, mention my name. Farewell, keep well, give Francis my regards and give Tati [Myriam], whom I will never meet now, a big fat kiss from me. Write to Mme Foulbourgh, Montmelian (Savoie) Centre Montfort, to send you my suitcase and my pictures. Ask her to tell you what it will cost. She cannot speak German. There isn't much in it, but

---

98 Serge Klarsfeld, *Le calendrier de la persécution des Juifs de France, vol. 2: juillet 1940—août 1942* (Paris: Fayard, 2001), pp. 956–957; Eggers, *Unerwünschte Ausländer*, p. 471.

99 Translated by the author, YVA, O.75/2804.

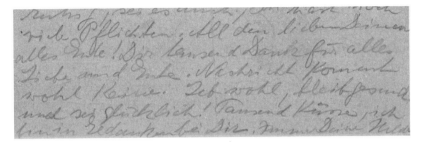

Fig. 13. Hilde's farewell to Leonie, August 29, 1943, YVA, O.75/2804.

perhaps you can make use of it. I am sorry that I cannot leave you more. When everything is decided I will try to write to you again. Farewell until then, 1000 kisses and thank you for everything, always. Your Hilde.[100]

The train arrived at Drancy on the morning of August 30, 1942. On September 2, 1942, Transport 27 left Drancy for Auschwitz with 1,000 Jews.[101] "Clara Hilde Neuberger, 17.7.96, Allemande" is named on the list of deportees.[102] The transport arrived in Auschwitz-Birkenau on September 6, 1942. One hundred and thirteen women and ten men were selected for labor in Auschwitz; all the other people on the transport were sent to the gas chamber immediately on arrival. At the age of forty-six, Hilde's chance of being selected for (momentary) survival was slim. Only thirty people from Transport 27 were still alive in 1945.[103]

Otto Neuberger was moved from the Jewish hospital on Collinistraße to the Jewish old people's home at B7, 3, on January 23, 1942. His third and last registration card records that he was "evacuated to the east" on August 21, 1942; this was a cynical euphemism for deportation, in this case to Theresienstadt (Transport XIII/1 1067). He died there on March 3, 1943, aged fifty-six.[104]

Francis Ehrmann served his time as a *prestataire* on a farm. Leonie and Myriam remained in the village of Bellac, and Myriam believes her

100 Ibid.

101 Klarsfeld, *Le calendrier de la persécution,* pp. 956–957.

102 Copy in the United States Holocaust Memorial Museum (UHSMM); http://ressources.memorialdelashoah.org/rechav_pers.php (accessed March 31, 2020).

103 Klarsfeld, *Le calendrier de la persécution,* pp. 1031–1032.

104 See https://www.holocaust.cz/databaze-dokumentu/dokument/96430-neuberger-otto-oznameni-o-umrti-ghetto-terezin/ (last accessed February 11, 2020).

father was deployed nearby. A local official, described by Myriam as "not a very nice person, but who did a good thing," warned those hiding in the village—Jews and refugees from Alsace and Lorraine who were avoiding conscription into the Wehrmacht—when the Germans were coming. In this way they escaped capture in the razzias carried out in the Vichy Zone in 1942. Leonie described the period of the razzias in her application for reparations:

> In August 1942, when the razzias began, I was forced to leave my room [in Bellac] and to go into hiding. I often wandered around for a long time, looking for a barn where I could stay for a time. Sometimes a farmer let me and my child sleep in a cow shed and gave me something to eat. The conditions were extremely primitive…I lived in this way like a wild hunted animal, always in the same area near BELLAC, until liberation in August 1944. And I also had terrible fears for my husband, who…lived in continual

Fig. 14. Hilde Neuberger Koch (1896–1943), *Shepherd playing the flute*, Gurs Camp, 1941. Watercolor and ink on paper, 22 x 26.7 cm.
Photo © Collection of the Yad Vashem Art Museum, Jerusalem (#19238/03). Gift of Myriam Nachsatz, Holon.

danger of deportation. I only heard from him occasionally, as he didn't know where I was.[105]

Workers from the Luxour tannery hid the Ehrmanns' papers and furniture and returned everything to them after the war. Leonie was able to retrieve Hilde's pictures from Mme. Foulbourgh in Montmélian. Together with her Chanukah gift to her niece Myriam, her three published works, her slim correspondence, and a handful of family photographs, these are all that remain to show that she once lived.

Conclusion

Recent Holocaust research has increasingly addressed the question of passivity versus agency in the attitudes and behavior of Jews under the Nazi regime. The fact that Hilde was Jewish made persecution inevitable for as long as she remained in Germany. Hilde and her husband, Otto Neuberger, had attempted to shape their own future by planning to emigrate to Palestine with Otto's children, but the stroke that Otto suffered robbed both Otto and Hilde of this redemption. Hilde's deportation, first to Gurs and then to Auschwitz, is on the face of it a fate that left little room for maneuver. But Hilde used her aloneness in Gurs to reassert her identity as an artist or *dessinatrice.* If we are to interpret this as an act of self-assertion, it is a remarkable gesture under extraordinary circumstances. The serene picture book that Hilde Koch created in the camp at Gurs for her niece Myriam for Chanukah in 1941, gives us a glimpse of a mindset that may have been part of a strategy for survival. Hilde's final letters to her sister depict a chaotic situation in which many things appeared possible. She was unwilling to abandon hope—even for a reprieve from the final deportation and the "long journey" (to Auschwitz), and perhaps ultimate survival. One of her chief concerns in this extreme situation was the preservation of "my pictures," which, again, required her own express agency.

This evidence of agency and persistent hope contrasts strangely with the effacement of Hilde Koch's professional identity both in family memory and in the public view; she left the commercial artists' professional group *Bund Deutscher Gebrauchsgraphiker* (BDG) around 1925, and no published work of hers has been found after that time. The

---

105   Translated by the author, reparation file for Leonie Ehrmann, HLA, Abt. 518, No.
        10631, pp. 6–7.

disparity between Hilde's short period of public visibility as a professional woman and her younger sister Leonie's career, maintained for sixteen years before she married in 1934, is intriguing. Leonie never told her daughter Myriam that Hilde had published any of her work; we may never know if Hilde had possibly kept this fact a secret from her family.

This study demonstrates how rich and even surprising results can be when the intensive methods of microhistory are applied to biographical research, using international sources in several languages, and exploiting the potential of digital and online resources. Women artists of the past were largely ignored until recent decades, and very few Jewish women illustrators of children's books in Weimar Germany are known of today. This fragmentary biography retrieves the story of a forgotten illustrator, whose *oeuvre* has turned out to be more diverse than her three surviving publications suggest, and who, at least for a few years, moved in an illustrious professional circle. *Les Animaux* has also added another piece to the catalog of art produced in Gurs. Its light-filled scenes are unique among the grim realism and biting satire of previously known works from that camp.

Raging Hasidic Sermons: R. Kalonymus Kalman Shapira's Halting Retreat from Theodicy

James A. Diamond

R. Kalonymus Kalman Shapira was a Hasidic leader known as the Piaseczner *Rebbe*. In this capacity he delivered sermons to his community from the beginning of the war in the autumn of 1939, and subsequently during his confinement in the Warsaw ghetto, until the summer of 1942. Despite the horrific conditions and his personal loss, he continued to transcribe, edit, and revise his talks, identifying them collectively for posterity as *Sermons from the Years of Rage*.[1] They were ultimately buried with other of his writings in the "Oyneg Shabbes" Archives that were retrieved after the end of the war.[2] The sermons constitute a wholly singular testament to a theological, philosophical, and existential struggle to wrest meaning out of evil of such magnitude as to defy all reason and to destroy all meaning in the phenomenal world. Eliezer Schweid considered the sermons incomparably unique in that they document a theological struggle contemporaneous with the oppressive conditions of the ghetto, "both as a witness to and victim of all that transpired there."[3] Another assessment also considers them utterly incomparable, since the "*Esh Kodesh* is not a religious work written about how a community may retrospectively justify catastrophe, it is written precisely within the period of collective trauma. No comparable document from the

---

1 Though they were first published in Israel under the title, *The Holy Fire* (*Esh Kodesh*), for scholarly use it is imperative to now reference Daniel Reiser's critical edition, *R. Kalonymus Kalman Shapira, Sermons from the Years of Rage*, 2 vols. (Jerusalem: Yad Vashem, 2017). All references to this work will be to volume 1, cited as *Sermons*.

2 For a fascinating and comprehensive account of these archives, see Samuel Kassow, *Who Will Write Our History? Rediscovering a Hidden Archive from the Warsaw Ghetto* (Bloomington: Indiana University Press, 2007).

3 Eliezer Schweid's chapter, "Hasneh Bo'er Ba'esh-Vehasneh Einenu Ukal?" (Hebrew), in his *Bein Hurban LiYeshua* (Tel Aviv: Hakibbutz Hameuchad, 1994), pp. 105–154, cited at pp. 105, 126.

Holocaust has yet been discovered, and thus *Esh Kodesh* remains sui generis."[4]

Most Orthodox responses to the Holocaust fall into the category of some form of reasoned argument, generally characterized as theodicy, or the age-old enterprise of justifying God's seemingly unjust governance of the world. That often entailed viewing the Holocaust as punishment "for our sins," though the specific sin varied.[5] This aspect of theology persists vigorously up to the present day.[6] However, though R. Shapira may resort periodically to what can be called theodicy, this is not what defines his sermons. R. Shapira's collection of rabbinic homilies constitutes an extremely rare extant testimony, if not a singular one, of an extended existential struggle, both in a personal capacity and as a communal leader, to wrest spiritual meaning out of steadily eroding circumstances that afforded not a glimmer of salvific hope.

No other Orthodox response compares to these sermons in their documentation of an extended theological struggle experienced contemporaneously with ongoing ghetto life and oppression until its end.[7] The imminent total physical destruction of an entire community, unprecedented in the *longue durée* of Jewish suffering and persecution, posed an acutely novel crisis for the spiritual leader. By late summer of 1941, for example, the *Rebbe* voiced the unimaginable prospect of devastation so extensive that "even if God has compassion and saves

---

4   Henry Abramson, "The Esh Kodesh of Rabbi Kalonimus Kalmish Shapiro: A Hasidic Treatise on Communal Trauma from the Holocaust," *Transcultural Psychiatry*, 37:3 (2000), pp. 321–335, cited at p. 323.

5   For a recent concise overview of various practical and theological Hasidic responses to the Holocaust, including that of R. Shapira, see the chapter "Khurban: Hasidism and the Holocaust," in David Biale et al., eds., *Hasidism: A New History* (Princeton: Princeton University Press, 2018) pp. 652–671. See also Pesach Schindler, *Hasidic Responses to the Holocaust in the Light of Hasidic Thought* (Hoboken: Ktav, 1990).

6   For example, Rabbi Elazar Menachem Schach (d. 2001), the most powerful and revered leader of the non-Hasidic (Lithuanian) community in Israel in the twentieth century, was a leading exponent of this theodicy into the 1990s; the sin in this connection was Zionism. Typical is his statement: "If we refuse to accept it as a punishment, it is as if we do not believe in the Holy One Blessed be He, God forbid." See Dina Porat, "'Amalek's Accomplices' Blaming Zionism for the Holocaust: Anti-Zionist Ultra-Orthodoxy in Israel during the 1980s," *Journal of Contemporary History*, 27:4 (1992), pp. 695–729, cited at p. 711.

7   As Daniel Reiser notes in "Esh Kodesh: A New Evaluation in Light of a Philological Examination of the Manuscript," *Yad Vashem Studies*, 44:1 (2016), pp. 65–97, "The uniqueness of this collection of sermons is its focus, from beginning to end, on the theology of suffering from the author's personal experience," cited at p. 68.

us there won't be anyone to fill the classrooms, there won't be enough students for whom to build institutions, and the community of the devout will be negligible."[8] In other words, there will no longer be future generations to whom Jewish traditions and thought can be passed on, threatening an end to the chain of transmission, the *mesorah*, which, for the *Rebbe*, ensures Jewish survival in body and soul.[9]

The sermons address a rapidly dying community that was becoming increasingly crushed in both body and mind; they abruptly end just prior to the *Grossaktion* (great deportations) of the ghetto population to the killing centers of the concentration camps in July 1942. As Daniel Reiser's new edition clearly evidences, although each sermon correlates to a certain date and evolving historical setting within the ghetto, R. Shapira's continuous revisions to the sermons complicate charting a clear-cut historical progression in his thought.[10]

Since these sermons emerge from profound physical, emotional, spiritual, and intellectual confoundedness with incrementally incomprehensible and unprecedented suffering in real time, they cannot be expected to develop the rigorous consistency of a philosophical or even a theological treatise. Martha Nussbaum's analogy between

8   *Sermons*, p. 210. Unfortunately, statistics compiled by the "Oyneg Shabbes" group itself in the ghetto a year after the great deportations starkly confirmed R. Shapira's prediction. As Kassow, p. 308, relates, in November 1942, 99.1 percent of children between the ages of newborn and nine were deported; this was down from 51,458 before the deportation to 498 following it. An entire generation of future students had indeed been murdered. For the importance of education even for a dying community, across the spectrum of Jewish life and belief, see the last essays of the leader of the "Oyneg Shabbes" group, Emmanuel Ringelblum, *Katavim achronim: Yachasei Polanim-Yehudim: Yanuar 1943 – April 1944* (Hebrew) (Jerusalem: Yad Vashem and the Ghetto Fighters' House, 1994), pp. 133–147. See also Dalia Ofer, "The Education of Jewish Children in Warsaw During the Nazi Occupation," in J.K. Roth et al., eds., *Remembering for the Future* (London: Palgrave Macmillan, 2001), pp. 289–301.

9   See *Sermons*, p. 302, where he asserts children are the guarantors of Jewish perpetuity. Elsewhere R. Shapira graphically expresses the idea that Jewish existence is contingent on educating the next generation, stating that failure to fulfill this sacred obligation by the elders will attract Divine condemnation, which will grievingly howl, "where are my children…where are the children of Abraham, Isaac, and Jacob"; *Hovat Hatalmidim [The Students' Obligation]* (Hebrew) (reprinted from first Warsaw edition, 1932 [Jerusalem: Gross Bros., 1970]), p. 8. Unless otherwise noted the English translations from Hebrew texts are my own.

10   See Reiser's introduction to *Sermons*, pp. 70–72. R. Shapira often addresses dire conditions in the ghetto that correlate to other dated eyewitness accounts, such as Chaim Kaplan's diary, *Scroll of Agony: The Warsaw Diary of Chaim A. Kaplan* (Bloomington: Indiana University Press, 1999).

much of ancient philosophy and the medical arts as conducting "therapeutic arguments" to address diseases of the soul can be applied to R. Shapira's sermons as well.[11] If, as she asserts, "the central motivation for philosophizing is the urgency of human suffering," then surely the sermons share that precise urgency. They present "arguments" whose evaluation, like those ancient schools of philosophy, "concerns itself not only with logical form and the truth of premises, but also with the argument's suitability for the specific maladies of its addressees."[12]

Thus, I follow Reiser's lead, who correctly classifies the sermons as "phenomenological," veering us away from "searching for a logical and clear progression" in its struggle with the meaning of suffering.[13] Rather than chart some steadily evolving theology, which the sermons really defy, in this article I note certain critical junctures along with new explications that both build upon and diverge from previous studies. As such I present a programmatic reading of the sermons' haltingly unprogrammatic, improvised widening of the door to alternatives that deviate from traditional theodicies, or from that enterprise of justifying God in the face of innocent suffering.[14] Moreover, although I do refer to historical dates periodically, my analysis intentionally refrains from correlating the sermons to specific events in the ghetto. As pertains to all Hasidic homilies, the very act of transcription surely transformed the original oral form of which no record remains. Thus, more importantly for his posthumous readers, R. Shapira envisioned a record of his own internal struggles and engagement "in a kind of reflective theological discourse rather than seeking to record history."[15] Though later there might be momentary withdrawals, relapses, or regressions, these critical

---

11 Martha Nussbaum, *The Therapy of Desire: Theory and Practice in Hellenistic Ethics* (Princeton: Princeton University Press, 1994).

12 Ibid., p. 15.

13 Introduction to *Sermons*, p. 60; and Daniel Reiser, "*Esh Kodesh*: A New Evaluation in Light of a Philological Examination of the Manuscript," supra note 7, especially pp. 93–97.

14 Erin Leib follows a similar approach in her doctoral dissertation, "God in the Years of Fury: Theodicy and Anti-Theodicy in the Holocaust Writings of Rabbi Kalonymus Kalman Shapira" (Chicago: University of Chicago, 2014). However, I trace a very different route, and when the sermons we cite converge, I diverge in their analysis and implications.

15 See Ariel Even Mayse's review of "*Torah from the Years of Wrath 1939–1943: The Historical Context of the Aish Kodesh* by Henry Abramson" *Studies in Judaism, Humanities, and the Social Sciences*, 2:1 (2018) pp. 124–130, on p.128.

junctures remain embedded in R. Shapira's consciousness, and from which, once contemplated, there is no turning back.

Reorienting the *Akedah* Toward Anti-Theodicy: First Juncture

One of the earliest sermons, in the autumn of 1939, born of extreme personal crisis, is one such juncture that opens the door to abandoning old theologies that justified God's countenance—or worse, imposition—of unwarranted suffering. The first sermon delivered after the death of the *Rebbe*'s only son during the German bombing of Warsaw relates to the biblical portion that begins with the death of Sarah. Its narrative sequence, which immediately follows the passage of the binding of Isaac (*Akedah*), spurred rabbinic interpretation to link the two events, depicting the drama of the *Akedah* as *causing* Sarah's death by virtue of her hearing the news that her son was about to be slaughtered.[16] R. Shapira prefaces his own version of that causal chain by drawing on Hasidic theology, which conceived suffering as remedial, as purging one's sins and strengthening the covenant between the sinner and God. However, citing his great-great-grandfather, a seminal Hasidic thinker, he draws an analogy between suffering and salt, which, while effective as a preservative of meat, must be finely measured or it could have the opposite corrosive effect. Likewise, suffering needs to be balanced with compassion in order to prevent it becoming purely destructive.

R. Shapira then builds on that idea and extends the traditional link between Sarah's death and what she had thought was the death of her son, or heart failure due to heartbreak, in a theologically startling direction. Sarah, he says, in fact intentionally surrendered her life in order to teach God the limits of corrective suffering, beyond which the torment simply becomes ruinous:

> Sarah our matriarch who took the *Akedah* so to heart to the point that her soul departed, **acted for the benefit of Israel, in order to demonstrate to God** [emphasis added, J.A.D.] the impossibility of tolerating excessive suffering, and should the person survive that

16 See Rashi on Genesis 23:2, which he cites, and Genesis *Rabbah*, chapter 58, section 5.

suffering by Divine mercy, nevertheless his strength, his mind, and his spirit has been broken and lost.[17]

That he considered Sarah to have committed suicide is clear from his exoneration of Sarah from what would normally be viewed as a transgressive act, for "since she acted for the benefit of Israel," she did not sin against those years she would have lived had she not cut her life short.[18]

I have discussed this theologically extraordinary exegesis elsewhere,[19] but critical for my analysis here is that R. Shapira at this early juncture begins to seriously challenge traditional reconciliations between God's goodness and innocent suffering. God has some theoretical notion of suffering as spiritually therapeutic, which led to administering it formulaically without regard to its dosage or the patient's tolerance. R. Shapira challenges God to set aside the Divine textbook, empirically monitor the side effects of his providential treatment plan, and change course accordingly. In this sense this sermon, as others we will mention, consists of what Nehemia Polen characterizes as an "activist, interventionist mode of interpretation," whose very "articulation will lead to the desired result."[20] It is a desperate appeal to rouse a seemingly oblivious God to live up both to His specific biblical promise as a guardian of Israel, and to His universal role as Creator and architect of historical events.[21] Though R. Shapira may retreat intermittently from

---

17 *Sermons*, p. 91.

18 There is a rabbinic source that attributes the reason for Abraham withholding the *Akedah* trial from Sarah to his fear that she might in fact commit suicide, but I know of no other source that makes R. Shapira's claim that Sarah actually went through with it. See *Midrash Tanhuma*, Vayera 22; *Yalkut Shimoni* 98. Don Seeman hesitates to characterize Sarah's death here as a suicide, but, rather, she "allowed" herself to die from grief. I don't believe this is a distinction with a difference. See Don Seeman, "Ritual Efficacy, Hasidic Mysticism and 'Useless Suffering' in the Warsaw Ghetto," *Harvard Theological Review*, 101:3–4 (2008), pp. 465–505, especially pp. 483–487.

19 See James A. Diamond, "The Warsaw Ghetto Rebbe: Diverting God's Gaze from a Utopian End to an Anguished Now," *Modern Judaism*, 30:3 (2010), pp. 299–331, and especially pp. 311–312.

20 See Nehemia Polen, "Hasidic Derashah as Illuminated Exegesis," in Michael Zank and Ingrid Anderson, eds., *The Value of the Particular: Lessons from Judaism and the Modern Jewish Experience: Festschrift for Steven T. Katz on the Occasion of His Seventieth Birthday* (Leiden: Brill, 2015), pp. 55–70, especially p. 56.

21 For a survey of the history of theological argument with and protest of God, see Anson Laytner, *Arguing With God: A Jewish Tradition* (Northvale: Jason Aaronson, 1990); for its origins in classical rabbinic literature, see Dov Weiss,

this theological protest, once he opened the door it remained latent in his thought until, as I will show, it emerges in its full-blown ramifications at the final juncture of the sermons.

Guiding Beyond the Intellect: Second Juncture

A sermon delivered on July 14, 1940, a few months prior to the official establishment of the ghetto in October, is a second juncture. It lays further foundations for constructing a theological edifice of overcoming the mind that can accommodate unparalleled suffering. R. Shapira would turn mind-numbing suffering into an "advantage" by considering it a gateway toward God's presence. Ego impedes the experience of Divine presence.[22] Consciousness of autonomy over one's thoughts constitutes an impediment to God's ingress into the human realm. This draws on a crux of Hasidic worship on which R. Shapira previously instructed his students in his pedagogical work, advising, "it is difficult for us to understand spiritual matters with our intellect for when we probe with our egos (*anokhiyut*) the result is 'I probe,' that is 'I' and my material ego."[23] Consciousness of thought as self-generated erects the material self as an obstacle to truly assimilating the spiritual. Thus, the disintegration of intellect overcomes an essential barrier between human beings and God.[24] Losing an independent grip on one's mind allows the Divine mind to suffuse the vacuum left behind.[25]

Pious Irreverence: Confronting God in Rabbinic Judaism (Philadelphia: University of Pennsylvania Press, 2017).

22 See, for example, Melila Hellner-Eshed, "Prayer from the Depths," in Lawrence Fine, Eitan P. Fishbane, and Or N. Rose, eds. *Jewish Mysticism and the Spiritual Life: Classical Texts, Contemporary Reflections* (Woodstock: Jewish Lights, 2011), pp. 137–144; on p. 140, the author analyzes a pertinent passage that calls for expanding the "contracted ego of the suffering supplicant" to access the "depths of divinity as oneness existing beyond language, beyond the discursive intellect, beyond time, and beyond all personal and national narratives."

23 *The Students' Obligation*, p. 94.

24 In *Avot* 2:4 there is a reflection of the first stirrings of this idea: "Do His will as though it were your will, so that He will do your will as though it were His. Annihilate your will in the face of His will, so that He may annihilate the will of others for the sake of your will."

25 This notion is a consequence of an essential principle in Hasidic theology, which views the material world as a veil for what is its essential divinity. See Rachel Elior, "Bein Tehiyah Ruhanit Litemurah Hevratit Bereishit Hahasidut" (Hebrew), in Moshe Hallamish, ed., *Alei Shefer: Studies in the Literature of Jewish Thought Presented to*

This theology traces its roots to medieval notions of "cleaving" (*devekut*), or union with God, and R. Shapira himself ironically co-opts Maimonides' rationalist Aristotelian epistemology in support of it.[26] Its Hasidic iteration again traces its way back to Dov Baer of Mezhirech's notion of mystical annihilation, concisely articulated by Joseph Weiss:

> As the contemplative Hasid annihilates himself, viz., his individual consciousness, the vacuum thus created within his soul is immediately filled by a new content. His soul is invaded by God, viz., the Divine *Shekhinah* [presence]…[27]

However, while the tools of self-annihilation consisted previously of devotional exercises, such as contemplation, prayer, physical postures, and other ascetic practices, R. Shapira adds the radically new means of suffering itself to the list in order to meet the radical newness of the moment.[28]

Rabbi Dr. Alexander Safran (Ramat Gan: Bar Ilan University Press, 1990), pp. 29–40, especially pp. 35–36.

26 For more on this notion, see my chapter, "Maimonides and Rabbi Kalonymus Kalman Shapira: Abandoning Reason in the Warsaw Ghetto," in James A. Diamond and Menachem Kellner, *Reinventing Maimonides in Contemporary Jewish Thought* (London: Littman Library of Jewish Civilization, 2019); and my chapter, "Raging Against Reason: Overcoming *Sekhel* in R. Shapira's Thought," in Don Seeman, Daniel Reiser, and Ariel Evan Mayse, eds., *Hasidism, Suffering and Renewal: The Pre-war and Holocaust Legacy of R. Kalonymus Kalman Shapira* (Albany: SUNY Press, forthcoming), pp. 263–298; as well as Moshe Idel, *Kabbalah: New Perspectives* (New Haven: Yale University Press, 1988), pp. 46–47.

27 See Joseph Weiss's chapter, "R. Abraham Kalisker's Concept of Communion with God and Man," in David Goldstein, ed., *Studies in Eastern European Jewish Mysticism* (Oxford: Oxford University Press, 1985), pp. 155–169, especially p. 156. See also, in the same volume, Weiss, "Contemplation as Self-Abandonment in the Writings of Hayyim Haika of Amdura," pp. 142–154.

28 Nehemiah Polen, in his pioneering study of the sermons, already briefly noted this aspect of madness as setting "the stage for a profound and absolute mystical surrender." See Nehemiah Polen, *The Holy Fire: The Teachings of Rabbi Kalonymus Kalman Shapira* (Lanham: Rowman & Littlefield, 2004), p. 138. However, Polen attributes this "surrender" to circumstances so extreme as to defy human comprehension, and thus it is the only means of dealing with "the way things are supposed to be" because God ordained them. See ibid., citing from a sermon delivered on March 7, 1942; *Sermons*, p. 278. Shaul Magid responds, "But from the perspective of paradigmatic thinking, or covenantal theology, if something is unparalleled that is precisely *not* the way it is supposed to be." See his chapter, "Covenantal Rupture and Broken Faith in R. Kalonymus Kalman Shapira's *Eish Kodesh*," in his collection, *Piety and Rebellion: Essays in Hasidism* (Brighton: Academic Studies Press, 2019), pp. 237–262, and especially p. 262.

R. Shapira builds on this theology and seizes on the verses that recount Moses' request of God to designate his successor, "who shall go out before them and come in before them, and who shall take them out and bring them in so that the Lord's community may not be like sheep that have no shepherd" (Numbers 27:17).[29]

Physically vanquished, the Hasidic *Rebbe* replaced the martial prowess demanded of Israel's desert leader with the spiritual ones that were the tools of his trade.[30] Utilizing his exegetical ingenuity in good rabbinic form, he links the term "before them" (*lifneihem*) with its appearance elsewhere, which introduces a set of laws as "the rules you shall set before them (*lifneihem*)" (Exodus 21:1). R. Shapira identifies the intellect as the term's referent, since laws must be understood in order to be followed. In other words, *before them* signals the discerning mind to which the laws are to be addressed. Since normal reasoning falls short of predicting the future, it is the *Rebbe*'s role to lead his community beyond what the mind can handle when it has reached its limits.

Thus, the verse in Numbers now depicts the leader as empowered with the ability to "take them out," that is take them out of their intellectual mode and "bring them in," to instruct them when and how they are permitted to employ their intellects.[31] Such a spiritually enabled leader is what the circumstances called for so that his community would not succumb to its anguish and despair, or, in the words of the verse, remain like sheep deprived of their shepherd. The dying community must look to their *Rebbe*/shepherd for guidance, but, in this case, the prospects of physical salvation or liberation were remote, and the historical biblical leaders, like Moses and Joshua, no longer presented realistic models. Even more dire and incomprehensible in the Hasidic worldview, the traditional means of spiritual advancement were becoming increasingly untenable, and so the *Rebbe*'s guidance aimed toward eking some virtue out of all that remained from that very incomprehensibility.

---

29 *Sermons*, pp. 146–148.
30 "Go out and come in before them" is a Biblical phrase that connotes military leadership; see, for example, Joshua 14:11; Samuel I 18:13, 29:6.
31 *Sermons*, p. 148.

Swerving from the *Tzaddik*'s Theurgy to the People's Song: Third Juncture

Another critical juncture in terms of R. Shapira's understanding of his own leadership role redirects it from guiding the people, "taking them out and bringing them in," to guiding God Himself. At the end of January 1942, the conditions in the ghetto had so deteriorated that a traditional mode of solace in the face of suffering was no longer viable. In the past suffering could be eased by "fortifying and cheering oneself up with the notion that things God forbid could be even worse than they are." However, "when suffering has intensified to the point where the person collapses and is totally shattered and there remains nothing left of his personhood to fortify then it is difficult to console himself with such thoughts."[32]

Clearly alluding to his own circumstances, R. Shapira creatively reread a problematic verse regarding Moses' leadership at the beginning of his mission to liberate the Israelites from Egyptian slavery. The Israelites initially "refused to listen to Moses due to their shortness of breath and crushing labor" (Exodus 6:9). As a result, "God spoke to Moses and Aaron and commanded them to the Israelites and to Pharaoh to release the Israelites from the land of Egypt" (6:13). Syntactical difficulties in reading this verse always attracted much commentary; most importantly was the question of the grouping of the Israelites and Pharaoh together as addressees of a common instruction from Moses "to release the Israelites." A traditional interpretation resolves the problem by reading the preposition "to" in the sense of "regarding." In other words, Moses and Aaron are instructed about the manner of their leadership vis-à-vis the Israelites that would lead to their liberation: "to lead them with gentleness and be patient with them."[33]

R. Shapira then applied his rabbinic/Hasidic acumen in a way that exudes the anguish he experienced personally and which was compounded by the suffering absorbed from his community. He read what are surely those conditions into this exegetical twist, shifting what is patently God's directive to Moses on how to guide the people into the reverse direction: "'To lead them gently' means that the leaders of

---

32 Ibid., p. 261.
33 For example, see Exodus *Rabbah* 7:3 and Rashi on this verse.

Israel must cause the upper realm to conduct itself with Israel out of gentleness and not with suffering."[34]

This Mosaic paradigm for leadership in extreme situations establishes the precedent that precipitously declining fortunes necessitate a different method of petitioning God for relief; from prayer and pleading to *demanding*: "When catastrophe is imminent and there is no time to spend in prayer then there must be action by way of fiat, 'the *tzaddik* decrees and God carries it out.'"[35]

This is the single instance in the sermons in which R. Shapira resorts to a power often ascribed in Hasidic theology to the *Rebbe*, or the *tzaddik*, which enables him to pull rank, so to speak, over God Himself.[36] All the more striking is its contrast with his generally muted treatment of the *tzaddik* in his overall written *oeuvre*, rarely mentioning the term, in contradistinction to most other Hasidic thought, especially in those of his grandfather and great-grandfather.[37] His exegesis actually instructs him to utilize a coercive rather than a supplicatory strategy, forcing God to radically transform His current governance manifest in the lived experience of His people from harshness to compassion, from punishing misery to comforting relief. R. Shapira employed exegesis itself as a theurgic act in the mode of an earlier Hasidic master, R. Levi Isaac of Berdichev (d. 1809), who extended the *tzaddik*'s power over God to the very act of interpreting sacred text. As noted by Arthur Green with respect to R. Levi Isaac, "As the Torah mirrors the changing cosmic situation, the cosmos itself is moved by the will of the *tzadiqim* as they interpret Torah."[38]

---

34 *Sermons*, p. 262
35 Ibid., p. 262, citing a rabbinic source that can be found in various formulations in Babylonian Talmud *Ta'anit* 23a; *Shabbat* 59b; *Moed Qatan* 16b; *Sotah* 12a; *Ketubot* 103b; *Zohar* 3:15a.
36 See, for example, Joseph Weiss, "The Saddik-Altering the Divine Will," in his *Studies in Eastern European Jewish Mysticism*, pp. 183–194; and Arthur Green's chapter, "Around the Maggid's Table: Tsaddik, Leadership, and Popularization in the Circle of Dov Baer of Miedzyrzecz," in his *The Heart of the Matter: Studies in Jewish Mysticism and Theology* (Philadelphia: Jewish Publication Society, 2015), pp. 119–166, especially pp. 130–136.
37 See Ron Wacks, *Lahevet Esh Kodesh: She'arim Letorato Shel Ha'Admor MiPiasts'enah*, (Hebrew) (Alon Shevut: Tevunot, 2010), p. 74.
38 See Or N. Rose's discussion in "Protest or Discernment? Divine Limitation and Mystical Activism in the Qedushat Levi," in Ariel Even Mayse and Arthur Green, eds., *Be-Ron Yahad: Studies in Jewish Thought and Theology* (Boston: Academic Studies Press, 2019), pp. 155–176, especially pp. 162–164.

Yet this same sermon abruptly swerves from the *tzaddik*'s theurgic powers to conclude more consistently with R. Shapira's overall conception of the *Rebbe* as a Socratic guide who draws out of his disciples their own potential to achieve spiritual perfection.[39] The *tzaddik*'s ability to overrule God's edicts is only a means to a latter end of raising the people to new spiritual heights that enables them to overcome their pain. Approaching God by way of demand rather than plea rouses the people to the potency of song and "to prepare themselves for the song and the melody when God will redeem them."[40]

The sermon continues with the biblical Egyptian paradigm, reading the preface to the song sung by the people at the splitting of the Red Sea as an enabling moment for all future generations to turn to song in the face of catastrophe. A textual "redundancy" provides the opportunity for the innocent, seemingly superfluous, term "saying" at the end of "Then Moses and the Israelites sang this song to the Lord, and they said, saying" (Exodus 15:1) causatively for all of future Jewish history: "Then they will sing [*yashir*], by way of their thoughts, Moses and the Israelites, who effected all future generations saying, that it will be said from the heart and the soul."[41]

In other words, conceiving of Moses and the Israelites as the archetype for all Jewish leaders and their followers, the *tzaddik*'s efforts must be consummated by the people's own spiritual practices, in this case by the use of song, in order to be effective.

There is nothing unusual in and of itself with the promotion of music for the fulfillment of sacred living in the writings of a Hasidic master, since Hasidism valued music as a crucial means for cultivating various dimensions of spiritual life.[42] However, it is critical to appreciate

---

39 See Isaac Hershkowitz, *Rabbi Kalonymus Kalmish Shapira, The Piasechner Rebbe: His Holocaust and Pre-Holocaust Thought, Continuity or Discontinuity?* (Hebrew) (MA Thesis, Bar Ilan University, Ramat Gan, 2005), pp. 16, 43, 128.

40 *Sermons*, p. 262

41 Ibid.

42 Moshe Idel, "Haperush Hamagi Vehate'urgi Shel Hamusikah Betekstim Yehudim Metekufat Harenasans Ve'ad Hahasidut," (Hebrew), *Yuval*, 4 (1982). For a concise overview of conceptions of music evolving in Jewish thought from the Biblical period to Hasidism, see Daniel Reiser, *Imagery Techniques in Modern Jewish Mysticism* (Berlin and Boston: De Gruyter, 2018), pp. 126–131. See also Dov Schwartz, *Kinor Nishmati: Hamusikah Bahagut Hayehudit* (Hebrew) (Ramat Gan: Bar Ilan University Press, 2013), and the bibliography he compiled on the role of music in Hasidism, pp. 144–151.

the spiritual role of music in R. Shapira's thought, as expressed elsewhere in his *oeuvre*, in order to understand its appearance at this specific juncture of the wartime sermons. Particularly important is the instrumentality of music toward achieving "nullification of self" and "cleaving one's soul to the supernal realms."[43] Others have analyzed the importance of music in R. Shapira's corpus, but here I focus on a pivotal dimension that they stress, which, in Nehemia Polen's words, "It is not just that *niggun* [melody] exerts power over our soul, but that *niggun* is the propulsive vehicle depositing the soul before God—God as conceived quite personally, even anthropomorphically."[44]

The unbearable suffering enveloping R. Shapira and his followers at the beginning of 1942 posed the clarion call for the type of turn to music that the *Rebbe* called for in his other works.[45] It penetrates so deeply as to evoke the self-generated song from the innermost recesses of being, as he anticipated at the end of this sermon in the ghetto. As he states in his prewar treatise,

> Turn your face to the wall, or just close your eyes and reflect again that you stand before the Throne of Glory. You have come with shattered heart to pour out your soul to God in song, the melody that emerges now from the deep recesses of your heart. You will spontaneously sense that your soul emerges with exultation. At first you were singing to your soul, to rouse it from its sleep. But slowly, slowly you feel that your soul has begun to sing on its own.[46]

43 See Aaron Wertheim, *Law and Custom in Hasidism* (Hoboken: Ktav, 1992), pp. 158–162.

44 Nehemia Polen, "Niggun as Spiritual Practice, with Special Focus on the Writings of Rabbi Kalonymos Shapiro, the Rebbe of Piaseczna," in Shlomo Zuckier, ed., *The Contemporary Uses of Hasidism* (New York: Yeshiva University Press, 2020), pp. 261–282, especially p. 270. See also the chapter on "Music and Dance," in Zvi Leshem, *Bein Meshihiyut Lenevuah: Hehasidut Al Pi Ha'admor MiPiaseczno* (Hebrew) (PhD diss., Bar-Ilan University, 2007), pp. 188–294.

45 See, for example, Leshem's citations from R. Shapira's *Bnei Mahshavah Tovah* and *Hakhsharat Avrekhim* (Hebrew) in Leshem, "Between Messianism and Prophecy," p. 190n646.

46 Cited by Polen, "Niggun as Spiritual Practice," p. 269, from *Hakhsharat Avreikhim*, 61b, as translated by Polen. For an eyewitness account of R. Shapira's musical celebration during a festival in June 1940, see Shimon Huberband, *Kiddush Hashem: Jewish Religious and Cultural Life in Poland During the Holocaust* (New York: Ktav, 1987), p. 64.

The soul could not be more shattered than it was at that time in the ghetto.

It is critical to bear in mind that this ghetto sermon was originally delivered at the end of January 1942, or in the middle of the Hebrew year 5702, the time R. Shapira admitted in a retraction he previously noted that the Jews had never experienced such consummate destruction in their history. R. Shapira graphically describes the dire state of existence after the middle of 5702, in another similar note appended in 1943, to a sermon he originally delivered in August 1941 (in the Hebrew year 5701). In that original sermon he still expressed hope of overcoming the crisis and insisted on persisting with the study of Torah and worship despite the suffering in order to "draw down physical and spiritual salvation and a total redemption for Israel."[47] However, the later note admits that his earlier hope was sustained by the still viable ability to "worry about those remaining, to weep over the future and how schools and *yeshivot* would be rebuilt, even to rebuke and to strengthen those still alive to pursue Torah and worship."[48]

That note laments a scene of devastation that had so worsened, to the point that, "there are no longer any words left that could lament over our suffering, there is no longer anyone to reproach, and no heart to awaken to Torah and worship."[49] It is difficult to find, if at all, a comparable expression of such hopelessness in rabbinic literature that completely gives up on the efficacy of Torah and *avodah*.

The original sermon delivered the previous year maintained the effectiveness of Torah study and prayer, if only at a superficial level, due to the physical constraints, to "sweeten the harsh judgment and draw down both spiritual and physical deliverance and a complete redemption."[50] The note acknowledges the utter futility of any conventional spiritual activism and abandons altogether the prospect of Jewish renewal, reconstruction, or survival in the natural course of history, for "there is no longer anyone to reproach, nor is there any heart left to awaken to worship and Torah." There is only utter destruction, and nothing remains to renew. The vestigial hope is for the end of history, when only a "total redemption and the resurrection of the dead" will materialize.[51]

47 *Sermons*, p. 211.
48 Ibid., p. 212.
49 Ibid.
50 Ibid., p. 211.
51 Ibid., p. 212.

The devastation was so crushing that no longer was there any religious role for human beings, and death was so pervasive that only resurrection can affect renewal.

Most likely R. Shapira refers to the fact that total physical annihilation is imminent. Elsewhere he locates Israel's immortality in the perpetuation of children, for "as long as this world exists Israel's eternality consists in children and future generations." However, "when history has spent itself our eternality is accomplished by way of resurrection of the dead."[52] Thus, looking forward only to resurrection implies the cessation of birth, of children, and of physical continuity. The lifeblood of a Hasidic community has been drained, and its spiritual leader, the *Rebbe*, has lost his raison d'etre.

In light of this perspective on resurrection, I return to Shapira's sermon that depicts the "Song at the Sea" as a prototype of inducing song as an expression of impending salvation for all future confrontations between Jews and disaster. The expression of joy over the ultimate defeat of the Egyptian slave masters took the form of spontaneous song at the splitting of the Red Sea. A prominent rabbinic *midrash* considers a future tense of "sing" in the preface to the song, "then Moses and the Israelites will sing [*yashir*] this song" (Exodus 15:1), to be the biblical substantiation of resurrection of the dead—that is, a song will be sung in the distant future culmination of history.[53] Since he himself exegetically focused on a future tense of this song, it is difficult to imagine that the rabbinic precedent for this sense of futurity did not resonate in R. Shapira's mind. One shudders therefore to think that R. Shapira may have entertained the possibility that song can never again surface until the end of history and the resurrection of the dead. Song can emerge from the depths of being, from one's soul, but it is the body that expresses such penetrating music. Only resurrection of the dead holds out any hope of reviving song when currently "there is no heart left to awaken."

The sermon ends with a rare flourish of Yiddish in the transcription "*es zol zikh zogen shirah*" ("Song will be proclaimed").[54] Yiddish would most certainly have been the language of the oral delivery, and so, while contemplating the worst, this fragment from its original version may reflect the glimmer of hope that was intended for the dwindling

---

52 Ibid., p. 301.
53 Babylonian Talmud, *Sanhedrin* 91b.
54 *Sermons*, p. 262.

audience. Since song is a particularly social and communal activity, it is not too speculative to imagine that those last words were directed to Shapira's community in their lingua franca in order to rouse the members to a unified chant, which might alleviate, if only for an instant, their overwhelming pain. As Reiser points out in a recent discussion of the elevated status of Yiddish within Hasidism,

> the integration of isolated Yiddish sentences within Hebrew hasidic sermons and stories—that is, the integration of the spoken language within the written language—exemplifies the living dialogue present within the text, as well as the importance accorded to this dialogue within hasidic culture.[55]

Thus, the *Rebbe* interpolates this Yiddish sentence in order to recapture that moment and preserve "the living dialogue present within the text."

Finally, this juncture in the sermons paves the way toward further deepening the role that suffering plays in the minimization of the intellect so that there could be an influx of divinity into the world. The notion that music surpasses the intellect as an instrument of unification between human beings and God already germinates in Shapira's prewar thought. One consequence of spiritual decline is the inability to articulate deep spiritual experiences in personal innovative ways, which for R. Shapira would be most soulfully expressed by a "new song" (*shirah chadashah*), "because his perception is limited."[56] The best one can do is in a sense plagiarize prophetic poetry,

> for it is difficult to compose new song and articulate through the power of divine inspiration [*ruach hakodesh*] what his soul viewed in the supernal realm, rather he praises and venerates only in the melodious language of our holy ones, imbuing them with his own perception, that of the descendants of prophets [*bnei hanevi'im*].[57]

R. Shapira pursues this line of thought by considering novel insights (*chiddush*) generated by intellect and reason—the normal modes of interpreting Torah, expressing the greatness of God, and how to worship and gain proximity to God—as watered-down distillations of "a spark of new song [*shirah chadashah*] residing within the interior of one's being."

55 Daniel Reiser, "The Sanctification of Yiddish Among Hasidim," *AJS Review*, 44:1 (2020), pp. 1–19, especially p. 7.
56 *The Students' Obligation*, p. 102.
57 Ibid., p. 102–103.

The exigencies of a historical decline in spiritual capacity, as well as the political, social, and economic woes of exile have arrested the emergence of that spark in the form of song, making it "impossible to draw out in song the greatness of God evoked by his soul, rather that spark stirred his mind to formulate by way of reason how to approach God." That musical spark is the spiritual force masked by its weakened form in reason, "that spark is hidden buried beneath his intellect."[58]

Finally, and critically for understanding the full thrust of the role that song plays in the wartime sermon, "that spark of the *shirah chadashah* is what draws the light and the perception of the *bnei hanevi'im* into this world and what reveals it in this place."[59] Thus, the intellect acts as a suppressant of that internal latent spark of Divine light whose vehicle for entry into the material world is song. R. Shapira resorted to all that was left in his theological tool box. He attempted to coax that spark-bearing song's emergence out of the mind-numbing circumstances posed by ghetto life in 1942, when the mind was least likely to resist.

Annihilating Intellect on the Precipice of Annihilating the Body: Fourth Juncture

During the course of the sermons in the ghetto R. Shapira builds on his prewar pedagogy with respect to studying Torah; this posited overcoming simple rational understanding, since the Torah reflects Divine knowledge that transcends human modes of comprehension. Once one plumbs the supra-rational depths of the Torah, there is a merging of the human and Divine intellects, achieving a recognition that what one knows is really what God knows. Thus, he asserts, regarding the divinization of studying Torah,

> since Torah emanates from heaven, when you study Torah it ascends to heaven, you ascend to God and in Him you unite… your soul and mind belong to God and when you comprehend something from the Torah then the Divine intellect, as it were, exists in you now and this is the essence of Torah and *mitzvot*, that God desires them, and is there any unification greater than this…[60]

58 Ibid., p. 103.
59 Ibid.
60 See *The Students' Obligation*, pp. 61–62.

The intellect, and humanity's confidence in its own ability to make sense of the world, must in fact be abandoned in order to gain access to the Divine mind.

For R. Shapira in the ghetto, suffering itself replaces the study of Torah as an instrument of "unification"; only then can one make sense of what is an insurmountably senseless world. In other words, suffering itself can evoke a mystical experience of union with God (*devekut*), which involves what Moshe Idel describes as central to major figures of Hasidism, "some form of obliteration of the human personality by means of the experience of a self-inclusion of the mystic in the divine realm."[61] Suffering evokes an absorption into God similar to what R. Menahem Mendel of Vitebsk, one of those central figures cited by Idel, considered the effect of self-effacement on the mystic: "they are stupefied and this is the matter of their annihilation [*bittulam*], since they self-annihilate themselves and they become enveloped [*nikhlalim*] in the sources of their influx…"[62]

R. Shapira thus considers that the forces of evil responsible for the mind-crushing suffering in the ghetto, which physically targeted the Jews, aim at diminishing God's presence as well. His pedagogical writings identify hatred of Israel, or antisemitism, with hatred of God. Thus, all the "suffering and pain caused to Israel conceal the Divine light, Heaven forbid." Because hatred for Jews is ipso facto hatred for God, "the more one exerts himself to reveal the light of God the more oppressed and afflicted he becomes."[63] In the ghetto R. Shapira transforms that very suffering into an instrument of revelation and reverses its aim, which is to suppress godliness in the world, into increasing its presence in the world. In addition, Isaiah's messianic vision that R. Shapira hoped for in his pedagogical work—when "the world will be filled with the knowledge of God" (Isaiah 11:9)—becomes an opportunity in the ghetto for its concrete realization. As R. Shapira envisions, "In the future when the demonic side ceases there will no longer be evil and destruction in

---

61 See Moshe Idel, "Universalization and Integration: Two Conceptions of Mystical Union in Jewish Mysticism," in Moshe Idel and Bernard McGinn, eds., *Mystical Union and Monotheistic Faith: An Ecumenical Dialogue* (New York: Macmillan Publishing, 1989), pp. 27–57, especially p. 33.

62 Ibid., p. 40, citing from *Sefer Peri Ha'aretz* (Hebrew) (Jerusalem: HaMesorah, 1970), p. 64.

63 *The Students' Obligation* p. 123.

all my sacred mountain for the world will be filled with the knowledge of God."[64]

Before the war R. Shapira had resigned himself to the inevitable clash of civilizations between Israel, the purveyor of godliness in the world, and its enemies, who seek to suppress that godliness. That conflict is bound to persist until history ultimately runs its course; when oppression will cease and therefore liberate the force that can introduce the Divine light unimpeded. Isaiah prefaces his vision of a world suffused with knowledge of God with a historical period when there will no longer be "hurt or destruction." However, R. Shapira's revolutionary new theology, confronting a radically new evil and suffering, frames that very suffering as the liberating force that obliterates the "I" to such an extent that there is no longer any partition between the human and the Divine.

The impact of overcoming normal modes of cognition extends beyond the mind into the world of conduct, promoting an ideal realization of compassion for others. Analogous to R. Shapira's instructions on achieving metaphysical knowledge, another sermon, delivered in July 1941, idealizes a type of compassion for the suffering of others that originates out of "the very core of one's being," and not simply out of a "knowledge of it alone."[65] A reasoned objective appreciation of the needs of others remains stunted. Just as the mind must be crushed in order to allow the Divine mind entry, so does the heart need to be agitated to the point of dissolving, so that the Divine heart, or compassion, which has already effected some decree of relief but remains dormant and stuck in the upper world, is drawn down to the material world.[66] Once again the *Rebbe* prods his followers themselves to induce a Divine decree out of an inert state, for

> a decree for the salvation of Israel can hesitate to materialize because it is above and cannot descend to this world and clothe itself in corporeality, thus when a man acknowledges not simply with his knowledge that other Jews need support, but rather he exerts compassion with his entire essence, then his prayers draw down salvation to this world as well.[67]

64 Ibid.
65 *Sermons*, p. 198.
66 Ibid.
67 Ibid.

That Divine decree stalled in the upper realm becomes embodied by the intensified compassion that involves one's entire being so that it can realize itself in the embodied world. The self, or the ego, must be overcome in both the realms of the abstract mind and practical ethics so that no obstacle remains between the Divine mind and the human mind and between Divine and human compassion that impedes God's entry into the world. The more one strips oneself of ego and abandons the possessive "mine" in relation to the mind, the more one ascends from reasoned knowledge to prophetic knowledge, or knowledge that is Divine and stripped of its materiality.[68]

Theological Anomaly: Fifth Juncture

At the end of June 1942, just a few weeks before the sermons go silent, as ghetto life becomes dire, R. Shapira's theology becomes more daring. This relatively lengthy sermon oscillates between disparate ideas which I will outline, followed by an explication of what I discern as its thematic unity.[69] As always, a question fuels *midrashic* reasoning; in this case one related to the tradition that credited Miriam's saintliness with the well that accompanied Israel in its desert wanderings.[70] Taking the well as a Divine source of life, or "sacred living water" (*mayim chayim kedoshim*), R. Shapira accounts for what uniquely qualified Miriam as the facilitator of Israel's spiritual nourishment in the desert. Since God is the source of everything, all men's actions are really God's. Despite that, God's magnanimity considers human actions autonomous, "as if he himself performs them" for the sake of reward.[71] However, as a woman, Miriam was classified juridically/Halachically as one "who performs but is not commanded to perform"; that is, her worship of God was *sui generis* unmotivated by any divinely sanctioned obligations. Her worship therefore belongs to her alone, and "since the source of her *avodah* is in

---

68 See *The Students' Obligation* p. 93.

69 For another close reading of this sermon that discerns a different unifying thematic thread, see Nehemiah Polen, "Miriam, Moses, and the Divinity of Children: Human Individuation at the Cusp of Persistence and Perishability," in Seeman, Reiser, and Mayse, *Hasidism, Suffering and Renewal*, pp. 234–262; Polen evaluates this sermon as possibly "the single most profound Hasidic teaching delivered and written at the very precipice of destruction," p. 261.

70 Babylonian Talmud, *Ta'anit* 9a.

71 *Sermons*, p. 299.

her and it streams from her, therefore the well that is the source which streams the sacred living waters was on her account."[72]

As the sermon develops, R. Shapira digresses, citing an ancient tradition related to the Ten Martyrs tortured by the Roman emperor Hadrian, which is another rabbinic paradigm of suffering. He prefaces it with a desperate plea in Yiddish, which demands of God an immediate rescue:

> the screams of agony of the young and the old that shout out "save us, save us" [*ratevet* in Yiddish] resound with both their own screams and those of all of us aimed at God the Merciful Father–*rateve, rateve* as long as there is some breath remaining in us.[73]

He appeals to God as Father since it is the children who are threatened with extinction; since children embody all Jews that have lived in the past, all of Jewish history verges on the precipice of passing into oblivion. Mention of these screams then compels R. Shapira to confront God with a horrifying logical extension of the martyrs' tradition:

> And in truth it is baffling how the world can endure after so many of these screams. It is reported in relation to the Ten Martyrs that the angels screamed "This is Torah and such is its reward!" A voice from heaven responded "If I hear one more sound I will deluge the world with water." Now that these screams of innocent pure children, and great holy sages of Israel, who are greater than angels, are killed and slaughtered solely because they are Jews fill the space of the entire world and yet the world does not revert to water and persists as if He does not care?[74]

From here I move to the sermon's climactic conclusion, and then return to link these seemingly disjoint thoughts along a unified thematic chain.

---

72 Ibid., p. 300. For the tension between pure spiritual devotion and normative obedience to God's commands, and the superiority of the former in terms of proximity to God, see Arthur Green, *Devotion and Commandment: The Faith of Abraham in the Hasidic Imagination* (Cincinnati: Hebrew Union College Press, 1989), pp. 20–24.

73 Ibid., p. 304.

74 *Sermons*, pp. 304–305. The boldness of this protest is reflected by its softening, as cited recently in a journal article in which the words "as if He does not care" were changed to "and nothing happens"; see Amos Goldberg, "Harebbe MiPiasetzna: Gibbor Ve'anti-Gibbor," (Hebrew), *Bishvil Hazikaron*, 20 (1997), https://lib.cet.ac.il/pages/item.asp?item=16226 (accessed July 26, 2020). I thank Daniel Reiser for this reference.

In order to assimilate Divine will and knowledge into one's being, there must first be a passionate desire for it. Miriam's passion for God was so strong that it buttressed the people's own passion sufficiently to attract "those supernal lights that Moses drew down." Although Moses channeled the Divine light down to earth, it was Miriam's herculean yearning for God that acted as the conduit between that light and the people whose longing for God was too shallow to bond with it. Miriam's death therefore severed the link between the Divine light and the people, leaving it to Moses to somehow reestablish that link by forging some commonality between him and the people in order to elevate them. That was accomplished by "lowering himself to their level by committing a sin relative to his stature, thus they complained about water so Moses struck the rock twice."[75]

Miriam's legal classification as one not obliged to perform a commandment, and therefore not within the prescriptive category under which males are subsumed, actually strengthened her voluntary performance, enabling her to draw the light down to the people. Moses, on the other hand, inverts that process by assuming the same legal category of the people in order to draw them up to the light together with him, "for sometimes it is necessary for the *tzaddik* to sin relative to his stature in order to benefit the community."[76]

R. Shapira constructs this sermon along a unified theme of what I describe as theological anomaly. There is a connective thread of unconventionality, or nonconforming modes of religious worship, which strings together those disparate exegetical insights into a unified whole.[77] First, Miriam's "nonconforming" righteous conduct that ensures her community's spiritual and physical survival operates outside the

---

75 *Sermons*, p. 306. For an analysis of this segment of the sermon, see Uziel Fuchs, "Miriam Haneviah Ve'eshet Ha'admor: Derashot Harebbe MiPyasetsnah Al Miriam Haneviah (Hebrew), *Masekhet*, 3 (2005), pp. 65–76.

76 Ibid. The topic of sinning for the sake of heaven is a large one and assumes various iterations in Kabbalah and Hasidism. For just one concise overview, see Samuel Dresner, *The Zaddik: The Doctrine of the Zaddik According to the Writings of Rabbi Yaakov Yosef of Polnoy* (New York: Schocken Books, 1974), pp. 191–221.

77 Polen follows a different, though related, theme of ways of "reserving a space for human initiative, enabling agency and creative movement, unencumbered by the overwhelming weight of omnipresent divinity…," in *Miriam, Moses, and the Divinity of Children*, pp. 259–260. A substantial part of his analysis focuses on a section of the sermon dedicated to the religious dimension of children as the "face of the *Shekhinah*," which I do not examine in this article.

confines of Judaism's Halachic, or normative, framework. In fact, R. Shapira's appraisal of Miriam's non-prescriptive performance as superior to a prescriptive one flies in the face of an explicit rabbinic assertion to the contrary.[78]

Second is R. Shapira's adaptation of the angelic exchange with God over the fate of His martyrs. R. Shapira switches briefly to his community's mother tongue in another rare preservation of what was surely its original Yiddish. I believe that this momentary lapse into the community's vernacular must be read in light of rabbinic traditions related to Aramaic, the vernacular of the classical rabbinic period. The general consensus is that Aramaic is considered to be beyond the angels' linguistic facility, and so it is questionable whether Aramaic is permissible for prayer.[79] The Talmud concludes that while Aramaic is forbidden for private prayer, it is permissible for communal prayer. Rashi, the most prominent of medieval exegetes, explains that an individual needs angelic mediation for prayer in order for it to reach its destination, and therefore must pray in the language comprehensible to angels; communal prayer, on the other hand, connects directly and can bypass angelic intermediaries.[80] Yiddish, as the folk language of R. Shapira's community, had replaced the Aramaic vernacular of his ancient rabbinic predecessors, conveying the potency of communal prayer. In this case he substitutes the original angelic weeping with the Yiddish pleas of *rateve* (save us), the language of immediacy that emanates from the communal screams of "the young, the old…of all of us." Here, too, the *Rebbe* steps outside convention—in this case, outside the tradition of transcribing oral Yiddish sermons into Hebrew for publication, by a conscious insertion of Yiddish echoing its original form.[81]

78 Babylonian Talmud, *Kiddushin* 3la; *Baba Kamma* 38a. See also Nehemia Polen, "Miriam's Dance: Radical Egalitarianism in Hasidic Thought," *Modern Judaism*, vol. 12:1 (1992), pp. 1–21, especially pp. 7–8; he characterizes R. Shapira's exegesis as "daring in the context of traditional Jewish thought."

79 On the topic of angels not knowing Aramaic, see Babylonian Talmud, *Shabbat* 12b; *Sotah* 33a; and Joseph Yahalom, "Angels Do Not Understand Aramaic: On the Literary Use of Jewish Palestinian Aramaic in Late Antiquity," *Journal of Jewish Studies*, 47:1 (1996), pp. 33–44.

80 Babylonian Talmud, *Sotah* 33a.

81 I do not make any historical claims here about the use of Yiddish in prayer. In my opinion, the combination of the particular midrash that R. Shapira adapts, the role of angels in it, the rare turn to Yiddish in the written text, and the general theme of the unconventional that I identify in this sermon together suggest the analogy that I have drawn between Aramaic and Yiddish.

Finally, once Miriam dies, Moses replaces her as the medium of spiritual ascendance, but, in his case, by diluting the pure grade of his own proximity to God, so that he could occupy some common ground with his people. Moses achieves this degrading by the most extreme form of unconventional or anomalous worship, by transgressing Judaism's normatively binding conduct. Moses' ability to elevate the people stems from erasing any class distinction between himself and them by descending to their lower level of spirituality. The power of Miriam's spiritual agency, on the other hand, had derived precisely from her distinct normative class, which did not consider the commandment she performed to be obligatory. She acted outside the prescriptive norms of Halachah.

Since R. Shapira's sermons all relate to his own and his community's immediate predicament, there is no doubt that Moses here stands in for the *Rebbe* himself.[82] The question is what "sin" could R. Shapira have contemplated for his own time as a reenactment of the Mosaic exodus experience. It is not inconceivable that despair had set in so deeply it was now up to the *Rebbe*, the *tzaddik*, to resort to his own powers to elevate whatever glimmer of divinity might be mired in the quagmire of despair. Perhaps R. Shapira is alluding to his own periodic capitulations to that same despair noted previously and reflected in envisaging the obliteration of both individual selfhood and national/religious existence. Hasidic theology considered sadness and despair cardinal sins, tantamount to "the conscious psychological manifestation of lack of faith and confidence in man's spiritual ability."[83] Since it is the *Rebbe*'s responsibility to preserve and shore up the faith of his community, sadness would be precisely the commission of a sin "relative to his stature."[84]

However, there is another possibility, which is substantively integral to the sermon itself. R. Shapira's precedent for this kind of antinomian

82 A few sermons mention the term "*itpashtuta demoshe*," a Zoharic term connoting an eternal recurrence of Moses; see Yehudah Liebes, *Perakim Bemilon Sefer Hazohar* (Hebrew) (PhD diss., Hebrew University, 1977), pp. 303–304, where he points out that Moses is reincarnated in specific individuals.

83 See Rivka Schatz Uffenheimer's chapter, "Despair, Sadness, Regret, and Their Connection with Sin," in her book *Hasidism as Mysticism: Quietistic Elements in Eighteenth-Century Hasidic Thought* (Princeton: Princeton University Press, 1993), pp. 93–110, especially p. 95.

84 For other examples of the types of "sin" in which the *tzaddik* would intentionally engage in order to descend to the people, see Dresner, *The Zaddik*, pp. 208–210.

behavior for the good is Moses' own sin when he struck the rock that was to miraculously provide water in the desert. Though what precisely was Moses' sin has been the subject of much argument in the rabbinic tradition, what is important here is that it concerned water.[85] I believe that R. Shapira contemplated his own adaptation of the Martyrs' *midrash* as the sin he committed that he could use for his community's benefit. It also involved a contravention of God's command, particularly related to water. Just as Moses' act may have reflected some lack of faith in God's omnipotence as related to water—in his case to convert a rock into a spring—so R. Shapira's shock at God's obliviousness to the cries of agony similarly questions why God remains insensitive to suffering and does not transform the world into a deluge of water.[86] R. Shapira replaced angelic weeping with the cries of the suffering, and therefore revived what God demanded must cease. Though of course not a formal violation of a Halachic norm, R. Shapira's revivification of that angelic criticism is a direct infringement of God's original injunction to the angels to desist from further critiquing Divine "justice." It thus constitutes a sin "according to his stature"; that is, relative to the *Rebbe*'s extraordinary piety, which the *Rebbe* committed for the benefit of his community.

Abandoning God's Long-Term Vision: The Final Juncture

The previous sermon's desperate resort to whatever theologies R. Shapira could muster—including the unorthodox—laid the groundwork for what is the final critical juncture in R. Shapira's struggle with what had by then evolved into terminal suffering. His very last sermon, delivered on the Sabbath prior to *Tisha B'Av*, the day commemorating the destruction of the First and Second Temples, just days before the mass deportations commenced, focuses on the power of witnessing events over merely possessing theoretical knowledge of them. R. Shapira once again recalls the Biblical exodus, the paradigm of divinely instigated

---

85 See, for example, the alternatives engaged by Samuel David Luzzato; they were so numerous that he refused to offer another for fear of fabricating and compounding Moses' sins. See *Commentary of Shadal on the Torah* (Hebrew) (Tel Aviv: Dvir, 1966), pp. 472–477.

86 For Moses' sin at the waters of Merivah as an archetype for all future *tzaddikim* enjoining a descent for the sake of the community, see Dresner, *The Zaddik*, pp. 201–202.

relief from oppression and suffering. In perhaps what is his boldest exegesis, he considers the impetus for God's decision to liberate the people earlier than planned to be His direct observation of suffering rather than indirect knowledge of it. In other words, God was so affected by actually seeing the people's suffering that He abandoned His original plan, which had called for a much longer period of enslavement, and initiated the process for immediate liberation.

Though I have discussed this sermon elsewhere, here I accentuate its direct subversion of a surgery metaphor, a classic trope of theodicy to which many resorted precisely in response to the evil of the Holocaust. Its standard use by major rabbinic figures both during and after the war analogizes God to a doctor conducting surgery in front of observers who have no knowledge at all of medicine.[87] Ignorant of its ultimate benefits, the onlookers consider the operating theater to be a torture chamber. The analogy responds to the age-old problem that innocent suffering raises with respect to God's goodness and providence. God is the surgeon; the sufferer is the patient undergoing surgery; and those theologically troubled by innocent suffering are the observers who, since they cannot fathom God's knowledge, are oblivious to its ultimate reward. However, rather than rationalizing the Divine imposition of suffering, which rests on the impassible abyss between human ignorance and God's inscrutable knowledge, R. Shapira transforms that same model into a rejection of its justification and instead calls for God to immediately discard His long-range beneficial plans in exchange for immediate relief.

In R. Shapira's version the patient is a child, and the observer is a father who fully understands the benefits of the surgery. Thus, there is in fact no divergence between the observer/father's knowledge and the surgeon's/God's knowledge as presented in the traditional version. R. Shapira then fleshes out the import of his modified rendering:

> although the father is aware of the great benefit surgery would have for his son he still would not be able to stand and watch as the surgery is performed since knowledge of pain does not compare to

---

87 See Diamond, "The Warsaw Ghetto Rebbe," pp. 319–320. For numerous examples of major rabbinic authorities who resorted to the surgeon analogy in order to justify theologically the enormity of the Holocaust, see Gershon Greenberg, "Menahem Mendel Schneersohn's Response to the Holocaust," *Modern Judaism*, 34:1 (2014), pp. 86–122, especially p. 117n19. See also Yehuda Bauer's chapter, "Theology, or God the Surgeon," in his *Rethinking the Holocaust* (New Haven: Yale University Press, 2001), pp. 186–212, especially pp. 198–209.

seeing it, and therefore despite the benefit, he would not tolerate seeing it because the knowledge of the benefit would dissipate and all that he would feel would be his son's pain.[88]

God's early release of Israel from slavery, because He "saw" their suffering forms the precedent for what R. Shapira is calling for in the ghetto in his last recorded sermon. R. Shapira inverts the essential dramatic elements of the common surgeon parable, which originally called for the subordination of the human mind and will to those of God, into its precise converse.

An Overarching Juncture: Ghetto Experience Poses a Theological Novum

Over the course of his internment in the ghetto, R. Shapira finally acknowledged the unprecedented nature of the suffering, as distinguished from previous tragic experiences. However, it is important to consider a note of retraction that he appended, at the end of 1942, to a sermon he had delivered approximately a year earlier during Hanukkah in December 1941. Though others have noted this remarkable change in R. Shapira's theological consciousness, it is crucial to examine its significance anew, as an overarching juncture within the setting of the intermittent junctures I have laid out.

In the original sermon Shapira contested those who believed that the suffering in the ghetto far outstripped previous Jewish catastrophes, rendering them useless as precedents for how to deal with the current situation. However, by late 1942, R. Shapira could no longer in good faith subscribe to his earlier stance. In a remarkable gesture of intellectual honesty and theological courage, he appended a note to his earlier sermon, admitting that the unremitting brutality, decimation, and utter bleakness of the ghetto's future had proven him wrong. Reconsidering the uniqueness of Jewish suffering under the Nazis, which he had previously dismissed, he now confessed that as far as,

> the monstrous torments, the terrible and freakish deaths which the malevolent murderers invented against us, the House of Israel, from that point on [the middle of 1942] - according to my **knowledge of**

---

88 *Sermons*, p. 314.

> **rabbinic literature and Jewish history** [emphasis added, J.A.D.]
> in general, there has never been anything like them.[89]

Shapira carefully measured the catastrophe's uniqueness against both history *and* rabbinic literature—what he would have considered the very essence of Jewish thought, or for him thought simpliciter. The suffering of the Holocaust presented a novum for Shapira—not just factually or empirically, according to his knowledge of "Jewish history in general," but rabbinically unparalleled as well.

The historical precedents he referred to in the earlier version of the sermon—the destruction of the Temples and later the bastion at Beitar by the Romans—signify far more than mere past events. These had been rabbinically constructed as the quintessential Jewish tragedies to which the classical rabbis responded legally and theologically in order to maintain and perpetuate their faith. These events thus form living theological, as well as historical, archetypes to which all Jews are meant to turn for some sense of psychological and theological comfort and spiritual sustenance in times of pain and distress. Yet by the end of 1942, the extraordinary needs of the moment rendered this old paradigm outdated and inadequate.[90] What is this "terrible truth" other than what Emil Fackenheim, one of the profoundest Holocaust philosophers, proposed; he characterized the Holocaust as a historical novum.[91]

The Holocaust is a manifestation of evil so heinously novel as to "rupture" philosophical and theological thought. Thus, the Hasidic *Rebbe*, whose life and thought were literally filtered through the lens of the vast midrashic corpus of his rabbinic predecessors, remained completely vulnerable to the theological challenges of the radical evil

---

89 Quoting from Polen's translation in *Holy Fire*, p. 35. The original appears in *Sermons*, p. 242 (*Hanukkah* 1941 [5702]). The critical mark he used to note this revision specifically instructs maintaining the original as well in any future transcription of the sermons; see ibid., note 12.

90 For a comprehensive review of scholars who grappled with the theological adequacy of analogies between the ancient Temple's destruction and the Holocaust, see Jonathan Klawans, "Josephus, the Rabbis, and Responses to Catastrophes Ancient and Modern," *The Jewish Quarterly Review*, 100:2 (2010), pp. 278–309.

91 Fackenheim made a succinct statement intended to challenge professional philosophers about novum in the history of evil at an American Philosophical Association symposium in 1985; see Emil Fackenheim, "The Holocaust and Philosophy," *The Journal of Philosophy*, 82:10 (1985), pp. 505–514. Shapira's amendment is one of only two passages from his sermons that Fackenheim cites in his entire corpus.

of his own day.[92] The importance of this retraction—which surely took root after creeping encroachment on his thought over time—cannot be overstated, for all Orthodox theology in response to the Holocaust turns on the question of its uniqueness. As Eliezer Schweid, a seminal contemporary Jewish philosopher, stated in his overview of religious responses, "The refusal to admit the uniqueness of the Holocaust is then the main characteristic of Orthodox theological argumentation."[93] R. Shapira could no longer in good conscience offer healing based on tired old theodicies that rang hollow in the shadow of looming inevitable physical destruction.

Conclusion: The Sermons Reach Full Circle

The final juncture discussed above arrives full circle back to where we began with the first juncture and R. Shapira's novel account of Sarah's suicide. There, too, R. Shapira's theological protest against excessive suffering rested on apprising God of human needs by diverting His focus from theory to practice. To appreciate the extent of this final sermon's theologically revolutionary intent, it is instructive to examine a previous adoption of "the God as doctor" metaphor at an earlier juncture during the first cycle of sermons at the end of 1939. R. Shapira then entertained the idea that God ultimately cures illness, but since He created a world "that operates by way of causality and nature," His cure follows the natural course of medicinal therapy. That often entails a lengthy regimen of toxic medicine, in this case Jewish suffering in the ghetto, and requires some time for relief to take effect: "Since God created the world to operate by way of causality and nature there are often phenomena that play out gradually, persisting and lingering until the solution arrives..." However, when the sick person faces the kind of imminent danger that could not tolerate an extended period of treatment, "God decrees an

---

92 The sermons are unique, as Don Seeman aptly characterizes them, in "their unprecedented depiction of psychic collapse and the desperate struggle by their author to overcome his gathering silence and despair," in "Ritual Efficacy, Hasidic Mysticism and 'Useless Suffering' in the Warsaw Ghetto," pp. 465–505, especially p. 481.

93 Eliezer Schweid, "The Holocaust as a Challenge to Jewish Thoughts on Ultimate Reality and Meaning," *Ultimate Reality and Meaning*, 14:3 (1991), pp. 185–209, especially p. 187.

end to the prolonging and lingering and heals immediately thereby revealing Heavenly sovereignty."[94]

At that earlier stage R. Shapira expressed faith in a Divine providence that would closely monitor the suffering in the ghetto, watching for a time when the community could no longer endure the suffering, or, in his theological language, the toxicity of God's "treatment" schedule. At that point R. Shapira anticipated that Divine intervention would surely interrupt the natural causal continuum in order to rescue the community from its imminent collapse. However, by the summer of 1942, when a miraculous end to the ghetto's collapse failed to materialize, despite the terminal conditions that should have already triggered it, R. Shapira could no longer sustain that faith. The healer God needed to be jolted out of adherence to an outmoded form of medicine that was fixated on an ultimate outcome to the disregard of the present danger. R. Shapira returned to this specific analogy in order to subvert its traditional use and turn it back on God as a demand for an immediate end to the suffering, rather than a justification of God's imposition of its application. Perhaps it summoned an end—not to R. Shapira's faith, but to theodicy altogether.

---

94 *Sermons*, p. 98, delivered on December 9, 1939.

The Shaping of Holocaust Memory and the Eichmann Trial: Jacob Robinson—Jurist, Historian, and Human Rights Activist

Zohar Segev

D
r. Jacob Robinson (1889–1977), an attorney by training, emigrated with his family from Lithuania to the United States in 1940. In New York he played a central role in American Jewish organizations' matrix of rescue and information-gathering during the Holocaust. After the State of Israel was established, his public and political efforts also centered on Israeli matters of interest. While the accounts of his perigrinations in Europe, the United States, and Israel, and his intensive and diverse public activities in varied settings are fascinating in and of themselves, in this article I focus on Robinson's life story and introduce his personal papers. These contain an abundance of valuable information about his activities in the context of the Holocaust and the establishment of the State of Israel. Robinson favored the creation of a Jewish state in *Eretz Israel* but did not see it as a be-all and end-all cause. He worked to bring it about but also to rehabilitate Diaspora Jewish life after the Holocaust, seeing these as complementary, not contradictory, goals. The Jews' steadfastness during the Holocaust and their patterns of response to the Nazis' terrifying murder operations, he believed, were proof positive of the power of Diaspora Jewry throughout the generations and were a clear indication of the survivability of Jewish communities even after the State of Israel came into being. The following discussion elucidates how Robinson's actions to commemorate the Holocaust and to organize research on the topic, especially on the Eichmann trial, may be understood in terms of this worldview.

Jacob Robinson was born in Seirijai, a small Lithuanian shtetl, as the eldest of seven offspring of David and Bluma Robinson. His family nurtured the embodiment of the tradition of engagement in study, teaching, and interpretation of the Jewish world of knowledge.

Robinson's father was an Enlightenment Jew and a teacher. By virtue of his family background and status in his profession, Robinson *père* became his community's spokesman and representative vis-à-vis the authorities of two empires, the Russian and the German, in line with the changing political realities. Jacob Robinson began his studies in the traditional Jewish manner and went on to complete high school at the gymnasium of Suvalkai. His dramatic decision to stray from the traditional Jewish educational frame was influenced by his uncle, Efim Semenovich London, one of the first Jews to engage in medical research in Tsarist Russia. Robinson earned a Master of Laws degree at the University of Warsaw in 1914. That year he also married Clara, his high school girlfriend, and immediately afterward, with the eruption of World War I, he was inducted into the Russian army and sent to the Eastern Front. About a year later, in September 1915, the Germans took Robinson prisoner in the Vilna area and kept him incarcerated there for three years. As a result of his polyglot talents and his ability to conduct public activity, Robinson became the unofficial spokesman of the Jewish and Russian POWs vis-à-vis the Germans. The latter recognized his unique stature by granting him the status of an officer, exempting him from physical labor, and tasking him with ordering newspapers and books for the camp. In 1919, with the war over, Robinson returned to independent Lithuania and embarked on a ramified public career that combined both the Zionist and Lithuanian arenas. He established the Hebrew gymnasium in Virbalis and served as its principal from 1919 to 1922. Afterward (1923–1925) he was one of the first editors of the Yiddish-language Zionist daily *Di Idishe Shtime*.

Robinson was a leading figure in the struggle for the creation of a corpus of laws in Lithuania that would assure the Jews' right to organize autonomously in matters of education, culture, and religion. Concurrently he engaged in building an intra-Jewish legal and political system in Lithuania. His crowning achievement at this time was the founding of the National Council of Jews in Lithuania (Der Idisher Natsional-Rat in Lite), the supreme executive institution of Jewish autonomy. It was granted broad powers, from imposing taxes for the functioning of community institutions to the creation of community-level education systems.

For many years Robinson chaired the Union of Zionist Organizations in Lithuania, participated in managing the pioneering training farm there, and attended multiple Zionist congresses. He acted on behalf of Jewish causes in the European arena as well. In 1925–1931, he was a prominent spokesperson at the Congress of European Nationalities, an umbrella organization for minorities in Europe that furthered these populations' common interests in the broader European setting.

Robinson was a member of the Seimas, the Lithuanian parliament, from 1923 until its de facto dissolution pursuant to the military coup in 1926. In this capacity he chaired the Jewish faction and led the Minorities' Bloc. He waged an especially vigorous struggle against days-of-rest bills that proposed to compel Jewish artisans and merchants to close their businesses on Sundays and Christian holidays in addition to the Jewish Sabbath and festivals that they observed. Due to his public activity and legal prowess, Robinson was named legal advisor of the Lithuanian Foreign Ministry. He represented Lithuania in the legal conflict surrounding the northernmost region of Eastern Prussia, the Memel land. Although this area had been awarded to Lithuania under the Versailles accords, Germany sought to reclaim it. Robinson represented Lithuania in this matter before the international court in The Hague and was a central player in the Lithuanian Foreign Ministry's success in swaying the court to its stance. During the 1920s Robinson also acted on the European scene for the rights of the Jews and of minorities in general and delivered the keynote speech at a conference of fifty minority representatives in Geneva in October 1925. Concurrent with his public activity, Robinson handled his brother Nehemia's legal affairs from 1927 onward.[1]

In 1940, before the Soviet Union annexed Lithuania, Robinson managed to emigrate with his family to New York, where he acted

---

1   Egle Bendikaite and Dirk Roland Haupt, "Jacob Robinson: Elements of his Curriculum Vitae and Aspects Exemplifying his Continued Relevance in Our Times," in Egle Bendikaite and Dirk Roland Haupt, eds., *The Life, Times and Work of Jokūbas Robinzonas—Jacob Robinson* (Sankt Augustin: Academia Verlag, 2015), pp. 39–66; Omry Kaplan-Feuereisen and Richard Mann, "At the Service of the Jewish Nation: Jacob Robinson and International Law," *Osteuropa*, 58 (2008), pp. 157–170. Many biographical details about Robinson appear in the introduction to his papers in the Yad Vashem Archives (YVA); see the Robinson papers in the Yad Vashem Archives in Jerusalem, Division O.65. For further information about Robinson, see Avraham Tory, "Lezekher Ne'edarim: Dr. Yaakov Robinson z"l" (Hebrew), *Hapraklit*, 32 (1978), pp. 125–126; Avraham Tory, "Dr. Yaakov Robinson," in Avraham Tory, ed., *Terumat Yehudim MiLita Levinyan Ha'aretz U'Medinat Israel* (Hebrew) (Tel Aviv: Association of Former Lithuanian Academics, 1988), pp. 43–45, and "Robinson, Yaakov ben-David," in Natan Goren et al., eds., *Yahadut Lita*, Vol. C, Book A, *Ishim* (Hebrew) (Tel Aviv: Am Hasefer, 1967), p. 231.

mainly under the auspices of the World Jewish Congress (WJC). This organization had been founded in 1936, and, although defined as an international Jewish body, was strongly dominated by its American components. For example, its founder and first president was the Reform Rabbi Stephen S. Wise, one of the most important American Zionist leaders and a Democratic Party activist. The dramatic realities of Jewish existence in the 1940s amplified the importance of the American elements in the WJC and transformed the organization, functionally, into an American Jewish body, albeit with unique attributes in the American Jewish philanthropic constellation. However, the WJC had been established in an international format; many of its foundational processes had taken place in Europe, and its activity focused on fighting for European Jewry. This made it easier for European Jewish activists such as Robinson, who had been exposed to WJC ventures in Europe, to fit into its purviews after they emigrated to the United States.

Robinson valued his activity in the WJC beyond its importance as a source of income and an avenue for his public endeavors. Other Jewish émigrés from Europe who came from a background of Jewish and Zionist public activity also joined the WJC organizational setup in New York, and Robinson initiated joint public activity with, and became personally close to several of them. These included Aryeh Tartakower, chairperson of the WJC Rescue Committee and subsequently professor of sociology at the Hebrew University, and one of the founders of Israeli sociology; Aryeh Leon Kubowitzki (subsequently Kubovy), chairperson of the WJC Rescue Committee and later Israeli ambassador to Czechoslovakia and Argentina and the second chairperson of the Yad Vashem Directorate; Nahum Goldmann, a prominent Zionist activist and future president of the WJC and the World Zionist Organization; and Benjamin Akzin, a leading Zionist activist in the United States and a future professor of political science at the Hebrew University.[2] As I demonstrate below,

2 On Robinson's connections with these personalities, see Benjamin Akzin, *MiRiga LiYerushalayim: Pirke Zikhronot* (Hebrew) (Jerusalem: Zionist Library, 1986), p. 348. For further evidence of these relationships, see minutes of the meeting of the World Jewish Congress Central Committee, April 20, 1944, Jerusalem, Central Zionist Archives (CZA), Division C6, File 403 (C6/403). Robinson's connection with Goldmann was especially conspicuous. See letter from Nahum Goldmann to Robinson, June 6, 1950, Robinson Papers, YVA, O.65/59. Robinson's relationship with Akzin developed despite the latter's Revisionist background, which differed from Robinson's. It may be understood in view of changes in Akzin's worldview until it corresponded to Robinson's, for example, with regard to the standing of

Robinson and the WJC leaders saw themselves as representatives of world Jewry on the eve of World War II, during the war, and after the war ended, and, as such, acted for the establishment of a Jewish state and the rehabilitation of Jewish life in the Diaspora as complementary goals.[3]

Central to Robinson's activity with the WJC was the Institute of Jewish Affairs, founded at the initiative of Robinson and his brother Nehemia in 1941, as a joint project of the WJC and the American Jewish Congress. The Institute moved its activity to London in 1965, and reconstituted itself as the Institute for Jewish Policy Research in 1994. It dealt with a wide variety of matters relating to worldwide Jewish life in and after World War II, including information about the Holocaust, reconstructing Jewish life in Europe, arranging for compensation for European Jews after World War II, prosecuting war criminals, and advancing human rights in the postwar world.[4] Robinson headed the Institute until 1947, while also lecturing in international law at Columbia University; he was succeeded by his brother, Nehemia Robinson.

At the conference in San Francisco (April–June 1945) at which the Charter of the United Nations was drafted, Robinson participated in a WJC delegation that had observer status. In 1947, he was named advisor to the UN Commission on Human Rights. Some time later he represented the State of Israel at the UN.[5]

The next stage in Robinson's public activity was closely associated with the Nuremberg trials. Robinson became the Jewish affairs advisor to Justice Robert Jackson, the chief American prosecutor, and played an

Diaspora Jewry and the importance of international organizations in post-World War II political arrangements; see Akzin, "Prelude to the Jewish State," December 1, 1948, CZA, A401/37.

3   On the World Jewish Congress, see Yitzhak Schwarzbart, *25 Shanim Besherut Ha'am Hayehudi: Sekira Al Pe'ulot Hakongres Hayehudi Ha'olami, August 1932–Februar 1957* (Hebrew) (Tel Aviv: World Jewish Congress, 1957). For an expression of the centrality of and total economic dependency on the United States, see letter from Nahum Goldmann to Stephen Wise, Jacob Rader Marcus Center of the American Jewish Archives (AJA), Cincinnati, December 17, 1936, Division 361, Box 1A, File 1, and continuation, AJA, 361, 1A/1. On the worldview of the WJC leadership, see, for example, "The Program of the World Jewish Congress," published by the World Jewish Congress head office in New York, November 1946, no exact date given, AJA, 5A/6.

4   Founding document of the Institute of Jewish Affairs, including a breakdown of officers and departments, 1941, no exact date given, AJA, 361, C68/1.

5   See WJC press release pursuant to Robinson's appointment as advisor to the UN Commission on Human Rights in 1947, no exact date given, AJA, 361, C14/26.

important role in grounding the Jewish aspects of the Nazis' criminality. The experience that Robinson amassed at these trials and the copious information in his possession about the fate of the Jews during the Holocaust, pursuant to his work at the Institute of Jewish Affairs, led to his joining the prosecution team at the Eichmann trial in 1960.[6]

After the State of Israel was established, Robinson shifted his public and political efforts to Israeli contexts. He acted in the service of the state and represented Israel in international forums while continuing to live most of the time in New York.[7] His unique case shows that he perceived postwar Jewish existence as a combination of an active Diaspora and the Jewish state.[8]

Documenting the Holocaust

Robinson saw much importance in documenting the Holocaust and often took action to keep the memory of the Holocaust alive. The first stage of his activity in this context took place within the setting of the Institute of Jewish Affairs in New York. The information about the mass murder of European Jewry and the Nazis' "Final Solution" scheme transformed the Institute's research program in several ways. From 1942 onward, Robinson's activity and that of the Institute's researchers no longer focused on writing position papers and action plans for the postwar era but on gathering information about the fate of European Jewry, cataloging, editing, and disseminating it to the public and to leaders in the Allied countries. The research that took place under Robinson's baton yielded the first comprehensive and organized tableau of the totality of the Nazis' assault on European Jewry.

The situation in Europe made the research process especially difficult. The Institute's researchers and representatives in Europe faced enormous logistical challenges in their attempts to gather information immediately after the war wound down. Importantly, as representatives of

---

6   Mark A. Lewis, "The World Jewish Congress and the Institute of Jewish Affairs at Nuremberg: Ideas, Strategies, and Political Goals, 1942–1946," *Yad Vashem Studies*, 36: 1 (2008), pp. 181–210.

7   On Robinson in this context, see remarks by the professor of international law and Israeli diplomat Shabtai Rosenne, "Sanegoro Hagadol Shel Am Yisrael, Lezikhro Shel Yaakov Robinson" (Hebrew), *Gesher*, 4:3 (1978), pp. 91–101.

8   For Robinson's remarks in this spirit, see confidential document of Jacob Robinson about the Institute of Jewish Affairs, March 29, 1939, AJA, 361, A9/6.

a philanthropic organization that had no official status vis-à-vis the Allied administrative and military systems in Europe, they had to wait until the end of 1945 to receive free and unlimited access to the DP camps.[9] Just the same, although the Institute and its researchers were at arm's length from the horrors of the war, they acquired up-to-date information about developments in Europe due to intensive contact between the WJC board in New York and the organization's offices in Europe.[10]

A summary of the Institute's research was published in several thick tomes during the war. The Nazis' actions against the Jews, from their rise to power in 1933 to 1943, were described in three books written by the Institute's team, headed by Robinson: *Jews in Nazi Europe* (November 1941), *Hitler's Ten-Year War on the Jews* (August 1943), and *Starvation over Europe* (1943). At the same time Aryeh Tartakower and the Institute's researcher Kurt Grossmann published a study on the Jewish refugee problem: *The Jewish Refugee* (1933–1944).[11]

The Institute's promotion of Holocaust research was part of a comprehensive move by Robinson to systematize and organize Holocaust research worldwide and, particularly, in the United States. In Robinson's opinion the situation in the early postwar years had made professional documentation impossible, had caused important primary material to be lost, had induced wastage of resources due to redundancy, and had ruled out the dissemination of the information to the public at large. Robinson wished to change this situation. He took up the matter in a classified letter to the well-known historian Prof. Salo Wittmayer Baron of Columbia University in mid-October 1946.[12] The topic of the Holocaust had preoccupied Baron both personally, because he himself had emigrated from Eastern Europe to the United States before the Holocaust, while his close family members remained in Europe, and as a historian, as manifested in his testimony at the Eichmann trial.[13]

---

9   Letter from Robinson to Wise, June 25, 1947, YVA, O.65/37.
10 Space limitations do not allow me to describe the masses of information that reached the WJC offices in New York from Europe. For a broad discussion of the matter, see Zohar Segev, "What Did the World Jewish Congress Know about the Fate of European Jewry at the End of 1942? Sources and Interpretations," in Dina Porat and Dan Michman, eds., *The End of 1942, a Turning Point in World War II and in Comprehension of the Final Solution* (Jerusalem: Yad Vashem, 2017), pp. 339–360.
11 All the aforementioned were published by the World Jewish Congress in New York.
12 Letter from Robinson to Baron, October 14, 1946, YVA, O.65/37.
13 Robert Liberles, *Salo Wittmayer Baron, Architect of Jewish History* (New York and London: New York University Press, 1995), pp. 266–282, 322–337.

Perhaps Robinson approached Baron also in view of their acquaintance before they had migrated to the United States. During Robinson's activity with the League of Nations, Baron had been legal counsel to the League committee that oversaw the implementation of international covenants on minority rights.

Robinson began the letter with a review of archives that had documented the Holocaust in general and those in the United States in particular.[14] His conclusion was that only American Jewry could fund the information-gathering process. By implication American Jewry bore great responsibility for this, and Holocaust research activity must be concentrated in the United States. A budget large enough to set up and run a modern cataloging system based on microfilm preservation of documents was needed. Only thus could the documents be shared with the various organizations and disseminated among the research community with relative simplicity. Such a matrix would also allow the information-gathering institutions in Europe to forward relevant materials to the research hub in the United States.[15]

Redundancies, budget constraints, and lack of professionalism, however, had created a situation of total chaos. Robinson thought it essential to transform the way the work and research were being done by establishing a central research institute in the United States that would receive material from all over the world for cataloging and accessibility to researchers and the public. The institute's researchers would publish two series of books: collections of documents in an annotated scientific publication; and a series of research monographs titled *Zakhor* ("Remember"). The research institute, Robinson stressed, must make room for non-Jewish historians and should not be situated in New York but nearby, allowing researchers the benefit of proximity to this important metropolis while enjoying the quiet and peace of mind that would make optimal research activity possible. Robinson wanted to found the institute at once and to budget it at $300,000 per year.[16]

Historians disagree as to what degree the murder of European Jewry was part of the historical memory of World War II in the second half of

---

14 Letter from Robinson, October 14, 1946, YVA, O.65/37. For a fascinating and comprehensive discussion of the processes of documenting information on the Holocaust in Europe, see Laura Jockusch, *Collect and Record, Jewish Holocaust Documentation in Early Postwar Europe* (Oxford: Oxford University Press, 2012).
15 Robinson letter, October 14, 1946, YVA, O.65/37.
16 Ibid.

the 1940s. They are, however, of one mind about the complex challenge and difficulties that arose in imparting knowledge of the Nazi murder of European Jewry to the Jewish and, more generally, the American population.[17] According to the historian Tony Kushner, historians and contemporaries alike wanted to believe that the liberation of the camps in 1945, and the accrued information about the Final Solution would, as a matter of course, reveal the Holocaust of European Jewry to the public at large and establish its importance in the collective historical memory of World War II and the Nazi regime. This assumption, Kushner claimed, proved erroneous for several political and psychological reasons. The dramatic power of the information about the extermination process itself made the information hard to accommodate, causing the general public mind to repress it in the early postwar years. Thus, Kushner stresses, early on the Jews were almost totally excluded from U.S and British media reportage about the Nazis' murders, atrocities, and extermination scheme.[18]

In examining Robinson's endeavors shortly after the end of World War II, I find that, as a Jewish public activist immersed in the non-Jewish world, he agreed that integrating Holocaust memory into the realities of American life immediately after World War II was no simple, easy, or self-evident process. Robinson believed in the need for comprehensive and intensive public and educational activity among the Jewish community and others to make sure the Holocaust of European Jewry (as it came to be defined) would be engraved onto the collective memory of both Jews and non-Jews in the context of World War II. Robinson's research method at the Institute of Jewish Affairs shows that thorough and probing historical research into the Holocaust was the basis for Robinson's postwar efforts to shape consciousness of the Holocaust among Jews and non-Jews alike. Historical research also served him as a foundation on which the process of bringing war criminals to justice could be advanced.

At the same time Robinson realized that any documentation process, however thorough and profound, would be limited if its findings remained within the walls of the research institute. He saw it as his duty,

17 For a broad discussion of this issue, accompanied by an explanation of the complexity of the matter and a presentation of leading studies, see Lawrence Baron, "The Holocaust and American Public Memory, 1945–1960," *Holocaust and Genocide Studies*, 17 (2003), pp. 62–88.

18 Tony Kushner, *The Holocaust and the Liberal Imagination: A Social and Cultural History* (Oxford, UK, and Cambridge, USA: Blackwell, 1994), pp. 205–278.

as a researcher and a public figure, to present the findings and the data to the public at large. To do so, he did not settle for conservative publishing media (books and articles); instead, he acted to create additional means of presentation and exposure. He manifested this, *inter alia,* by initiating an exhibition on the fate of the Jews in the Holocaust that made its debut in Atlantic City in November 1944, as part of the WJC Emergency War Conference, and then toured across the United States. The Institute was responsible for the design, content, and construction of the exhibition. This first-of-its-kind venture, preceding the establishment of Holocaust memorial museums and commemorative centers in the United States,[19] was meant to syncretize the description of Jews' daily lives in Nazi-occupied Europe and the measures that the Nazis took to spread their anti-Jewish ideology. For reasons of limited space, it was decided to present visitors at the exhibition with only the most essential information about European Jewry before the Nazis' accession to power in Germany and anti-Jewish trends in medieval and modern Europe, in contrast to giving the broadest possible information about Jewish resistance during the Holocaust and Jews' participation in the Allied armed forces. The exhibits and their background material were to be shown in chronological order.[20]

True to the worldview that he had formed in the United States, Robinson saw the cause of remembering and studying the Holocaust in the Israeli arena as part of a global whole. Israel, he believed, deserved to play an important but not an exclusive role in Holocaust studies. Studying the Holocaust was too important to be confined to Israel's geographical boundaries; it was a central issue that, in his view, should be engaged by Jewish and non-Jewish researchers and opinion-shapers worldwide in the second half of the twentieth century. Importantly, Robinson dealt intensively with complex historical issues even though his formal training was in law and not history. Without denying it, he explained that he had been engaging in historical research for many years and that everything he said and wrote in this context was backed by primary sources.[21]

19 On the belated establishment of Holocaust memorial museums and centers in the United States, see Rochelle Saidel, *Never Too Late to Remember: The Politics behind New York City's Holocaust Museum* (New York: Holmes & Meier, 1996).

20 Institute of Jewish Affairs staff meeting, March 13, 1944, AJA, 361, C.2/98.

21 Robinson's responses to criticism after the Eichmann trial, November 11, 1965, YVA, O.65/38.

A typical example of Robinson's initiatives in this matter after the attainment of Israeli statehood in 1948, was his activity to convene the Conference on the History of the Jewish Catastrophe,[22] a joint venture of Israeli, European, and North American research institutes, academic institutions, and scholars. While arguing in favor of international collaboration in Holocaust research, Robinson advocated holding the conference in Jerusalem in order to assure the centrality of Israel in Holocaust research.[23] While stressing the importance of including non-Jewish researchers and research institutes in the conference, Robinson wanted to make sure that the Jewish research centers, foremost in Israel and the United States, would continue to lead the way in this field and would establish the guidelines for Holocaust research. The crucial need to hold the colloquium in Jerusalem, in his estimation, derived from the intended creation of an international academic team of Holocaust scholars centered in the Israeli capital.[24]

Ultimately the event took place in 1968. The delay may well have traced to technical difficulties and struggles among members of the Yad Vashem Directorate over the role of academic research at Yad Vashem. Robinson's involvement in the context of the conference shows that in his activities at Yad Vashem, as with those in the United States, he sought to combine public commemoration of the Holocaust with academic research at the highest level.[25] Robinson also wanted to make certain that the research would not be limited to the narrow context of the Holocaust theme; instead, he believed, it must fit into the broadest aspects of Jewish historical research. Therefore, he proposed that the conference in Jerusalem coincide with a colloquium of the World Union

---

22 Preparatory meeting for an international conference on the history of the Jewish catastrophe, 1964, no exact date given, YVA, O.65/76.

23 Ibid.

24 Ibid.

25 The conference was held on April 7–9, 1968. In English it was titled "Jewish Resistance during the Holocaust"; in Hebrew, the expression "Jewish steadfastness" was used. Boaz Cohen notes the difference between the English wording and the broader Hebrew concept. In regard to the conference, see Boaz Cohen, *Israeli Holocaust Research: Birth and Evolution* (London and New York: Routledge, 2013), pp. 208–225. Robinson visibly favored empowering the research element at Yad Vashem and did the same when he testified before a commission of examination, appointed in 1964, that probed the directions in which Yad Vashem was heading. See Cohen, *Israeli Holocaust Research*, pp. 165–179.

for Jewish Studies in the city and that researchers in other disciplines, such as sociology and psychology, be invited as well.[26]

Robinson's efforts regarding holding the event in Jerusalem were part of a total endeavor to empower research at Yad Vashem. One may find a salient manifestation of this in the decision by the minister of education to task him with examining the research component at Yad Vashem after voices within and outside the institution had criticized the conduct of its research array and the quality of the studies produced. The result was the "Robinson report," issued in 1960, in which Robinson leveled caustic criticism. He stated that the relations between Yad Vashem's researchers and the Israeli academic system in general—and the Hebrew University in particular—were incomplete and insufficient; even collaboration and joint research within Yad Vashem were sometimes nonexistent. Robinson demanded corrective action and urged Holocaust research to expand into fields such as antisemitism and totalitarianism—the exclusion of which from the research agenda, he opined, was detrimental to Holocaust research.

Robinson's report did not dampen the controversy over the question of research at Yad Vashem. Robinson attempted to systematize relations between Yad Vashem's research function and the Hebrew University, expand academic supervision of research work at Yad Vashem, and create an infrastructure for high-quality research in the future. These initiatives encountered major difficulties for reasons of budgetary shortfall and divergent perspectives among several leading personalities at Yad Vashem. The latter singled out a different field of endeavor at the institution—activity in the public contexts of Holocaust remembrance—as worthy of reinforcement. Throughout the 1960s, Robinson's hand remained evident in designing the research function at Yad Vashem and regularizing relations with the Hebrew University. His involvement, although unofficial, emanated from his post as the academic advisor of an interuniversity academic committee that had been established in 1967, to take up this issue.[27]

---

26 Robinson's efforts to broaden the purview of Holocaust research were the tip of an ongoing polemic on the issue. For a broad discussion of the matter, see David Engel, *Mul Har Ga'ash: Hokre Toldot Israel Lenohah Hashoa* (Hebrew) (Jerusalem: Zalman Shazar Center, 2010), pp. 206–257.

27 Cohen, *Israeli Holocaust Research*, pp. 158–164. In 1957, Yad Vashem and the Hebrew University jointly established the Institute for Research into the Destruction of European Jewry and its History in the Last Generation. Yad Vashem's International

The effort to convene the international conference in Jerusalem is but one example of Robinson's vigorous activity toward improving and systematizing Holocaust research in Israel and the world over. Another significant example was his initiative to publish *Chronology of the Jewish History under Nazi Impact*. The working meetings and discussions that preceded the appearance of this book took place in the second half of the 1950s. In the minutes of the meetings, one senses the processes that shaped Holocaust research and teaching, as well as vacillations about basic questions that Holocaust researchers have been confronting to this day.[28]

Robinson's outlook on the need to create an international matrix for Holocaust research, with its main centers in Israel and the United States, found practical expression in the publication of the *Chronology* in New York in 1960, as a joint project of Yad Vashem and YIVO under the editorship of Robinson and the eminent Holocaust researcher Philip Friedman, a pioneer in this field in the United States. Their collaboration also resulted in both historians, one in Jerusalem and the other in New York, writing the introduction to the study. The forewords to the volume were written by Ben-Zion Dinur—historian, Israel's minister of education, Israel Prize laureate, and the first chairperson of the Yad Vashem Directorate—and Professor Salo Baron.[29]

Robinson's book from 1960, and his other published works later in that decade should be understood in the context of Raul Hilberg's *The Destruction of the European Jews*, which came out just one year later.[30] Robinson was almost certainly aware of Hilberg's study before it appeared in print. Hilberg had completed his PhD dissertation in 1955,

Institute for Holocaust Studies was founded in 1993. On the debate surrounding the research element at Yad Vashem, see Dan Michman, "Ha'im Yesh 'Eskola Israelit' Beheker Hashoa? Heker Hashoa Veheker Ha'antishemiyut Le'or Hashoa BiMedinat Israel" (Hebrew), *Zion*, 74 (2009), pp. 219–244.

28 Minutes of meetings of the preparatory staff, *Chronology of the Jewish History under Nazi Impact* (no exact date, YVA, O.65/4).

29 Jacob Robinson and Philip Friedman, eds., *Guide to Jewish History under Nazi Impact* (New York: Yad Vashem and YIVO, 1960). For additional publications in the same context, see Jacob Robinson and Yehuda Bauer, eds., *Guide to Unpublished Materials of the Holocaust Period* (Jerusalem: The Hebrew University Institute of Contemporary Jewry, 1970); Jacob Robinson, ed., *The Holocaust and After: Sources & Literature in English* (Jerusalem: Israel Universities Press, 1973); and Jacob Robinson, ed., *Holocaust: The Nuremberg Evidence* (Jerusalem: Yad Vashem and YIVO, 1976).

30 The book has been published in multiple editions; for example, Raul Hilberg, *The Destruction of the European Jews* (New Haven: Yale University Press, 2003).

and submitted his study to Yad Vashem's publishing department but was turned down.[31] While acknowledging the importance of Hilberg's research, Robinson acidly criticized him for not basing himself on Jewish sources; in Robinson's opinion this introduced bias to the study and blurred the connection between the victims' Jewishness and the Nazis' decision to exterminate them.[32] Robinson's remarks fit into broader criticism of Hilberg's claim that the passivity of the Jewish leadership during the Holocaust and its de facto collaboration with the Nazis helped enhance the Nazis' ability to exterminate European Jewry. Robinson's research in the second half of the twentieth century, in contrast, is set on broad foundations of rich Jewish source material on the Holocaust and, in effect, offers an alternative direction of research than that of Hilberg.

The Eichmann Trial

The Eichmann affair as a public event began on May 23, 1960, when David Ben-Gurion informed the Knesset that Adolf Eichmann was in custody in Israel. It ended on May 31, 1962, the day that Eichmann was executed by hanging.[33]

In early July 1960, amidst the preparations for Eichmann's trial, the chairperson of the World Zionist Organization, Nahum Goldmann, wrote the following to Jacob Robinson:

I am of the view that you should appear at Eichmann's trial as the general prosecutor on behalf of the Jewish people, given [your] knowledge of the era and also [your] talent and demeanor. I would also be interested in hearing your view on this matter before I

31 On Hilberg's difficulties in publishing his work and Yad Yashem's rejection, see Engel, *Mul Har Ga'ash*, pp. 157–161. Years later, in 2012, the book was also published in Hebrew under the scientific editorship of David Bankier and Bella Gutterman: Raul Hilberg, *Hurban Yehudei Eropa* (Jerusalem: Ben-Gurion Research Institute for the Study of Zionism and Yad Vashem, 2012).

32 Engel, pp. 158–183; for a positive response to Hilberg by Robinson, see p. 167.

33 For a discussion of Ben-Gurion in the context of the Eichmann trial, see Michael Keren, "Ben Gurion's Theory of Sovereignty: The Trial of Adolf Eichmann," in Ronald W. Zweig, ed., *David Ben-Gurion, Politics and Leadership in Israel* (London: Frank Cass, 1991), pp. 38–51. On the Eichmann trial, see Hanna Yablonka, *Medinat Israel Neged Adolf Eichmann* (Hebrew) (Jerusalem: Yedioth Ahronoth and Yad Izhak Ben-Zvi, 2001), pp. 1–67; on the trial and its repercussions, see articles in Richard J. Golsan and Sarah M. Misemer, eds., *The Trial that Never Ends: "Eichmann in Jerusalem" in Retrospect* (Toronto: University of Toronto Press, 2017).

discuss it with Mr. Rosen [the minister of justice], Ben-Gurion, and others.

As is known, Robinson did not receive the appointment—it went to Gideon Hausner—and the complex and tangled discussion of whom to appoint overshoots the limits of this article. My purpose in quoting Goldmann's letter is to demonstrate Robinson's deep involvement in the Eichmann trial.[34] He was made "Special Consultant to the Attorney General," and no doubt possessed the legal training, comprehensive knowledge of the Final Solution, and the experience accrued from his participation in the Nuremberg trials. Presumably this unique combination led to his recruitment for involvement in the preparations for the trial and at the trial itself. In her book about the trial, Hanna Yablonka notes Robinson's conspicuous role.[35] Robinson's papers bring to light additional levels of his involvement and add another layer for research into this complex affair.

Robinson's papers demonstrate his centrality in shaping the legal process and weaving the web of arguments that demonstrated the necessity of trying Eichmann in Israel. After Eichmann's capture and the intention of prosecuting him in Israel were announced, an international debate arose concerning the entitlement of the State of Israel to carry out the legal proceeding. Robinson plotted the course of Israel's response. In the summer of 1960, he published a comprehensive article on the issue in the influential journal *Commentary*.[36] He began by advising his readers that most UN resolutions after World War II instruct the organization's member states to try Nazi war criminals who had committed crimes against humanity. The Government of Argentina had neither honored the relevant resolution nor had it advanced any judicial process involving Eichmann. Therefore the Government of Israel, in accordance with the resolution, was compelled to operate on Argentinean soil and bring this Nazi criminal to trial in Israel. Eichmann had not been prosecuted at Nuremberg because he had managed to escape, but he had been declared a war criminal and the perpetrator of crimes against humanity. This, by implication, established the duty and the right of the Government of Israel to take legal action against Eichmann. A trial of this kind,

34 Letter from Nahum Goldmann to Robinson, June 6, 1960, YVA, O.65/59.
35 Yablonka, *Medinat Israel Neged Adolf Eichmann*, p. 115.
36 Jacob Robinson, "Eichmann and the Question of Jurisdiction," *Commentary*, 30 (1960), pp. 1–6.

Robinson stressed, could not be held in Argentina as it had proven its reluctance to do so. International law, he continued, allows a state to adjudicate crimes committed elsewhere, and the International Court of Justice at The Hague did not have jurisdiction over the type of crimes that Eichmann had committed. The German extermination machine, Robinson stressed, had had no territorial attributes; this strengthened the reasoning in favor of holding the trial in Jerusalem. Since the State of Israel has the world's largest concentration of Holocaust survivors, Robinson contended, that is precisely where the trial should take place.[37]

Although clearly in favor of Israel as the place of jurisdiction, Robinson was mindful of the difficulties that a trial in Jerusalem would create.[38] In early November 1960, he wrote to Minister of Justice Pinchas Rosen a strictly classified document titled "Preliminary List of Problems in Need of Imminent Discussion and Decision."[39] The letter takes up basic questions on the conduct of the Eichmann trial in Israel and shows how deeply involved Robinson was in designing the course of the proceeding. Well aware of the political and public significance of the trial, Robinson began this document as follows:

> This trial has already stirred and will yet stir much interest worldwide. Consequently, as we try the defendant, the great and small world (by which I mean the Jewish world) will judge the State of Israel and its judicial arm on the basis of accepted principles in enlightened countries.[40]

Robinson reasoned that his remarks would demonstrate the need for decisions on several basic questions that, he said, would make it possible "to set the trial within the narrow frame of eradicating the criminal phenomena of World War II without transgressing the accepted fundamentals of law in enlightened countries."

How can justice be done, Robinson asked, when the defendant provokes such stormy emotions in Israel? How will witnesses who live abroad arrive? If they do, how should we relate to those who come from Nazi party circles? In this context Robinson mentioned the ban on Nazis from entering Israeli territory. How should the trial be kept from

---

37 See Robinson's remarks in Robinson, "Eichmann and the Question of Jurisdiction."
38 Ibid.
39 Letter from Robinson to Minister of Justice Rosen, November 6, 1960, marked "top secret," YVA, O.65/75.
40 Ibid.

becoming too lengthy? Should other countries and organizations that were harmed by Eichmann's deeds be allowed to be involved in the trial? Should the defendant be judged for what he did throughout Europe, or should the focus be trained on specific countries? How should an appropriate balance be struck between documents and testimonies at the trial? It is impossible, Robinson stressed, to judge the defendant in a vacuum; thought should be given as to how to link him to his superiors. Notwithstanding the importance of the documents, witnesses should be called to the stand. He explained:

> The documentation per se yields an account neither of Jewish suffering at large, nor of Jews in different geographic areas, nor in the concentration camps and the extermination centers, nor, of course, in the experience of the individual—the victim of the entire Nazi enterprise—and it totally overlooks the special cruelty that was applied to children, women, the elderly, and the disabled. This knowledge is not needed to create a dramatic atmosphere but to balance the testimonies. Jewish witnesses will be needed and here, as always, problems of their quantity and quality will arise.[41]

The matter of concern in Robinson's letter to the minister of justice transcends judicial issues. Robinson wrote not only as an attorney but also as a Jewish public activist familiar with the international political system and immersed in academic and intellectual circles that might take a keen interest in the trial. He wished to make sure that Eichmann's trial would serve Israel's political and public interests and not create a stumbling block. The question of the acceptability of the trial abroad was especially important to Robinson, who pursued his quotidian affairs in the New York public, intellectual, and political domain. In his letter to the minister of justice, Robinson went on to stress:

> I am not an expert in public relations but there is no overlooking the fact that this trial will reverberate widely abroad and, in a certain sense, its power and influence will hinge on the effectiveness with which public relations will be organized. The question one hears not only from non-Jews but also from Jews, "What is all this labor to you?," needs a full and convincing answer, especially for that upper stratum in the enlightened world that takes an interest in

---

41 Ibid.

this problem from a historico-judicial or moral perspective, that will satisfy its needs in a manner befitting those types of people.[42]

Robinson strongly favored Israeli jurisdiction but was severely troubled by the complex interrelations of law and history that arose in the context of the Eichmann trial. He did not overlook the fact that, while only Eichmann would be on trial from the purely judicial standpoint, the proceeding would carry much broader significance. He asked:

> Who is being tried?
> a. the German people?
> b. the National-Socialist regime?
> c. antisemitism (at large or in its Nazi form)?
> d. the SS?
> e. the "Final Solution" and its perpetrators (and the former Mufti of Jerusalem Haj Amin al-Husseini as well)?
> f. the defendant as an initiator, participant, and perpetrator?

Then he warned: "The greatest danger that lurks for us in this trial is the blurring [of] the boundaries between criminal law and history. It is of course impossible to perceive the defendant's trial without [understanding] the historical background of the time in which he lived and acted."[43]

Robinson wished to integrate the essential historical background into the trial but not to make it the first and last word. Therefore he suggested that a precedent from the Nuremberg trials be used: The prosecutor in Nuremberg, Robert Jackson, had invited Chaim Weizmann, the future first president of the State of Israel, to describe to the court the general background of the Jewish issue in Europe in the Nazi context. Similarly, Robinson now proposed that a reliable witness or witnesses be summoned, along with experts, to describe the events from a broad perspective. While mindful of the educational importance of inserting the historical aspect into the trial, he maintained:

> It bears mentioning that the working methods of a criminal judge are so different from those of a historical researcher that one doubts the very possibility of a criminal court's dispensing historical justice and not only criminal justice. Just as the court cannot resemble the

---

42 Ibid.
43 Ibid.

throne of history, it is unfit to serve as a bureau of statistics. Today there is no need whatsoever to examine what was determined in Nuremberg. It is not our brief to challenge it. That will be done by those who have an interest in reducing the number of victims and vindicating the criminals.[44]

Practically speaking, the desire to set the trial of Adolf Eichmann in its broad historical context was reflected in the decision by the prosecution team to call a historian to the stand as an expert witness. Robinson played a central role in choosing this expert, and, in fact, only after his final approval was it decided to assign this duty to Salo Baron of Columbia University.[45]

Gideon Hausner, the prosecutor, wrote the following to Robinson with regard to "historical testimony" at the trial of Adolf Eichmann: "I ask again that the sole consideration in regard to the 'historical testimony' be [its] utility for the cause itself. And if you have doubts about inviting Prof. Baron after meeting with him, please let me know and we will look for a way to revert to the previous plan."[46]

The Hausner–Robinson correspondence sheds no light on the "previous plan." Robinson did meet with Baron in New York, and they decided that Baron would give his testimony in Hebrew. Robinson prepared Baron for the cross-examination pursuant to the testimony, and additional meetings were set up before Baron set out from New York for Israel to assume his task. Robinson's conclusion was that, "Baron is the [best]-qualified man to prepare the testimony and defend it."[47]

Notwithstanding Robinson's consent to Baron as a witness and despite the preparatory meeting between the two, Robinson expressed pointed criticism of Baron's testimony after the fact.[48] In Robinson's papers one finds two levels of remarks about the testimony. In the first,

44 Ibid.

45 See Baron's testimony at the trial: State of Israel, Ministry of Justice, Israel State Archives, Trial of Adolf Eichmann, *Reshumot Mishpat: Hayo'etz Hamishpati Shel Memshelet Israel Neged Adolf Eichmann,* Vol. 1 (Hebrew) (Jerusalem: Israel State Archives, 2003), pp. 143–162.

46 Letter from Gideon Hausner to Robinson, January 12, 1961, YVA, O.65/41. See also official letter from the consul general in New York to Baron, inviting him to testify at the Eichmann trial, February 7, 1961, YVA, O.65/41.

47 Letter from Robinson to Gideon Hausner, January 19, 1961, YVA, O.65/41.

48 For suggestions of other candidates for the "historical witness" role at the Eichmann trial, other critics of Baron's testimony, and the main points of Robinson's critique, see Yablonka, *Medinat Yisrael neged Adolf Eichmann,* pp. 100–106.

Robinson harshly criticized historical imprecisions in the testimony
on the basis of a painstaking review of each paragraph. A pronounced
example is his response to Baron's statements about Europe during
World War II. "The response was as full of errors as a pomegranate,
too many to count," Robinson wrote. "Here are a few examples: Italy
joined the war not in May 1940 but in June. Two lines later, it is stated
first that Germany took over the Balkans with the Bulgarians' aid, but
Hungary replaces Bulgaria in the same breath."[49]

One may set some of Robinson's critique of Baron's testimony in the
framework of the complex relationship between the historian and the
judicial system as manifested in the former's role as an expert witness.
A historian usually testifies as an expert witness in legal proceedings
concerning mass murders and acts of genocide. His/her role in such
a proceeding comprises two main tasks: to provide documents and
primary sources in support of the various testimonies and to equip the
court with comprehensive historical background that is essential for
understanding the issues being litigated. In the case of the Eichmann
trial, historical research institutes such as Yad Vashem and its team of
historians interacted with the prosecution in order to set the indictment
on solid ground. The purpose of Baron's testimony was to advise the
court of the broad historical background of European Jewry and to
describe in general contours its fate during the Holocaust. Historians
and lawyers are not oblivious to the intrinsic difficulties that arise when
historical testimony is introduced into a judicial process. The historian's
testimony as an expert witness may generate tension between factual
presentation and the historian's personal interpretation.[50]

One who peruses the minutes of Baron's testimony at the trial does

---

49 Letter from Robinson to the minister of justice and attorney general concerning
    Baron's testimony, May 14, 1961, YVA, O.65/41.
50 For support of the participation of historians in legal proceedings, see Rebecca Gidley
    and Matthew Turner, "Judicializing History: Mass Crimes Trials and the Historian
    as Expert Witness in West Germany, Cambodia, and Bangladesh," *Genocide Studies
    and Prevention*, 12:3 (2018), pp. 52–67. See also Erich Haberer, "History and Justice:
    Paradigms of the Prosecution of Nazi Crimes," *Holocaust and Genocide Studies*,
    19:3 (2005), pp. 487–519. On resistance to the involvement of historians in legal
    proceedings, see Henry Rousso, *The Haunting Past: History, Memory and Justice
    in Contemporary France* (Philadelphia: University of Pennsylvania Press, 2002). For
    further discussion of the matter, see Lawrence Douglas, *The Memory of Judgment:
    Making Law and History in the Trials of the Holocaust* (New Haven: Yale University
    Press, 2001).

find several instances of tension between Baron's remarks as a historian and the judges' demands. The judges had to elucidate the professor's statements in their own words and ask Baron to be more forthcoming and precise in his remarks.[51]

In my estimation, Robinson's critique of Baron's testimony at the Eichmann trial crosses the bounds of the debate over the historian as a witness. Fascinatingly, it focuses on issues relating to the essence of Jewish nationhood. According to Robinson, Baron underweighted the complexity and formal wealth of diasporic Jewish national existence: "[Baron offers] no answer at all about the forms of the national movement and, as for youth, the description is truncated and faulty." In addition, in Robinson's opinion, Baron omitted the Jews' enormous contribution to human civilization, offering "a sparse review of Hebrew literature and the Jews' contribution to general culture, artistic treasures, and libraries, and not a word about 'human civilization.'"[52] Robinson took particular offense at Baron's use of superlatives to describe the successes of the Jewish people. To buttress his argument, Robinson actually counted what he considered the overstatements in Baron's testimony, such as "exceptional, one should be amazed, I was amazed, very wonderful, very horrific, with all the efforts that their strength permitted, and of the highest order."[53] The witness, Robinson thought, presented a boastful and overstated Jewish national perception. Importantly, he did not object to the very mention of these matters in Baron's testimony but only to the exaggeration. By prior agreement between Hausner and Robinson concerning this testimony, Baron's remarks in court were to combine a general presentation of basic facts and historical, national, and cultural testimony.

Robinson's remarks about the testimony reflect vehement criticism of what he considered the factual missteps in Baron's performance. His main objection concerned Baron's presentation of Jewish nationhood and diasporic Jewish existence. Thus Robinson challenged Baron's historical and national outlook by invoking Chaim Weizmann's testimony before

---

51 For critical remarks by the panel of judges toward Baron's testimony, see, for example, *Minutes*, pp. 145, 146, 150, 153, 154, 161.

52 Letter from Robinson to the minister of justice and attorney general concerning Baron's testimony, May 14, 1961, YVA, O.65/41.

53 All quotations in this context are taken from Robinson's letter to the minister of justice and the attorney general concerning Baron's testimony, May 14, 1961, YVA, O.65/41.

the Peel Commission rather than that of an expert historian. His criticism of Baron was not only historical but combined history, ideology, and national perspectives. In Robinson's eyes, the witness Weizmann, unlike the witness Baron, had presented the combination of history and ideology that best reflected the main outlines of modern Jewish existence. As reinforcement of the estimation that Robinson's criticism was not limited to historical inaccuracies, one may cite the concluding paragraph of his letter to Gideon Hausner in regard to Baron's testimony: "What bothers me at this moment is [whether there is] some possibility of fixing the mistakes (in the broad sense of this word)."[54] Robinson, a lawyer who was trained to use words precisely, chose to conclude his letter by emphasizing a more sweeping issue than just historical errors and imprecisions of various levels of importance.

Baron's testimony and Robinson's criticism should be understood in view of the primacy of the Diaspora in Baron's historical *oeuvre*. Baron had published trailblazing studies, and many historians see him as the doyen of this field. Baron objected to the "lachrymose conception," which sees Jewishness in the Diaspora as reflected only in persecution and suffering. He presented a more balanced and optimistic perception that stresses the successes and achievements of Jewish communities, particularly in the spiritual domain. Nevertheless, Robinson chose to attack Baron in the latter's métier of all places.[55] Robinson inveighed against what he called the "overstated Jewish national perception" in Baron's testimony. In his opinion, Baron disregarded various complex manifestations of Jewish nationhood. In fact, Robinson maintained that Baron had not presented Jewish life in its diasporic form as a realistic option, had refrained from describing the richness and dynamism of Jewish life in Europe, and had failed to describe points at which Jewry touched and intersected with the non-Jewish world.

Robinson's critique of Baron's testimony at the Eichmann trial should be understood in light of his own broad worldview. Robinson, although a Zionist, wanted Jewish life to continue in its diasporic form as well. As he saw it, Jews continue to maintain rich and intensive Jewish life as individuals; as a community, they are an inseparable part of the non-Jewish world in their countries of residence. Robinson applied this

---

54 Ibid.
55 On Baron's historical project, see Robert Liberles, "Salo Baron Kehoker Toldot Am Israel" (Hebrew), *Zion*, 55:3 (1990), pp. 333–340.

paradigm in his own life by supporting the establishment of the State of Israel and participating in its institutions while still going about his daily life in New York. Robinson attacked the testimony precisely in Baron's area of expertise in reference to the Diaspora. One may only surmise why, when placed on the stand, Baron stressed elements that effectively contradicted his studies and the life he actually led in New York. Perhaps the impressive combination of the Holocaust, the establishment of the State of Israel, and Baron's invitation, as a Jewish historian living in New York, to give the main historical testimony at the Eichmann trial amplified his Zionist and Israel-centric national sentiments at the expense of the meaningfulness of Diaspora Jewish life.

Some time after the trial, Baron sent Robinson a conciliatory letter that acknowledged the latter's massive contribution to the Eichmann trial. This may indicate that Baron himself assessed Robinson's arguments as having been correct. Instead of merely attaching an official letter to the return of a book that Robinson had lent him in order to prepare for the trial, Baron wrote, among other things, "Now that your arduous labors are over and you can relax I wish to congratulate you upon your part in the historic trial."[56]

One example of how Robinson implemented his worldview was as Israel's representative to UN frameworks, as noted above. In this capacity he sought to create a web of international agreements that would allow Jewish communities to continue to exist around the globe. His efforts found salient expression in his involvement in the Convention Relating to the Status of Refugees (1951), which was called in the first half of the 1950s in order to regulate the refugee problem that had come about after World War II. The conferences leading up to the convention began in 1950; the convention took place in Geneva in the summer of 1951. The participants established the identity of those entitled to refugee status, defined refugees' rights, and determined the documents that refugees would need in order to cross international borders. The resolutions of the convention were ratified in a special session of the General Assembly in April 1954; most of them define refugees' status and rights to this day. Special attention was devoted to the question of the post-World War II Jewish refugees in the debate preceding the signing of the accord in 1954. Robinson played an important role at the convention and strove prodigiously to improve and settle the status

56 Letter from Baron to Robinson, July 6, 1962, YVA, O.65/41.

of refugees generally and Jewish refugees in particular. In the Jewish context, Robinson wished to make sure Jewish refugees would be given access to new immigration countries and, if interested, to return to their original lands of residence. As Israel's representative, Robinson of course supported the establishment of a Jewish state in *Eretz Israel* within the construct of the political arrangements that followed World War II. Concurrently, however, he sought to spin a web of international accords that would assure the option of not immigrating to Israel and carrying on in Diaspora communities for those who so desired. Robinson did not see the State of Israel as the sole guarantor of world Jewry. Members of Jewish communities elsewhere, he argued, should be protected by a structure of international agreements under UN auspices.

Another set of players that should defend the interests of Jews around the world under the UN umbrella, he believed, was that of the international Jewish organizations. Robinson did not see the activity of such entities as an infringement on Israeli sovereignty; rather, the organizations were positive actors that would enhance the Jews' ability to live as individuals and in community settings outside of Israel. Robinson's support of the activity of Jewish organizations on behalf of world Jewry was part of a broad worldview that favored the involvement of nongovernmental organizations, including Jewish ones, in UN activity as agents of peace and international cooperation. This could be seen in Robinson's attitude toward the appearance of representatives of the Jewish Agency and the Arab Higher Committee, the main political representative body of the Arabs in Mandatory Palestine, before the UN institutions as the UN debated the initiative that would become the 1947 partition resolution. It was important for these representatives to appear before the UN institutions, Robinson reasoned, not only to further the struggle for Jewish statehood but also to set an important positive precedent for the involvement of NGOs in UN activity.[57]

---

57 Robinson's struggle to settle the status of Jewish refugees can be found in his reports to the Israeli Ministry of Foreign Affairs: Israel State Archives, Mission of Israel in Geneva, reports from Dr. Robinson, File *het-tsadi*-18/4, January 23 and 30, 1950; February 6 and 21, 1950. For a discussion of Robinson's disagreements with relevant Israeli government officials with regard to the 1951 Refugee Convention, see Rotem Giladi, "A 'Historical Commitment'? Identity and Ideology in Israel's Attitude to the Refugee Convention 1951–1954," *The International History Review*, 37 (2015), pp. 745–767. See quote in Jacob Robinson, *Palestine and the United Nations, Prelude to Solution* (Washington DC: Public Affairs Press, 1947), p. 103. For a broad discussion of NGO operations at the UN, see Robinson, pp. 88–105.

Robinson and Hannah Arendt

At the end of his remarks on Baron's testimony, Robinson mentioned "fixing the mistakes."[58] Robinson was keenly aware of the historical and public importance of the Eichmann trial. From his standpoint, "fixing the mistakes" had to be done not only in court but also in the public arena after the trial. In 1965, Robinson published his book *And the Crooked Shall be Made Straight: The Eichmann Trial, the Jewish Catastrophe and Hannah Arendt's Narrative,* in response to Arendt's *Eichmann in Jerusalem: A Report on the Banality of Evil.*[59]

Arendt observed the Eichmann trial as a correspondent for *The New Yorker.* Her submissions were published in five issues of the magazine and then collected and edited into the book *Eichmann in Jerusalem* in 1963. In it Arendt subjects the Eichmann trial to acerbic criticism. She opposes Jerusalem as the jurisdiction, arguing that the trial should have been heard before an international tribunal.[60] She also assails the way the trial was conducted, citing as an example the defense's inability to call German defense witnesses due to concern that they would be arrested in Israel under the Nazis and Nazi Collaborators (Punishment) Law (1950). According to Arendt, Eichmann was put through a show trial in which the goals deviated from sound court proceedings.[61] Arendt pays much attention to analyzing Eichmann's actions during the Holocaust. While not absolving him of responsibility for his horrific deeds, she portrays him as a bureaucratic product of the German murder machine. She synopsizes her complex attitude toward Eichmann in a passage that refers to the immediate prelude to his execution by hanging: "It was as though in those last minutes he was summing up the lessons that this long course in human wickedness had taught us—the lesson of the fearsome, word-and-thought-defying *banality of evil.*"[62] She has been subjected to particularly trenchant criticism for this attitude.

Arendt also uses her writings about the Eichmann trial as a

---

58 Letter from Robinson to the minister of justice and attorney general concerning Baron's testimony, May 14, 1961, YVA, O.65/41.

59 Hannah Arendt, *Eichmann in Jerusalem: A Report on the Banality of Evil* (New York: Viking Press, 1963; revised edition [London: Penguin, 1968]); Jacob Robinson, *And the Crooked Shall be Made Straight: the Eichmann Trial, the Jewish Catastrophe, and Hannah Arendt's Narrative* (New York: Macmillan, 1965).

60 Ibid., p. 277.

61 Ibid., pp. 22–27.

62 Ibid., p. 263.

springboard for the examination of important Holocaust-related issues. Particularly salient is her criticism of the patterns of activity of Jewish community leaders in Europe, especially the Judenräte, during the Holocaust. Arendt depicts them as collaborators with the Nazis and claims they made a perceptible contribution to the Nazis' success in implementing the Final Solution.

The publication of Robinson's response to Arendt's work should be understood in view of his acute sensitivity to the public resonance of the Eichmann trial abroad. *And the Crooked* is indeed a stinging indictment of Arendt's treatise. Further study of both works and of Robinson's papers, however, points to a more complex reality. A central portion of Arendt's critique of the Eichmann trial revolves around the design of the proceeding as a "show trial" that Ben-Gurion used to influence the political and ideological shaping of the State of Israel. Such a situation, she says, obviates the very possibility of a sound judicial proceeding.[63] Statements by Robinson during the preparations for and during the trial show that he entertained a similar concern. Robinson acknowledged the public and educational messages of the proceedings but wished to avoid a show trial and thus demanded strict adherence to sound and orderly judicial process. By implication he reasoned that any other measure would impair the historical meaning of the trial and trigger piercing criticism abroad. In his book, understandably, Robinson did not reveal his apprehensions; instead, he wrote vehemently against defining the Eichmann trial as a show trial. His comments include the following:

> According to Miss Arendt, the Prime Minister of Israel, David Ben-Gurion, "had in mind" a "show trial" in Jerusalem (p. 2). She also says that he was the "invisible stage manager of the proceedings" (p. 3). She offers no support for these serious accusations... [64]

Robinson was also aware that the choice of Jerusalem as the jurisdiction would send waves of tumult through the international community. In Chapter 2 of his book *War Crimes Trials and International Law*, he expresses unmitigated support of the choice of Jerusalem and of an Israeli court, acting under the laws of the State of Israel.[65] He finds Arendt's opposition to trying Eichmann in Jerusalem groundless; he states that

63 Ibid., pp. 14–38.
64 Robinson, *And the Crooked,* p. 108. With regard to Robinson's concerns, see his letter to Minister of Justice Rosen, November 6, 1960, YVA, O.65/75.
65 Robinson, *And the Crooked,* pp. 60-100.

his position is backed by the jurisprudence of international law. In this case, too, study of Robinson's papers reveals that he acknowledges the less than self-evident nature of the issue and admits that the prosecution team and the Government of Israel should have addressed the matter with gravitas *ab initio*, thus creating a worthy judicial infrastructure that would show the world methodical reasoning in support of trying Eichmann in Jerusalem. Robinson is mindful of the difficulty that this involved and stresses the need to bring in public relations people to bolster the media campaign.[66]

Robinson and Arendt disagreed ferociously on other issues relating to the Eichmann trial. In particular Robinson rejected Arendt's criticism of the leaders of the Jewish communities in Europe. Arendt's definition of them as collaborators with the Nazis, Robinson charged, is rooted in a total misunderstanding of realities in the Holocaust era. In his opinion one might trace this misunderstanding to Arendt's exposure only to German sources in regard to the process used to exterminate European Jewry. The Jewish documents, he advised, tell a totally different story. Robinson reacted similarly to Arendt's description of Eichmann's actions during the Holocaust, claiming it revealed an egregious misunderstanding of Eichmann's centrality in the extermination of European Jewry, effectively belittling his murderous role and its importance.[67]

Robinson wrote his book in English for Jewish and non-Jewish readerships in the United States and, particularly, in New York.[68] In the preparations for the trial and during the proceedings, Robinson was severely concerned about how the American intellectual elites would respond: "It will be necessary to pay particular attention to that upper stratum of the enlightened world that takes an interest in this problem from a historico-judicial or moral perspective and to meet its needs in a manner appropriate to this kind of people."[69]

It should be recalled that although Robinson was active in Israel and held important posts in its institutions, the center of his life was in New York. Even before the Eichmann trial, Robinson was aware of the powerful impact of Holocaust remembrance on shaping the Jewish

---

66 Letter from Robinson to Minister of Justice Rosen, November 6, 1960.

67 Robinson, *And the Crooked*, pp. 58-59.

68 In this context Robinson's response to the criticisms of his book in the American press is noteworthy. See his letters of October 24, September 12, and November 11, 1965, YVA, O.65/38.

69 Letter from Robinson to Minister of Justice Rosen, November 6, 1960.

world after World War II. The Eichmann trial was especially important in this process, and Robinson wanted to make sure that the trial would not impair American Jewry's ability to retain its place within the tangled tapestry of American Jewish life while maintaining a meaningful relationship with Israel. Thus the acceptability of the Eichmann trial in non-Jewish social, intellectual, and cultural circles had to be assured. Any presentation of the Eichmann proceedings as a show trial deviating from international jurisprudence would obviously harm the cause. For this reason Robinson placed special emphasis on these issues in his battle with Arendt, even though he knew they were complex.

In Robinson's estimation, barbed criticism of the Jewish leadership during the Holocaust era represented more than a grave misunderstanding of history; it had pernicious implications for the ability of world Jewry to use Holocaust remembrance as a reconstructive mechanism after the catastrophe. The possibility of a favorable reception for Arendt's book in the United States, from his perspective, might jeopardize or, at the very least, disrupt the Jews' integration as a community into the American sphere. Therefore, he had no option but to rebut the book with an appropriate response.

In the context of the Eichmann trial, Robinson targeted both Baron's testimony and Arendt's book in connection to their attitudes toward the Diaspora, as Robinson felt that these might undermine the existential foundations of the postwar and post-Holocaust Jewish communities. Robinson believed that the Jews' steadfastness during the Holocaust and their patterns of response to the Nazis' murderous actions were solid proof of the power of Diaspora Jewish existence throughout the generations and signaled clearly that world Jewry would continue to survive and thrive.[70]

Although Robinson's purpose in publishing his book was to dispute Arendt's conclusions about the Eichmann trial in front of a broad readership, the structure of the book did not serve this cause. *And the Crooked* is a highly detailed document that tears down Arendt's claims and strives to impress its readers with her errors, contradictions, and ignorance. The main argument of Robinson's critics was that his choice of focus—on minutiae and not on the overall picture—gravely diminished the ability to mount an effective response to Arendt. Robinson was

---

70 Jacob Robinson, "On the Jewish Catastrophe – Where Does it Stand Today," *Proceedings of the World Congress of Jewish Studies*, 1 (1965), pp. 15–20.

aware of the criticism but pronounced it factually groundless. *And the Crooked*, he said, elaborated on all of the main issues in his controversy with Arendt, such as the Jewish resistance and its place in the Holocaust, and Eichmann's role in the Final Solution. The point-by-point discussion of Arendt's errors is crucial, he insisted, to uncover her ignorance, reveal the shaky basis of her outlook on the Eichmann trial, and, more generally, on the fate of the Jews in the Holocaust.[71]

Even if Robinson was right and coped effectively with Arendt's sweeping allegations, his raft of arguments "drowns" in the profusion of details specified in the book. Robinson's response to his critics implies that he realized this but attempted to stress the breadth of his claims.[72] Although Robinson was deeply and broadly versed in the Holocaust, his legal training and the official nature of much of his historical writing, carried out as part of his activity in bodies such as the Institute of Jewish Affairs, lend his writing a persnickety legalistic complexion that the public at large found off-putting. Interestingly, similar difficulties come to light in Robinson's books from the early 1960s. In these works Robinson stressed the Jewish perspective on the Holocaust and offered an approach different from that of Hilberg, who, his critics allege, muted the connection between the victims' Jewishness and the Nazis' decision to murder them. As in Robinson's writing in the context of the Eichmann trial, the tenor of these early works made them inaccessible to the public at large, causing them to be almost totally crowded out of the public consciousness. However, there is a difference between the public's disregard of Robinson's writings and the major impact of the direction of Holocaust research that he spearheaded in Israel and the United States. Studies on the shaping of Holocaust research emphasize Robinson's contribution in this regard.[73]

---

71 Robinson's response to criticism of his book, *New York Herald Tribune*, October 24, 1965, YVA, O.65/4.

72 Robinson's response in *New York Review of Books*, November 11, 1965, YVA, O.65/4. For another response by Robinson in a similar vein, see *New York Review of Books*, October 12, 1965.

73 Another eminent example of Robinson's writing style is his criticism of Baron's testimony at the Eichmann trial. Again he produced a detailed document that examines the testimony meticulously and presents a detailed list of what Robinson considers errors. This manner of writing makes it very hard to illuminate the main arguments that transcend his discussion of specific historical errors. On the enormous influence of the Robinson–Hilberg tussle on Holocaust research, see Engel, *Mul Har Ga'ash*, p. 183. For the same discussion in the American context, see

In contrast to Robinson's book, *Eichmann in Jerusalem* is written in a totally different style, much more accessible to readers at large. One may presume that this is the reason that Arendt's opus gained much wider diffusion. It penetrated the core of the exchange on the Eichmann trial and the Holocaust and has maintained that position in the intellectual and public discourse surrounding these events. Robinson's book, in contrast, has been almost totally sidelined in the debate over the trial and the Holocaust.

The social, cultural, and intellectual contexts of the discussion of Arendt's book are too broad to treat in this article. One may surmise rather confidently that *Eichmann in Jerusalem*, like *And the Crooked*, was addressed to the New York social, political, and intellectual circles in which each author moved. Although Arendt was active in Jewish and Zionist settings in Europe before she emigrated to the United States, one cannot find similar patterns in her activity in New York.[74] Thus both of these important books, which made definitive contributions to the shaping of public memory of the Eichmann trial, were written about a trial held in Jerusalem but for readers in New York.

Conclusion

Robinson's public activity reflects a fascinating and singular model of Jewish nationhood. Robinson opposed "the negation of the exile," viewing the Diaspora as an important and evolving part of Jewish existence, particularly after World War II. The establishment of the State of Israel did not change his worldview. For Robinson the Diaspora was not a vestigial appendage of sovereign Jewishness in the Land of Israel but an organizational and ideological political entity that interrelates with Israel in complex and valuable ways.[75] Robinson maintained an

Nancy Sinkoff, *From Left to Right, Lucy S. Dawidowicz, the New York Intellectuals, and the Politics of Jewish History* (Detroit: Wayne State University Press, 2020), pp. 176–188. As for Robinson's important contribution to shaping Holocaust research in Israel, see Cohen, *Israeli Holocaust Research*, pp. 158–164.

74 The research literature on Arendt is too copious to present here. For an example, see Elisabeth Young-Bruehl, *Hannah Arendt: For Love of the World* (New Haven: Yale University Press, 2004).

75 Robinson expressed his worldview in a work plan that he wrote: Robinson, Action Plan for the Institute of Jewish Affairs, 1941, no exact date given, AJA, 361 3/5-A. He wrote in a similar vein in the weekly journal of the World Jewish Congress, February 21, 1941, AJA, 361 1/86-C.

ongoing dialogue between activity in the Jewish world and important contributions to the construction of the post-World War II world, from the struggle to bringing war criminals to justice to shaping key issues in human and minority rights at the UN and other international organizations.[76]

The question of Diaspora coexistence with the State of Israel is a constant theme in Robinson's public activity as well as his academic and public writings. It was in this spirit that Robinson established the Institute of Jewish Affairs as a practical manifestation of Jewish existence in the Diaspora and labored to create a legal infrastructure that would assure the survival of Jewish and non-Jewish minority and diasporic groups. Robinson pursued Jewish survival in this format during his public career in the first half of the twentieth century, preceding Jewish statehood, and after statehood was attained in 1948. This worldview also greatly influenced his public activity within the framework of the Eichmann trial and the public polemics that followed. In the Israeli reality of the 1950s and 1960s, it was an exceptional ideological and public demarche—one that offered an alternative to the conventional Zionist and Israeli outlook of the time.[77]

The tension that enveloped the question of maintaining a Jewish Diaspora after the founding of the State of Israel reflects the hardships that diasporic communities everywhere face in the modern era. In order to maintain community identity in their lands of settlement, members and leaders of such communities have to create a hybrid ethnic identity that is at once national and universal. The national element is needed in order to maintain the group's separate identity in dispersion; the universal parts allow members of the community to proceed with their lives as a community in the land in which they settled.[78]

A diasporism that sustains this hybrid outlook often evokes resistance in the community members' homeland. Studies on relations between origin country and diaspora stress the desire of leadership in

---

76 For a broad and important discussion of Robinson's activity at the UN, see James Loeffler, *Rooted Cosmopolitans: Jews and Human Rights in the Twentieth Century* (New Haven and London: Yale University Press, 2018), pp. 147–151.

77 On this matter, see Zohar Segev, "Tsiyone Artzot HaBrit BiMedinat Israel Bishnot Haamishim—Opozitzia Politit Ve'alternativa Liberalit" (Hebrew), *Iyyunim Bitkumat Israel*, 12 (2002), pp. 491–519.

78 For a discussion of this nature, see Susanne Lachenicht and Kirsten Heinsohn, eds., *Diaspora Identities: Exile, Nationalism and Cosmopolitanism in Past and Present* (Frankfurt and New York: Campus Verlag, 2009), pp. 7–15.

the homeland to harvest the economic and political advantages of the diaspora while rejecting any entitlement of the diaspora leadership to involvement in the homeland. Recourse to diaspora resources by the parent country is particularly salient at moments of crisis and in the initial stages of nation-building, when the homeland's resources are especially limited.[79] Ben-Gurion and most of the *Eretz Israel* leadership in the first half of the twentieth century embraced a policy that reflected this reality in the years of distress preceding statehood and in the challenging time that followed.[80] Ben-Gurion took great pains to make all the organizational systems of the world Zionist movement, in which American Jewish leaders were visibly and strongly dominant, subordinate to the Government of Israel, transforming American Jewry into a community that provides only economic and political support for the State of Israel. Robinson opposed this policy and sought to design an alternative.[81]

The papers of Jacob Robinson demonstrate how deeply responsible he felt for the fate of Jewry during and after World War II. The purpose of his efforts to disseminate information about the Holocaust transcended the bounds of the Holocaust question itself. As his involvement in the Eichmann trial reveals, he wished to use the memory of the Holocaust to shape the Jewish people and, indeed, the world at large after the war. Robinson saw Holocaust remembrance as an instrument with which to amplify American Jewry's ethnic identity and promote global trends that were antithetical to the Nazi ideology and actions. One

79 Myra A. Waterbury, "Bridging the Divide: Towards a Comparative Framework for Understanding in State and Migrant-Sending State Diaspora Politics," in Rainer Bauböck and Thomas Faist, eds., *Diaspora and Transnationalism: Concept, Theories and Methods* (Amsterdam: Amsterdam University Press, 2010), pp. 131–148.

80 For a broad discussion of this issue, see Ariel L. Feldestein, *Ben-Gurion, Zionism and American Jewry, 1948–1963* (London: Routledge, 2006).

81 In the context of American Jewry, it should be kept in mind that diasporic communities can define a given country as a homeland even if they themselves or previous generations of community members had not actually migrated from it to their country of residence. A country becomes a homeland external to the ethnic diaspora when those in the diaspora and their economic and political elites, on the one hand, and the leaderships in the homeland, on the other, so define the diaspora-homeland relationship. See Rogers Brubaker, *Nationalism Reframed: Nationhood and the National Question in the New Europe* (New York: Cambridge University Press, 1996), pp. 57–67. For further discussion of various issues in diasporic nationhood, see Rogers Brubaker, "Myths and Misconception in the Study of Nationalism," in John A. Hall, ed., *The State of the Nation: Ernest Gellner and the Theory of Nationalism* (Cambridge and New York: Cambridge University Press, 1998), pp. 272–306.

may find a practical manifestation of this commitment in his decision, shared by the institutions of the World Jewish Congress, to accede to the UN request and allow him to prepare the research foundation for the UN bodies' discussions of human rights. The fact that Robinson was approached for this task indicates not only the commitment of the World Jewish Congress as an organization, and of Robinson as an individual, to the cause of human rights, but also the international system's acknowledgement of his contribution to the struggle for human rights after World War II.[82]

Translated from the Hebrew by Naftali Greenwood.

---

82 Minutes of meeting of Institute of Jewish Affairs team, November 27, 1946, AJA, 361, 8/68-C. Robinson's activity within the UN institutions in 1946 was part of comprehensive WJC involvement in UN activity on this topic. See, for example, "Memorandum of the World Jewish Congress for the Forthcoming Third Session of the Human Rights Commission," March 24, 1948, AJA, 361, 10/68-C.

"Who Owns This Holocaust Anyway?"
The Homosexuals' and Lesbians' Memorial Ceremony at Yad Vashem, 1994[1]

Amit Kama and Sharon Livne

Preface

On May 30, 1994, at 3:00 P.M., a group arrived at Yad Vashem in Jerusalem with the intention of holding a ceremony in the Hall of Remembrance, the official and central venue for Holocaust commemoration, and the site on which the state memorial ceremonies take place on Holocaust Martyrs' and Heroes' Remembrance Day. It would seem that this would be a rather straightforward matter, as many groups plan to honor the memory of their loved ones at Yad Vashem and commune with their grief in ceremonies carried out there. This event, however, was different for several reasons. The first concerned the participants' identity. They were Jewish homosexuals and lesbians[2] from Israel and abroad, mainly from the United States but also from Europe, who had come to Yad Vashem in order to remember and commemorate homosexuals and lesbians whom the Nazis had murdered.[3] The second singular factor was the

---

1   The authors wholeheartedly thank Prof. Ofer Ashkenazi, Prof. Moshe Sluhovsky, and the reviewers of this article for their astute remarks and useful suggestions.

2   The terms prevalent today—gay, queer, and LGBT (lesbian, gay, bisexual, and transgender)—are not used in this article. Our purpose is to avoid anachronism; that is, an after-the-fact historical bias from a time when these terms had not yet come into common use in Israel. No attempt, of course, is made to exclude or disregard these identities nor the current ways of naming them; the sole purpose is to preserve the spirit of the time.

3   Nazi doctrine prohibited homosexuality. The official attitude toward German homosexuals was harsh and often culminated in murder. A monument in their memory, not far from the Holocaust memorial, has been installed in Berlin. The accusation of "homosexuality" was also employed as a tool for political tussling (for example, against the SA chieftains who were murdered on the "Night of the Long Knives"). Notably, the Nazis were more tolerant of lesbians than of homosexuals, because homosexual men were deemed guilty of offending Aryan masculinity (See

reaction it engendered. There was a demonstration held against it as it proceeded, and it stirred a tumultuous public debate. In the course of the controversy, the acceptance and visibility of the Israeli homosexual and lesbian community and the public debates surrounding it made reference for the first time to the fate of homosexuals and lesbians under Nazi rule and the question of marking them specifically within the limits of conventional Holocaust remembrance in Israel. Although the organizers wished to hold a ceremony like any other, theirs was understood and interpreted in the Israeli public as a challenge to the state-sanctioned paradigm of Holocaust remembrance that was prevalent during those years. The third aspect of the ceremony was the tension it caused between the organizers' goal of preserving the conventional memorial narrative and upholding the rules of protocol—and thus nurturing a connection with the core of Israeli society (as with the community's struggles at large)—and their wish to emphasize what they defined as the double victimhood of Jewish homosexuals and lesbians, who had been persecuted by the Nazis because of both their sexual orientation *and* their Jewishness.

In this article we discuss the complex relations of culture and memory, polarized political discourse, and conventional wisdom as to the right way of Holocaust commemoration. We examine several questions: Why did the ceremony trigger such a turbulent discourse and stir such acrid objections to the inclusion of this community in Holocaust remembrance? Why did the presence of homosexuals and

also the preface to the United States Holocaust Memorial Museum in Washington bibliography on this topic at https://www.ushmm.org/collections/bibliography/gays-and-lesbians.). Yet homosexuals did not face the total persecution that the Jews suffered, because no overall policy on this matter was developed or implemented in the German-occupied countries; it was left to local forces. We debated at length as to whether to include an extensive discussion of these issues in this article, given the ramified research devoted to it in recent years, but decided that, in order to keep to the space limitations of the article and in order to stay on topic—that is, to focus on the ceremony itself—further elaboration here is not needed. For literature on these issues, see, for example, Boaz Neumann, *Historiyot Hadashot Shel Hanazism* (Hebrew) (Tel Aviv: Modan and the University on the Air, 2019); Moshe Zimmermann, "Nirdefe Hamishtar Hanazi: Homosexualim Veasotsialim" (Hebrew), in Yair Oron and Sarit Seibert, eds., *Hakorbanot Halo Yehudim Shel Hamishtar Hanazi* (Hebrew) (Ra'ananna: Yair Oron and Sarit Seibert,, 2016), pp. 161–173; John Connelly, "Gypsies, Homosexuals and Slavs," in Peter Hayes and John K. Roth, eds., *The Oxford Handbook of Holocaust Studies* (New York: Oxford University Press, 2010), pp. 274–294, especially pp. 281–283; Günter Grau, *Hidden Holocaust? Gay and Lesbian Persecution in Germany 1933–45* (Chicago: Fitzroy Dearborn, 1995).

lesbians at Yad Vashem evoke questions regarding the sanctity and desecration of Holocaust remembrance? What were the overt and covert goals of the homosexual/lesbian community in holding the ceremony? Finally, how did the media portray the climate of opinion surrounding the event? This article is based on an analysis of the tumultuous public discourse that unfolded at the Knesset rostrum and in the media.

"Out of the Closet, into the Living Room"[4]

In early June 1994, an international homosexual/lesbian conference (the fourth) took place at Giv'at Haviva in Israel. The 150 Jewish homosexuals and lesbians from twelve countries who attended[5] heard lectures on a range of topics, became acquainted with Israel, enjoyed some leisure time, and did some sightseeing. The conference was initiated by Keshet Ga'ava (the Congress of Gay & Lesbian Jewish Organizations, an umbrella body of Jewish gay and lesbian organizations established in 1976 that, among other things, organizes conferences around the world[6]) and the SPPR.[7] The day before the conference began, the organizers made reservations for a memorial ceremony that would take place under the accepted rules at Yad Vashem. This plan was in keeping with the way various groups tended to hold official ceremonies at Yad Vashem, and with the importance of the site as a main stop on the tourist itinerary when visiting Israel.

The conference organizers invited the participants to a ceremony specially dedicated to "those slaughtered in the Holocaust—including our homosexual and lesbian brothers and sisters."[8] The event was meant to be dignified and restrained, and to this end the organizers applied for,

---

4   In Hebrew: "Min Ha'aron El Hasalon," the title of a column written by Liora Moriel, chairperson of the Society for the Protection of Personal Rights (SPPR), in the society's newsletter, *Nativ Nosaf*. In Moriel's view the expression captured the SPPR's goal at the time: integrating into quotidian Israeli social life in a way that would underscore homosexuals' and lesbians' being like anyone else (personal communication, April 21, 2009).
5   The number is based on *World Congress Digest*, the newsletter of the World Congress of GLBT Jews, 1994.
6   See its website: www.glbtjews.org/our-history (October 16, 2020).
7   The SPPR, established in 1975, was then the only homosexual/lesbian organization in Israel. Today it is called Ha'aguda Lema'an Halahatab—The Aguda: The Association for LGBTQ Equality in Israel (the Aguda).
8   *Nativ Nosaf* (Hebrew) (Spring 1994), p. 6.

and even received, permission from Yad Vashem to hold it in accordance with the accepted rules.[9] It took place under the moderation of the chairperson of the Aguda, Susan Kirchner, the president of the World Congress, Beth Cohen, and the Reform cantor Michael Mandel. The organizers intended to include in the ceremony a memorial prayer for "our homosexual brothers and our lesbian sisters, of our people and of other peoples, who were murdered in the Holocaust, so that we may pray for the remembrance of their souls."[10]

It was not the first time that the homosexual/lesbian community had sought to memorialize and commemorate the Nazis' homosexual and lesbian victims. About two months before the event in question, at a Holocaust Remembrance Day ceremony, two members of the Aguda had laid a wreath at Yad Vashem. Each year on this day dozens of wreaths are placed there by Israeli leaders, Holocaust survivors, students, and representatives of various organizations. As the ceremony proceeds, the name of the individual, the organization, or the institution that places the wreath is called out. Although Yad Vashem allowed the Aguda to lay a wreath, it vehemently demanded that the organization refrain from adding the expression "for the sake of homosexuals, lesbians, and bisexuals." This directive was followed, and, despite its forbearance in this matter, the Aguda took pride in having being allowed, like all others, to lay a wreath at the state memorial ceremony.[11] The optics of the moment, however, were somewhat imaginary, because the purpose of the Aguda's wreath was not mentioned.

The pride evoked by this achievement originated, *inter alia,* in the extensive exposure that the homosexual/lesbian community was receiving at this time. Profound revisiting of the public's attitudes toward homosexuals and lesbians, far-reaching changes in legislation and case law, and the community's growing presence in the public sphere were hallmarks of the early 1990s.[12] Amit Kama[13] distinguishes between two eras: the era of silencing that preceded 1993, when a Knesset

---

9   "Tekes Shel Homosexualim Velesbiyot Beyad Vashem," *Divre Haknesset* (Hebrew), June 1, 1994, pp. 7,781–7,790.
10 Rahel Sofer, "Tekes Yahid Bemino" (Hebrew), *Yedioth Ahronoth*, May 30, 1994.
11 "Zer Lezikhram," *Nativ Nosaf*, 12 (1994), p. 6.
12 Einav Morgenstern, Yaniv Lushinski, and Alon Harel, eds., *Zekhuyot Hakehila Hage'a Be'Israel: Mishpat, Netiya Minit Vezehut Migdarit* (Hebrew) (Tzafririm: Nevo, 2016).
13 Amit Kama, *Ha'iton Veha'aron: Defusei Tikshoret Shel Homo'im* (Hebrew) (Tel Aviv: Hakibbutz Hameuchad, 2003).

subcommittee on the prevention of discrimination on grounds of sexual orientation convened; and the current era, which followed. At the Knesset subcommittee meeting, a symbolic but substantive turnabout had taken place, after which the homosexual/lesbian community's struggle for equal rights found its way to the national political agenda. Its struggles since then have borne fruit in both personal and public life, and the common motif has been an effort to gain acceptance as equals in society and its institutions.[14] The community's cause was marked by the goal of acceptance into the core of the general society in order to become part of the social fabric. This assimilation, known as homonormativity or homonationalism,[15] is expressed in multiple respects, such as military recruitment, parenting, marriage, and integration into the public sphere. The ceremony discussed here, too, is an epitomic manifestation of the intent of assimilating and accepting the hegemonic "rules of the game," not only by holding the ceremony but also by the organizers' acceptance of Yad Vashem's demands verbatim (except for a minor revision of the wording of the prayer, which we discuss below).

Cease and Desist[16]

Three days before the planned event, the *Jerusalem Post* published a paid manifesto from the self-styled "Supreme Rabbinic Court of America," signed by nineteen American and Israeli rabbis.[17] The signatories inveighed against Jews who self-defined both as Jews and as homosexuals or lesbians. They also warned against holding the ceremony at Yad Vashem. Vituperating against "homosexual abominations," they threatened an all-out boycott of El Al, the airline with which the conferees would be flying to Israel; the Israeli Ministry of Tourism, for allowing homosexuals and lesbians to visit the Holy Land; and Yad

14 Amit Kama, "Parading Pridefully into the Mainstream: Gay & Lesbian Immersion in the Civil Core," in Guy Ben-Porat and Brian Turner, eds., *The Contradictions of Israeli Citizenship: Land, Religion and State* (Abingdon: Routledge, 2011), pp. 180–202.

15 Aeyal Gross, "Hapolitika Shel Zchuyot Lahatab: Ben (Homo) normativiyut Ve(homo) le'umiyut Lepolitika Queerit" (Hebrew), in Aeyal Gross, Amalia Ziv, and Raz Yosef, eds., *Sex Aher: Mivhar Ma'amarim Belimudim Lahatabi'im Vequeeri'im Israeli'im* (Tel Aviv: Resling, 2016), pp. 183–245.

16 This expression appears five times in the manifesto of the "Supreme Rabbinic Court of America."

17 *Jerusalem Post*, May 27, 1994, p. B3.

Vashem, for sanctioning a ceremony that would "desecrate" the place. The ceremony would befoul the memory of the martyrs, the signatories contended; it would put the venue to mockery and disgrace; and it would "[profane] the name of God." It might even devalue the fortunes of Judaism around the world and humiliate the faith in the eyes of Jews and non-Jews alike. The manifesto went so far as to link AIDS to the homosexuals' sins. The public was urged to turn out and cry out.

The organizers responded to the manifesto with dismay: a dignified representative event had become polemical and incendiary in one stroke. No one knew how this tribunal had even found out about the planned ceremony. Tension enveloped the intended participants and the organizers; no one knew what to expect. On the day of the event, the newspaper *Yedioth Ahronoth* ran an article featuring an interview with Cantor Michael Mandel,[18] noting that the ceremony would be taking place that afternoon. Members of the homosexual/lesbian community were frightened, and a debate broke out over the wisdom of having advertised the event. It was now clear that a public tempest would soon erupt.[19] Several Israeli members of the community, who had until then sought to refrain from visiting Yad Vashem on this "touristy" occasion, were now eager to secure their place on the planned bus ride to Jerusalem.

In addition to the police and some representatives of the media, a handful of demonstrators awaited approximately 150 people who were scheduled to participate in the ceremony. Although the demonstrators' numbers are not documented, it is almost certain (as the media reported) that they did not exceed a dozen. They belonged to two main groups: Holocaust survivors and their offspring; and activists in Kach, a radical Orthodox, ultranationalist political movement and party (from 1971 to 1994, when it was banned from national elections due to its incitement of racism). The participants began the ceremony as the conventional Yad Vashem rules dictated: they turned to place a wreath, embellished with a ribbon bearing the message, "In memory of our homosexual brothers and our lesbian sisters," next to the eternal flame in the Hall of Remembrance. Commotion then erupted. "Get out. Don't do that here! Lepers. AIDS is what you have coming," shouted Kach activist

18 Sofer, "Tekes Yahid Bemino."
19 One of the authors of this article was executive director of the Aguda at the time; some of the descriptions that have no other documented source are based on his recollections.

Avigdor Eskin. He was joined by Yossi Dayan, a fellow Kach operative, in chanting "perverts, perverts," and trampling on and defacing the memorial wreath. The Holocaust survivors demonstrating against the ceremony stood there with signs denouncing it, and a man who self-identified as a second-generation survivor filmed the affair with his camera. Apart from the participants and the opponents, police had arrived, as well as many from the media who had come to cover the event. Again and again Eskin managed to disrupt the ceremony. Despite being evicted over and over again, he managed each time to return and sustain his raucous protest.[20]

The assemblage of participants was shocked by the hate and the inflamed passions, which escalated to violence in the form of slapping and shoving. Many participants, humiliated by the screams directed at them, burst into tears,[21] and were frustrated by the fact that the police had failed to clear the demonstrators from the area.[22] The participants broke into a spontaneous rendition of Hannah Szenes's poem "A Walk to Caesarea" (*"Eli, Eli"*), and chanted it over and over in a sort of prayer. After the passions ebbed somewhat, two participants sang the "Partisans Song" in Yiddish: *"Zog nit keyn mol, az du geyst dem letstn veg"* ("Never say that you're going your last way").[23] However, when they began reciting the *Yizkor* and the *Kaddish* in the victims' memory, the rioting resumed, accompanied by invectives and obscenities. Ultimately the police managed to evict the demonstrators, and the ceremony ended shortly afterward. The demonstrators then waylaid the participants outside the Hall of Remembrance and attempted to assault them, but the police intervened. A few minutes later the participants, demonstrators, police, and media crews dispersed.

The spectacle at Yad Vashem made the evening news on both radio and television. The next day the homosexual/lesbian community was accused in the print media of having held a "sales-promotion

20 Ilana Baum, "Mehuma Beyad Vashem Be'azkara La'alizim Shenispu Bashoah" (Hebrew), *Yedioth Ahronoth*, May 31, 1994, p. 12.
21 ITIM, "Beshirat 'Eli, Eli' Higivu Homosexualim Velesbiyot Al Hafra'ot La'azkara Lekorbanot Hashoah Beyad Vashem" (Hebrew), *Davar*, May 31, 1994, p. 5; Gabi Zohar, "Sihat Hayom Im Ilan Sheinfeld" (Hebrew), *Ha'aretz*, June 1, 1994, p. 2a.
22 After the fact Avner Shalev, chairman of the Yad Vashem Directorate, reported that the police had come late. Asked to arrive at 2:45 P.M., they showed up at 3:15 P.M.. "Tekes Shel Homosexualim Velesbiyot Beyad Vashem," *Divre Haknesset* (Hebrew), June 1, 1994, pp. 7,781–7,790.
23 Baum, "Mehuma Beyad Vashem."

junket,"[24] "mobilizing the national symbol of Holocaust remembrance for political and media exigencies,"[25] and "[staging] a provocation for media attention."[26] The word "provocation" recurred as a slogan of sorts, with no attempt made to explain it properly. As we show below it seemed as though the participants' homosexual/ lesbian identity was in and of itself the determinant of how the ceremony would be perceived and construed in the public mind. The picture that emerged, however, was neither simple nor monodimensional, as the media also found room for sympathetic voices toward the community.

Sacred Memory

The Martyrs' and Heroes' Remembrance (Yad Vashem) Law was adopted in the summer of 1953. In his remarks, as he presented the bill to the Knesset, Minister of Education and Culture Ben-Zion Dinur asked rhetorically: "How shall we preserve the memory?" He answered that the law would make it possible to memorialize every person who had perished in the Holocaust by maintaining a ledger in which each Jew would be recorded. In addition, Yad Vashem would gather testimonies, documents, memoirs, and artifacts from the destroyed communities and the soldiers, partisans, and ghetto rebels. Dinur distinguished between "remembrance of Holocaust and heroism" and remembrance of "victims of the Holocaust" in order to emphasize one of the institution's main goals: to understand how the Holocaust had happened, why the Jewish people had not heeded the warnings and had not realized "the pace of the hate, the enmity, and the planning of the killing."[27]

In the years following its establishment, Yad Vashem did focus

---

24 Ibid.

25 Amos Carmel, "Bli Homofobiya Ubli Politika" (Hebrew), *Yedioth Ahronoth*, June 2, 1994, p. 3.

26 Haim Hanegbi, "Hahomo'im, Ehai" (Hebrew), *Ma'ariv*, June 3, 1994, p. 26.

27 Ben-Zion Dinur, remarks on presentation of the Martyrs' and Heroes' Remembrance (Yad Vashem) Bill, 5713-1953, *Divre Haknesset* (Hebrew), May 12, 1953, pp. 1,310–1,314. On various proposals for establishing Yad Vashem and the nature of the Holocaust Martyrs' and Heroes' Remembrance Day, the bitter disputes that surrounded these issues, and the diverse views that were expressed as they unfolded, see Roni Stauber, *Halekah Lador: Shoah Ugvura Bamahshava Hatziburit Ba'aretz Bishnot Hahamishim* (Hebrew) (Jerusalem: Yad Izhak Ben-Zvi, 2000); Mooli Brog, *Yad Vashem—Lemi? Hama'avak Al Demuto Shel Har Hazikaron* (Hebrew) (Jerusalem: Carmel and Bar-Ilan University, 2019).

on initial scientific research into the Holocaust and marginalized the aspect of memorialization, even though this was ostensibly integral to its raison d'être. Several years later, however, in the mid-1950s, an internal struggle ensued at Yad Vashem over whether it should devote exclusive attention to Holocaust research and how it should exercise its responsibility for commemoration. The capture of Adolf Eichmann in 1960 turned the Holocaust into a fixture of Israeli public life and prompted the heads of Yad Vashem to collaborate with members of Knesset and cabinet ministers in amending the Holocaust Martyrs' and Heroes' Remembrance Day Law (which had been enacted in 1959). In Hebrew this day was referred to as Yom Hashoah. They sought to attribute to this day the status of a *yom kadosh* (a holy day); it would start and end in the evening as per Jewish practice, and places of public entertainment would be closed.[28] The initiative behind the amendment was prompted by the widespread public disregard of Yom Hashoah, and the idea was to establish a state memorial setting that would unite Israeli society and allow the Holocaust to be understood on all its levels: its intrinsic melancholia, the heroism woven into it, and the things we must protect so that it does not recur. In the words of MK Baruch Osnia, the institution should communicate "anguish, intelligence, and a lesson."[29] The religious complexion of this memorial day, with its prayers and content, was also discussed.[30]

At that time the place of Yad Vashem as a memorial site was overshadowed by the Chamber of the Holocaust on Mt. Zion as the hub of commemorative activity on Jewish fast days and festivals.[31] Doron Bar claimed that various people at Yad Vashem understood that in order to realize the institution's responsibility for commemorating the Holocaust and sustaining its memory, ashes of Holocaust victims brought over from Europe would have to be interred in the institution's central memorial

28 Brog, *Yad Vashem—Lemi?*, p. 135.

29 Member of Knesset Baruch Osnia, remarks at a debate over the Holocaust Martyrs' and Heroes' Remembrance Day Law (Amendment), 5721-1961), *Divre Haknesset* (Hebrew), 31, March 8, 1961, pp. 1,264–1,268.

30 Debate over the Holocaust Martyrs' and Heroes' Remembrance Day Law (Amendment), 5721-1961, *Divre Haknesset* (Hebrew), March 14, 1961, pp. 1,314–1,317.

31 Alex Lavon, "Martef Hashoah Behar Tziyon: Ben Zekhira Amamit Lezikaron Mamlakhti" (Hebrew), *Israelim*, 3 (2011), pp. 71–91; Doron Bar, *Lekadesh Eretz: Hamekomot Hakedoshim Hayehudi'im Bimdinat Israel* (Hebrew) (Jerusalem: Yad Izhak Ben-Zvi, 2007), pp. 81–104.

structure.[32] At the time that the trial of Adolf Eichmann began, in April 1961, Yad Vashem dedicated the Hall of Remembrance, a structure resembling a basalt and concrete cube that evokes the sense of an ancient tomb. The hall itself is made of concrete; its ceiling is serrated; and its floor is a gray mosaic engraved with the names of concentration camps, death camps, and mass-murder sites. An eternal flame shaped like a goblet illuminates the interior; in front of it is a niche that contains the ashes of persons who had been murdered and which had been gathered at extermination camps and brought to Israel. Laid over the niche is a black stone, much like a tombstone, on which visitors lay wreaths at ceremonies. Since the place was constituted as a shrine, men who enter are asked to cover their heads or wear a *kippah*. The interment of ashes made it possible to consolidate and institutionalize the sanctity of the venue.[33]

Mooli Brog claims that, throughout the planning stage, participants in the planning sessions already used terms such as "holy place," "sanctuary," "hall of remembrance," and "meeting tent." This attests to inspiration drawn from the realm of sanctity. Thus Yad Vashem was designed and built as a shrine to the Zionist civil religion with a religious lexicon adapted to secular national use. In subsequent decades Yad Vashem's status as a unique and exclusive memorial site became an established part of Israeli public life. As part of this the perception of *mamlakhtiyut*, or a non-partisan national approach, which was typical of that time and which aspires to develop civic consciousness and responsibility in the public political domain, was realized.[34]

The ceremonies conducted at Yad Vashem from the 1960s to the 1990s settled into a standard format. An official agenda of remembrance—run by the establishment and committed to structuring an official narrative—determined the complexion of memorial ceremonies and presented a unifying policy that reflected contents that the establishment

32 Doron Bar, "Between the Chamber of the Holocaust and Yad Vashem: Martyrs' Ashes as a Focus of Sanctity," *Yad Vashem Studies*, 38:1 (2010), pp. 173–174.

33 James Young calls this "creating a new civil religion"; see James E. Young, *The Texture of Memory: Holocaust Memorials and Meaning* (New Haven: Yale University Press, 1993), pp. 243–263.

34 For more on state-level formality, see Avi Bareli and Nir Kedar, "Mamlakhtiyut Israelit" (Hebrew), *Policy Studies*, 87 (Israel Democracy Institute, 2011); Nir Kedar, *Mamlakhtiyut: Hatefisa Ha'ezrahit Shel Ben-Gurion* (Hebrew) (Beer-Sheva: Ben-Gurion Institute for Israel Studies, 2009).

and society found desirable and acceptable.[35] These ceremonies mirrored the way the state aspired to remember the Holocaust and bequeath this memory to posterity.[36]

Over the years Yad Vashem managed to instill the perception of Holocaust remembrance as such a sacred cause that only a state-level apparatus could oversee it adequately. It was tasked with creating an identity that transcends ethnicity, class, and politics, and shapes a unity in shared patterns of remembrance.[37] Holocaust remembrance in Israel's first half-century served as a receptacle for the Israeli melting pot, evoking an exalted respect that carried with it a charge of sanctity. The institution's epitomic objective was to unify all segments of the nation in collective remembrance of the Holocaust and its Zionist lesson.

Does Yad Vashem, however, engage in forming memory or just preserving it? Is Holocaust remembrance a spontaneous grassroots phenomenon, or is it structured by institutions and/or instrumentalized by institutions and political groups and interests? The processes of collective creation and preservation of memory are presumably interconnected, but, in the second half of the 1970s, the status of Holocaust consciousness began to fissure. First flickerings of openness to new themes and perspectives began to subvert the perception of the Holocaust as sanctified and state-related.[38]

According to Daniel Gutwein, in the 1960s and 1970s, the Holocaust was an instrument of social cohesion and political legitimacy.

---

35 Yohai Cohen, writing about the historical exhibits at Yad Vashem since the mid-1950s, regards these exhibits as intended to make the Holocaust accessible and relevant to the public at large. In the 1990s, he argues, Yad Vashem broadened the consensus by accommodating additional narratives under the aegis of the main narrative. These (including those of non-Jewish victims and of North African Jews) were admitted in order to defend the core values of the main narrative against social, historiographical, and political challenges. Yohai Cohen, "Shoah She'al Hakir: Dmut Hashoah Batatzuga Hahistorit Shel Yad Vashem 1956–2005" (Hebrew) (PhD diss., The Hebrew University of Jerusalem, Jerusalem, 2017).

36 Pierre Nora, "Ben Zikaron Lehistoria: Al Habe'aya Shel Hamakom" (Hebrew), *Zemanim*, 45 (1993), pp. 5–13; Maurice Halbwachs, *On Collective Memory* (Chicago: University of Chicago Press, 1992), especially pp. 37–40, 46–51.

37 Ayala Felsenthal, "'Tzrikha Hahanhala...Lehargish Ki Kan Yesh Ma'avak': Hantzaha, Hegemoniya Vezehut Le'umit—Mikre Hamivhan Shel Yad Vashem" (Hebrew) (M.A. thesis, The Hebrew University of Jerusalem, Jerusalem, 1997).

38 For more on the meaning of collective memory, see Mordechai Bar-On, "Lizkor Ulehazkir: Zikaron Kolektivi, Kehilot Zikaron Umorasha" (Hebrew), in Matityahu Meisel and Ilana Shamir, eds., *Defusim Shel Hantzaha: Asufat Ma'amarim* (Tel Aviv: Ministry of Defense, 2000), pp. 17–19.

The "nationalization of Holocaust memory" in those years served also to justify repression and negation of the Other. In the 1980s, Gutwein continues, a process of "privatization of memory" began; the Holocaust was now presented as a personal experience that focuses on Jews' fates as individuals.[39] Pursuant to Gutwein's theses, Hanna Yablonka defines the late 1980s and early 1990s as the years of maturation among the Israel-born generation in the way they coped with the Holocaust, amidst a growing recognition of the existential centrality it signified for them.[40] The Holocaust became salient in culture, art, education, and Israeli media, and evolved into a national ethos and a unifying consensus. At this time, Yablonka notes, a stream of Mizrahi Israelis from the sociocultural periphery flowed toward the established center; intersecting with the Holocaust became the missing link in attaching and gluing this population to the core of Israeli society. As evidence of this link, Mizrahi artists in the 1990s created an alternative to the canon remembrance in the form of films, plays, and rituals that allowed the Other also to play a role in Holocaust remembrance and the collective that was engaged in it.

One of the first Holocaust Remembrance Day ceremonies that made room for a range of narratives that had been excluded from conventional memorial events until then took place in 1995, at the Kedma School under the administration of Sami Shalom Chetrit. Alternative Holocaust Day ceremonies that have been held in Tel Aviv since 1999, which accommodate thinking about the Other in broad contexts of antisemitism, racism, and hate, may be seen as the continuation of that ceremony at Kedma. The main alternative event is the one held at the Temu-Na Theater, and, like the others, strives to produce dynamic, not lachrymose, remembrance in order to make the Holocaust relevant to the present and not only to the past. The organizers of the alternative ceremonies endeavor to demonstrate what Holocaust remembrance means in Israeli society and how the Holocaust affects the Israeli collective. Although public figures and Holocaust survivors initially decried the alternative ceremonies for ostensibly demeaning the

---

39 Daniel Gutwein, "Hafratat Hashoah: Politika, Zikaron Vehistoriografia" (Hebrew), *Dapim LeHeker Hashoah*, 15 (1998), pp. 7–52.

40 Hanna Yablonka, *Harhek Mehamesila: Hamizrahim Vehashoah* (Hebrew) (Beer-Sheva: Ben-Gurion Institute for Israel Studies, 2008), p. 272.

Holocaust, the new models have slowly made inroads, penetrating the social core, and giving rise to supplementary versions in various places.[41]

The ceremony under discussion here may exemplify an attempt by the homosexual/lesbian community to gain acceptance and fit into the collective circle of Holocaust remembrance and, by so doing, if only indirectly, to acquire social acceptance as well; that is, Israeli society's consent, in a sense, to the admission of homosexuals and lesbians as full-fledged members. In its aspiration to commemorate in ritual the homosexuals and lesbians whom the Nazis and their accomplices had murdered, the community attempted both to be included in the canon bastion of Holocaust remembrance as well as to create a new stratum of remembrance that until then had remained unexpressed in Israeli public life. Concurrently, it did not seek to construct an alternative ceremony but to vary the customary protocol with only the slightest change (adding the words "homosexuals and lesbians" to the wreath-laying and the *El Male Rahamim* prayer). Paradoxically, by holding this ceremony the community indirectly (and even inadvertently) challenged the official Holocaust remembrance while actually fervently wishing to be included in it.

Gal Hermoni and Udi Lebel distinguish between intra-paradigmatic rituals, which reenact a hegemonic narrative and do not represent a range of voices, and extra-paradigmatic rituals—alternatives that counter the paradigm of national remembrance.[42] The ceremony in question was intra- and extra-paradigmatic at one and the same time. The community aspired to an intra-paradigmatic ceremony that could catapult it to the center of the national remembrance stage, and this was why it wished to be part of it. The organizers took the first step (even before the alternative ceremonies began to take shape) within the official memory mechanism and thus expressed their wish to be enmeshed within it. The opponents of the ceremony, in contrast, regarded the ceremony as a pronouncedly, if not radically, extra-paradigmatic attempt to subvert the collective memory in its customary form. The homosexual/lesbian community tried to establish itself in the center of the collective memory of the

41 Liat Steir-Livny, "Hatekes Ha'alternativi BeTe'atron 'Temuna' Be'erev Yom Hazikaron Lashoah Velagevura" (Hebrew), *Dappim Leheker Hashoah*, 28 (2018), pp. 131–150.
42 Gal Hermoni and Udi Lebel, "Ketzad Zokhrim Dam? 'De-Politizatzia Kepraktika Anti-Hegemonit: Al Hapolitika Shel Hatekes Ha'alternativi 'Halel'" (Hebrew), in Sandra Meiri et al., eds., *Zehuyot Behithavut Hatarbut Ha'israelit* (Ra'ananna: The Open University of Israel, 2013), pp. 205–227.

Holocaust, whereas its opponents perceived the ceremony as a breach of protocol, an affront to the sanctity of the venue, and the product of the community's quest for alternative remembrance rather than its very inclusion in the canonized one.

A Graven Image in the Sanctuary

"From our standpoint, the homosexuals and the lesbians are laying wreaths in memory of Jews who perished in the Holocaust; if they are saying anything else, it's their own business," asserted the spokeswoman of Yad Vashem at the time, Billy Laniado. Her institution had not initiated the ceremony, she added: "The Hall of Remembrance has been open to the entire public for more than thirty years; it allows anyone who wishes to commune with the memory of the Jews who perished in the Holocaust to lay a wreath and utter a prayer, provided they do so respectfully." Yad Vashem, Laniado explained, had organized a standard memorial ceremony at the request of a travel agency (which had arranged the tourist aspects of the international conference) and had not realized that it was intended to commemorate homosexual victims until the Aguda's press release appeared.[43]

One cannot assume that Yad Vashem would have responded differently had it been another group. However, the response (spelled out below) makes it quite clear that the resistance was rooted in the identity of the victims and of the participants in the ceremony. After the event repudiations of the ceremony and its moderators were publicized. Avner Shalev, chairman of the Yad Vashem Directorate, was quoted as alleging that the homosexual/lesbian community and, foremost, the organizers of the ceremony had staged a provocation to promote their legitimacy.[44] MK Shaul Yahalom (National Religious Party) urged Dr. Joseph Burg, chairman of the International Council of Yad Vashem, to resign. "It's preposterous," Yahalom explained, "that a person of Burg's stature, a man who represents religious Zionism, should head an institution that allowed a group of deviants and perverts to defile Jewish sanctity, the

---

43 The press release was disseminated in response to the manifesto that had appeared in the *Jerusalem Post*; *Ha'aretz* (Hebrew), May 31, 1994, p. 1. Ilan Sheinfeld (personal communication, March 31, 2009) asserts that the Aguda corresponded with Avner Shalev about laying a wreath and holding a memorial ceremony.
44 *Hatzofe* (Hebrew), June 3, 1994, p. 5.

prayers of the Jewish people, and the memory of the Holocaust, in grave offense to tens of thousands of Holocaust survivors' families."[45]

Régis Schlagdenhauffen-Maika claims that representatives of Yad Vashem stressed the sacred aspect of the venue when the event was discussed and actually tended to favor the opponents' religious arguments. The opponents, who regarded homosexuality as an abomination and a sin, judged the ceremony to be in fundamental transgression of Halacha. According to Schlagdenhauffen-Maika, Yad Vashem is rooted in religious semiotics; therefore, its pronouncements in effect denied that homosexuals and lesbians were exterminated as such and not only due to their Jewishness. He elaborates: "The ambiguous statute of Yad Vashem, like the Shoah, considered by some as a 'civil religion,' excludes homosexuals from the 'right to remember.' Although this is a laical place, the weight of religious opinion explains this phenomenon."[46]

These pronouncements were the first products of a discourse that had begun to dominate the public debate over a perceived affront to the sanctity of Yad Vashem. As stated, elements of sanctity have been part of Yad Vashem since the 1960s, and constitute the institution's raison d'être. Therefore, the ceremony in question was perceived by its opponents as an act of desecration and defilement. Amos Carmel affirmed this—"The place was established to be a shrine for the Jewish people"[47]—and many in the political arena felt the same way. MK Avraham Shapira (United Torah Judaism), for example, was quoted in the *Hatzofe* newspaper: "It's stinging and shameful to legitimize deviants." Four deputy speakers of the Knesset protested "the desecration of the place and the grave offense to the emotions."[48]

As we elaborate below, many opponents of the event stressed that Jewish homosexuals had been murdered due to their Jewishness and not their sexual orientation, making such a so-called contentious ceremony unnecessary. To their way of thinking, the ceremony was a tasteless

---

45 Yehuda Golan, *Ma'ariv* (Hebrew), May 31, 1994, p. 13.
46 Régis Schlagdenhauffen-Maika, "The New Holocaust History Museum of Yad Vashem and the Commemoration of Homosexuals as Victims of Nazism," *Bulletin du Centre de recherche français à Jérusalem*, 16 (2005), pp. 244–261, here p. 261.
47 Carmel, "Bli Homofobiya Uvli Politika."
48 Amos Carmel, "Arba'a Misganei Yoshev Rosh Haknesset Ginu Et Tekes Ha'azkara Lahomosexualim Vehalesbiyot Beyad Vashem" (Hebrew), *Ha'aretz,* June 1, 1994, p. A6.

event that dishonored Yad Vashem and sabotaged the memory of the Holocaust. In their attempt to defend the Holocaust survivors' dignity and feelings, they even overlooked the violence that the Kach activists had perpetrated. The proponents of the event, in contrast, denounced the Kach people for their display of extremism and homophobia, called them fascists and racists, and found the parliamentarians' support of the opposition to the event bewildering. Even those who sided with the ceremony refrained from attacking the Holocaust survivors and their successor generation for opposing it, choosing to focus only on decrying the Kach activists and the resistance they had put up during the ceremony. They preferred to center their critique on the radical demonstrators and not clash with Holocaust survivors and their offspring.

Due to the public tumult that had erupted, MK Yael Dayan (Labor Party) sought an urgent parliamentary discussion of the event and its offshoots. On Wednesday, June 1, 1994, the Thirteenth Knesset convened for its 224th session. After the opponents of the ceremony briefly attempted to postpone the debate, the requisite motion for the agenda was passed. Facing an almost empty plenum, MK Binyamin Temkin (Meretz) began to speak. He tried to explain the fact, which the passions had obscured, that the Nazis had murdered homosexual Jews due to their sexual orientation and not necessarily because of their Jewishness.[49] MK Yahalom found Temkin's argument difficult to accept and repeatedly heckled him, including, "They were murdered because they were Jews!" and saying that the ceremony was nothing more than a publicity stunt. These interruptions prompted Knesset Speaker Szewach Weiss to call Yahalom to order twice. Temkin and then Dayan construed the event as an indication of a flawed social situation and an urgent problem. Both insisted that the Nazis had annihilated those who were different and Other. They decried the origins of the opposition to the ceremony and *a fortiori* the roots of the demonstration in certain groups that claimed exclusive ownership of the Holocaust and its memory. Speaking from the Knesset rostrum, Dayan said:

> We are dealing not with the Holocaust but with the right to be different and the duty to be equal; the pathetic, distortive, and distorted exclusivity of our victimhood; the commemoration of

49 See note 3 above.

Jewish victimhood expressed both politically and socially; the victim's right to be an executioner; and the sanctification of something that embodies all atrocities and all crimes save sanctity itself—all with the intolerable and unacceptable ease of defining anyone who circulates among the minions of the martyrs but fails to meet the archaic, unequal, and undemocratic Jewish criterion as a deviant, a pervert, fit to be stoned, a source of defilement.[50]

Two parliamentarians who took part in the debate were Holocaust survivors. MK Dov Shilansky (Likud) vented his rage on the organizers of the event:

> I, who had been in the ghetto and the camps, saw all along the way people who adhered to their faith in their last moments…No one stuck to their sexual orientations at those moments. What those who walked to the crematoria and the gas chambers had in common was their Jewishness and their faith. That's how Yad Vashem was built, too, and that's how it ought to be.[51]

The homosexuals and the lesbians, from his standpoint, had frayed a strand in the tapestry of Holocaust remembrance. Knesset Speaker Szewach Weiss took a different tack. Weiss, who had facilitated and even promoted events associated with the homosexual/lesbian community in the Knesset (for example, the groundbreaking establishment of a subcommittee for the prevention of discrimination on grounds of sexual orientation, chaired by MK Dayan),[52] charged,

> It concerns not only homosexuals and lesbians but anyone who has a different opinion, too…We in the Knesset are committed to the principle of the right to be different and the principled quality of the matter stands out specifically in this context of the Holocaust.[53]

Two Holocaust survivors, two worldviews. One defended Yad Vashem and Holocaust remembrance as something sacred; for him, it teaches one lesson only: the victims' Jewishness and faith. The other, by accepting those who are different, allows another lesson to be learned from the

---

50 "Tekes Shel Homosexualim Velesbiyot Beyad Vashem," *Divre Haknesset* (Hebrew), June 1, 1994, pp. 7,781–7,790.

51 Arik Bender, "Eikh Nizkor" (Hebrew), *Ma'ariv*, June 1, 1994, p. 8.

52 Aeyal Gross, "Hasipur Shel Danilovitz: 'Tnu Ladayal Lehitromem El-Al'" (Hebrew), *Ma'ase Mishpat*, 10 (2019), pp. 13–59.

53 "Tekes Shel Homosexualim Velesbiyot Beyad Vashem," *Divre Haknesset*.

Holocaust: "All of the Nazi racism was built on difference." Therefore, homosexuals and lesbians have every right to commune with the victims' memory in the Hall of Remembrance.[54]

The Ministry of Education, tasked by the government with oversight of Yad Vashem, asked the institution's directorate to respond. Avner Shalev's version of the sequence of events was read aloud by Deputy Minister of Education Micha Goldman, who did much to create the impression that the homosexual/lesbian community had indeed carried out a "publicity stunt," a breach of protocol, and a grave offense to the sensibilities of the Holocaust survivors as a collective. "The script of the memorial remarks," Shalev claimed, "was not only the traditional accepted script of the prayer. Every group of commemorators read the text that it saw fit and prayed the prayers that it saw fit, Jews and non-Jews."[55] He wished to stress that he considered it

> important in principle that Yad Vashem be open to all and not differentiate among groups of different outlooks or ways of behavior, if they wish to visit and commune with the memory of the Holocaust and its victims in a dignified manner that does not offend the accepted rules. We realize that there are groups of people that enrage, outrage, or infuriate some members of the survivor community, and we do everything we can to avoid hurting their feelings.[56]

Yad Vashem issued a statement saying that the way that various groups engage in commemoration in unofficial ceremonies would be reexamined during the next meeting of its executive committee and management.

Remembrance as a Social Demarcation Mechanism

The Knesset debate concluded with a vote on whether to pass the matter on to the Education Committee for discussion. An aye vote indicates that the issue matters; leaving it in the plenum signals that it has spent itself. Only thirteen Knesset members had attended the plenary session; six

---

54 Bender, "Eikh Nizkor"
55 "Tekes Shel Homosexualim Velesbiyot Beyad Vashem," *Divre Haknesset*.
56 Ibid.

voted in favor, six opposed, and one abstained. Thus, the matter would not be referred to the Education Committee.

"Who abstains?" asked MK Shilansky.

"I abstain, sir," replied MK Salah Tarif (Labor), who was chairing the session, "and you'll accept my abstention…I just won't meddle in such a sensitive matter."

"Mr. Chairman," said MK Yahalom, turning to Tarif, "well done!"

By not wishing to intervene in the "sensitive" topic, the Druze parliamentarian, Tarif, had thus accepted that only Jewish Israelis belonged to the circle of victims—i.e., only they had standing—and drew these boundaries emphatically. One may surmise that Tarif, due to his non-Jewish identity,[57] felt unable or unentitled to express a view. As we have shown, the Holocaust has been a pillar of Israeli nationhood and a strongly constitutive feature of the identity of those allowed to participate in remembering and memorializing it. The practical implication of this is a continual demarcation of social boundaries that strictly distinguishes between the Israeli Jewish in-group and the non-Jewish Israeli out-group. The roots of this differentiation stem from the Martyrs' and Heroes' Remembrance (Yad Vashem) Law itself, which clearly demarcates the borders of the in-group.

A society constitutes its identity by means of discourse invested with symbolic elements, thereby demarcating the borders outside of which are Others who are usually stigmatized.[58] So, too, the cultural, social, and political discourses revolving around the Holocaust allow Israeli society to understand the members of the in-group, who alone are allowed to participate in discussion of the topic. A symbolic rite of ownership unfolds here, determining not only who is entitled to take a stance but even who or what should be included in the concept of "Holocaust."[59] Accordingly, it is no wonder that MK Tarif abstained from participation in the Knesset plenum debate. Since the Holocaust is not

---

57 Another possible interpretation of Tarif's abstention might stem from an overall conservative and traditional perception of homosexuality. It should be noted that the debate spilled over from the topic of Holocaust remembrance to that of tolerance toward minorities. Presumably Tarif had an opinion on this issue but chose to refrain from expressing it publicly.

58 Amit Kama and Anat First, *Al Hahadara: Yitzugim Tikshorti'im Shel "Aherim"* (Hebrew) (Tel Aviv: Resling, 2005).

59 To prove the point, it is no wonder that the term "Holocaust" must not be applied to the Turks' genocide of the Armenian people; see Yair Oron, *Hakh'hasha: Israel Veretzah Ha'am Ha'armeni* (Hebrew) (Kefar Sava: Maba, 2005).

part of his and his group's genealogy, he seemingly has no right, in his way of thinking, to express his views about it or to shape its memory.

Until the 1990s the attitude toward the Holocaust and its remembrance was divided into two main periods. The first, from the establishment of the State of Israel to the 1960s, is what Gutwein calls the "split-memory period," in which Israeli society's response to the Holocaust was typified by a combination of contrasting emotions that included, all at once, empathy for the victims and their suffering and criticism of their behavior and use of their memory.[60] After the Eichmann trial, and all the more after the 1967 Six-Day War, an era of "nationalized memory" (Gutwein) began in which Israeli society manifested its response to the Holocaust in total empathy with the victims and established Holocaust remembrance as a common basis for an Israeli collective identity. This definition would increasingly strengthen and replicate national solidarity. It took until the late 1980s for criticism of this kind of Holocaust remembrance to be heard.[61]

Identification with the Holocaust is a fundamental element in the civil religion of Israel, and the observance of Holocaust Remembrance Day is enshrined in law. Thus, Holocaust memory and commemoration is demanded of all (and only) Jewish members of Israeli society and arguably constitutes an entry pass, so to speak, to membership within it. By accepting the broadly defined protocol of the Ashkenazi victim hegemony, the national identity is not only constituted but also demarcated. The use of the Holocaust as a unique and unifying event is incomparably important. Any attempt to fissure the modality of remembrance or to present, mention, or remember other groups within it may not be received kindly. This happened, as we have shown, in the case of the Mizrahim.[62] The urgent need among groups that were excluded and silenced—not only in the context of the Holocaust—to

60 Gutwein, "Hafratat Hashoah: Politika, Zikaron Vehistoriografia," pp. 8–9.
61 Yehuda Elkana's article "Bizkhut Hashikheha" in *Ha'aretz* (1988) marks the beginning of critical attention to the role of the Holocaust and its remembrance in Israeli society. The critical line was carried on in the early 1990s in Tom Segev's *The Seventh Million* (1991) and Moshe Zuckerman's *Shoah Baheder Ha'atum* (1993). See Yehuda Elkana, "Bizkhut Hashikheha" (Hebrew), *Ha'aretz*, March 2, 1988; Tom Segev, *The Seventh Million: the Israelis and the Holocaust* (New York: Hill and Wang, 1993); Moshe Zuckerman, *Shoah Baheder Ha'atum: "Hashoah" Ba'itonut Ha'israelit Betkufat Milhemet Hamifratz* (Hebrew) (Tel Aviv: privately published, 1993).
62 See, for example, Yossi Sukary, *Benghazi-Bergen-Belsen* (Hebrew) (Tel Aviv: Am Oved, 2013).

belong to Holocaust remembrance and, through it, to join the Israeli mainstream created a slow process of inclusion in the circle of Holocaust victims and survivors. The struggle for the inclusion in Holocaust remembrance of victims who were not Ashkenazi or heterosexual is being won amid small and large tempests in Israeli public life. Thus, the homosexual/lesbian ceremony at Yad Vashem is a paradigmatic example of the phenomenon.

The wish to deconstruct or (as per Gutwein) to privatize the memory is a Sisyphean, distressing, and painful process. As this wish percolates into the broad strata of Israeli society, it must cope not only with the place of the Holocaust and its memory but also with the existence of various narratives that challenge the way that Holocaust remembrance is perceived. Perhaps for this reason, in one of the most interesting Mizrahi responses to criticism regarding slight attempts to crack the standard image of remembrance, it was asserted[63] that they, the Mizrahim, lacked the legitimacy to speak out on how to commemorate the Holocaust because neither they nor their families had personally experienced it.

The homosexual/lesbian community, too, had diverse views.[64] It was riven by disagreements after the ceremony and its pursuant public tumult. The prevailing argument was that even if visiting Yad Vashem and holding the ceremony had been tactically justified, strategically the event had harmed the community's overarching objective of attaining social acceptance and assimilation. Some termed the event "traumatic";[65] others saw it as "constitutive." The ceremony participants' families and friends—even those who showed support and acceptance in daily life—also expressed severe displeasure with the decision to hold the ceremony at Yad Vashem of all places. The offense to the Holy of Holies of Israeli society was not accepted with understanding, even if some had parents or other kin who were Holocaust survivors. Families and friends confronted their loved ones and advised them that, while loving and acknowledging them, they considered holding the ceremony at

63 Yablonka, *Harhek Mehamesila,* p. 286.
64 Interestingly, the very elite that had created the patterns of Holocaust remembrance and its preservation was strongly represented in the Aguda leadership of those years. Many were university-educated Ashkenazim of the upper-middle socioeconomic class.
65 One of the community activists wrote to us (on July 8, 2019): "In my opinion, it was traumatic for all parties; that's why there was no event afterward" (personal email correspondance translated by the authors).

Yad Vashem nothing but a provocation. The message, simply put, was: anywhere else, okay; at Yad Vashem—no.

Media Coverage

The media, particularly the press, create and tell stories (in the current context, news reports) by phrasing them in accordance with a goal, chiefly political or ideological, that is not necessarily explicit but may be subsumed and embodied in the text proper. Media stories have always been set within an ideological frame, usually a hegemonic one.[66] The media discourse is not always an innocuous mirror of reality but rather, by necessity, the product of ideological labor.[67] Representing reality, therefore, intertwines with emphasizing certain facets and concealing others. This phenomenon, known as framing,[68] manifests in a process in which journalists choose how to represent, arrange, and organize the reality that they report. It takes place on two levels: choosing the event about which to report from a set of actual events; and describing it with the help of words or concepts that fit a particular worldview. The theory of media framing is derived from Erwin Goffman's conceptualization,[69] in which individuals and groups produce a discourse about reality and communicate it by identifying, selecting, and organizing content worthy of communicating and abetting its communication in the way it is phrased. These frames emphasize certain meanings and focus on them while disregarding others. Media-frame analysis is instructive of the systems of mass-media attribution of meaning and the hierarchies of importance embodied within it.

In order to gauge the states of mind that surrounded the event at Yad Vashem, we analyzed the framing methods that the media adopted in representing it, including quantitative measures of occurrence of

66 Paul Frosh and Anat First, *Yerivim O Shutafim: Yahasei Demokratia Vetikshoret* (Hebrew) (Ra'ananna: The Open University of Israel, 2012), pp. 1–39.

67 Stuart Hall, *Representation: Cultural Representations and Signifying Practices* (London: Open University, 1997); Douglas Kellner, *Media Culture: Cultural Studies, Identity and Politics between the Modern and the Postmodern* (London: Routledge, 1995).

68 Paul D'Angelo, *Doing News Framing Analysis: Empirical and Theoretical Perspectives* (New York: Routledge, 2010); Robert M. Entman, "Framing: Toward Clarification of a Fractured Paradigm," *Journal of Communication*, 43 (1993), pp. 51–58.

69 Erwin Goffman, *Frame Analysis: An Essay on the Organization of Experience* (London: Harper and Row, 1974).

verbal statements and mention of relevant participants, as well as semiotic and semantic analyses of the texts. The analyses included the entire population of texts: thirty-eight news items, articles, op-eds, editorials, and letters to the editor that were published in the print media in the days following the event, and a single coverage in a Voice of Israel newscast.[70]

With regard to the distribution of coverage among the Hebrew press, each of the three most circulated newspapers—*Maʿariv, Yedioth Ahronoth,* and *Haʾaretz*—published seven texts. In the political-party press, six news items appeared in *Al Hamishmar,* in comparison to *Davar,* which, although it had been a pioneer in writing about and on behalf of homosexuals and lesbians, devoted only four texts to the issue. In the *Jerusalem Post,* there were five texts, and in *Hatzofe,* there were only two. As a religious-oriented newspaper, it was obvious that the editors of *Hatzofe* preferred not to cover topics that are considered taboo in the religious world, or, in other words, were upholding "the public's right not to know."[71]

Particular aspects of the way the event was covered were also examined, including headlines, descriptions of the participants, the organizers, and the opponents, as well as interviews with various personalities. Finally, the ways in which the press conveyed its outlooks and positions regarding the event, and the public polemics that accompanied it, were also checked.

As the press employs headlines in order to grab readers' attention, they are very instructive as to the attitude of the press and the framing

---

70 Unfortunately, the recording of the *Popolitka* TV program that dealt with the matter on the day of the event was unobtainable. However, from mentions of the program in the press, one can identify the participants: MKs Yael Dayan (Labor) and Shlomo Benizri (Shas); two representatives of the Aguda; and a Holocaust survivor. The last related that he had been the victim of sexual abuse at the hands of a Nazi guard and deduced from this that the memorial ceremony also commemorated Nazi homosexuals, and therefore was illegitimate *ab initio.* The *Al Hamishmar* newspaper reported: "On the television program *Popolitika,* Holocaust survivor Eitan Porat claimed that one must not forget the children who were sexually abused by German homosexuals" (Aliza Hatuel, *Al Hamishmar* [Hebrew], June 1, 1994). Sheinfeld, the Aguda spokesman, alleged: "The gravest thing is that on television they showed a Holocaust survivor who had been exploited in his childhood by a Nazi sex pervert; thus they created a totally warped analogy between us and the Nazis" (Kobi Medan, *Al Hamishmar* [Hebrew], June 1, 1994).
71 Kimmy Caplan, *Rabot Raʾot Tzadik: Kavim Letoldolt Haʾitonut Haharedit BeIsrael, Lemeʾafyeneha Ulehitpathuta* (Hebrew) (Tel Aviv: Tel Aviv University, 2006), p. 18.

of the event. Although the headlines varied widely among and within the newspapers, three noteworthy phenomena are discerned: (1) most headlines, true to how the press usually operates,[72] emphasize the disturbance of the peace: "Riot" (*Yedioth Ahronoth,* May 31, 1994); "Disturbances" (*Davar,* May 31, 1994); and "fracas" (*Jerusalem Post,* June 1, 1994). These headlines do not attest to the newspapers' bias toward any protagonist; one may even surmise that the event would not have been covered at all had it not been for the opposition. (2) Several headlines stress the establishment's response and insinuate that the event was illegitimate: "Yad Vashem Dissociates from Homosexuals' Ceremony" (*Yedioth Ahronoth,* June 1, 1994); "Four Deputy Knesset Speakers Denounce Memorial Ceremony" (*Ha'aretz,* June 1, 1994). (3) *Davar,* despite lack of sympathy in the articles it published, is the only paper that stresses the participants' response to the opposition ("Homosexuals and Lesbians Respond by Singing *Eli, Eli*"—*Davar,* May 31, 1994). Perhaps it tried in this manner to encourage readers to sympathize with the participants' distress. As we show below, only the *Jerusalem Post* (June 1, 1994) expresses unequivocal support for holding the event and even suggests as much in the headline ("Desecrating Yad Vashem" in an unmistakable allusion to the opponents).

All the texts,[73] of course, mention the organizers, the participants, and those who opposed the ceremony, and demarcate them as two rival camps: participants versus opponents. Most of the texts describe the participants in neutral terms that carry no negative symbolic load: "homosexuals and lesbians" or "gays and lesbians [*sic*]." Seven texts do not mention lesbians, possibly reflecting the widespread and well-known phenomenon of excluding women from the media by and large. Three texts use derogatory and degrading labels: "perverts" (*Yedioth Ahronoth,* May 31, 1994); "deviants and perverts" (*Hatzofe,* May 31, 1994); and "people of uncommon sexual habits" (*Davar,* June 3, 1994). Interestingly, *Davar,* of all newspapers, published a homophobic opinion

---

72 Eli Avraham, *Israel Hasemuya Me'einei Hatikshoret: Hakibbutzim, Hahitnahaluyot, Arei Hapitu'ah Vehayishuvim Ha'arvi'im Ba'itonut* (Hebrew) (Jerusalem: Academon, 2000).

73 In the content analyses that follow, the texts are not differentiated by genre (news items, opinion pieces, editorials, and letters to the editor). In order to keep within the space limitations of this article, we chose to examine them on an overall basis. Nevertheless, we believe it is possible to deduce the genre of each text from its context and the quotations provided.

piece that invoked hostile images. In sum, only three of the thirty-eight texts used pejorative language. Arguably, then, the media did not consider the ceremony participants as stigmatized Others. Four texts identify the participants as Jews, as though this were not self-evident. Shosh Arar, in a letter to the editor in *Ha'aretz*, for example, defines the participants only as "Jewish worshippers" (June 6, 1994) and disregards their homosexual and lesbian identity.

Almost all the texts reference the opponents of the event and signify them as members of a social group demarcated by four measures: political affiliation with the Kach movement (N=16); place of residence (Kiryat Arba, N=8); Holocaust survivors or offspring (N=6); and religiosity (N=4). Namely, the opponents are usually signified by their political affiliation either directly or by insinuation. Haim Hanegbi, for example, writes explicitly in *Ma'ariv* (June 2, 1994) about "Kahanist thugs...a squad of professional Kahanists." Meir Shalev remarks pointedly in *Yedioth Ahronoth* (June 1, 1994) about "natural racists." The editorial in *Davar* (June 1, 1994) insinuates this by calling them "people of Kiryat Arba, Baruch Goldstein's town." In other words, the large majority of texts paint the opposition to the event in unmistakably political colors.

In 1994, the government of Israel outlawed the Kach movement by declaring it a terror organization. Thus, at the time of the event it was perceived in Israeli public life as unworthy of participating in the political "game" and taking part in the public sphere. By inference, then, identifying the opponents as Kach members endorses a sympathetic view of the ceremony. Furthermore, approximately three months before the ceremony, Baruch Goldstein (of Kiryat Arba) had carried out a murderous terror attack at the Tomb of the Patriarchs in Hebron. Thus, noting the opponents' place of residence may have helped to frame the opposition as another manifestation of religious fanaticism, making "Kiryat Arba" a semiotic shortcut[74] that newspaper readers could easily decode. This could also immediately evoke a social demarcation between the out-group of "provocative vandals" (Aliza Hatuel, *Al Hamishmar*, June 1, 1994), "sons of darkness," and "the monster in our midst" (Haim Hanegbi, *Ma'ariv*, June 2, 1994) and the in-group, the "sane" who march down the path of common sense, including homosexuals and lesbians ("The Homosexuals, My Brothers"; ibid.). Finally, although the Knesset

74 Richard Dyer, *The Matter of Images: Essays on Representation* (London: Routledge, 1993).

debate emphasized the religious aspect, the newspapers largely refrained from framing the opponents as religious.

The stark binary of out-group versus in-group that typifies all the texts is an added element in the newspapers' discussion of the urgent question that lies at the core of the event: Who is allowed to hold a memorial ceremony at the Hall of Remembrance? In other words, do heterosexual Jews have sole title to remembering and commemorating the Holocaust? What are the opponents so angry about, irrespective of where they express their views: *in situ* or in the public sphere? And what are the proponents, be they participants in the ceremony or journalists and parliamentarians, defending? The boundaries of the "sanctified" territory of the Holocaust are threatened because members of a traditional out-group (homosexuals and lesbians) have attempted to infiltrate the domain of the hegemonic in-group and find shelter under its wings. Furthermore, the very discussion of the matter strengthens the gradual inclusion of homosexuals and lesbians into the in-group's world, if only because the Others are now reconstituted as the political rivals (i.e., the Kach movement) and not members of a minority traditionally perceived as markedly Other (i.e., homosexuals and lesbians).[75] In other words, the media and political debate had redrawn Israel's social borders, perhaps for lack of choice. However, it could also be argued that the debate at hand was but an excuse or pretext for working through a deeper issue of what the nature of the *Homo Israelicus*[76] is. Are his/her identity and sexuality constituted as only heterosexual, or might they be flexible enough to accommodate homosexuals/lesbians and homosexuality as well? Two camps—the religious Right and the liberal Left—clashed over drawing the borders of legitimacy and utilized the ceremony for this purpose.

Several texts include interviews. There were fifteen interviews with organizers of the ceremony and participants, including several that name names and others that identify the interviewee only as a homosexual or a lesbian. Eight interviews were conducted with representatives of Yad Vashem, including Avner Shalev, chairman of the Yad Vashem Directorate; Joseph Burg, chairman of the International Council of Yad

75 Amit Kama, "From *Terra Incognita* to *Terra Firma*: The Logbook of the Voyage of Gay Men's Community into the Israeli Public Sphere," *Journal of Homosexuality*, 38 (2000), pp. 133–162.
76 Tamar Katriel, *Dialogic Moments: From Soul Talks to Talk Radio in Israeli Culture* (Detroit: Wayne State University Press, 2004), p. 188.

Vashem; and Billy Laniado, the institution's spokeswoman. Six interviews were held with MKs: Shaul Yahalom (National Religious Party), Shlomo Benizri (Shas), Binyamin Temkin (Meretz), Yael Dayan (Labor), and Szewach Weiss (Labor). Only three interviews were held with the opponents (including Holocaust survivors). As we show below, in this context, too, one may infer that the relatively strong voice allotted to the organizers and the participants—even if some remain nameless[77]—re-emphasizes the media's sympathetic framing.

Most of the texts (N=27) refer to the event noted in the headline or the body of the text in neutral language; i.e., a "memorial ceremony" or a "remembrance ceremony." In *Davar* (May 31, 1994), the ceremony is said to be "in remembrance of victims of the Holocaust," and *Ha'aretz* (June 1, 1994) prefers to mention "the memorial ceremony for homosexuals and lesbians." Two texts—"Prayer" (Haim Hanegbi, *Ma'ariv*, June 2, 1994) and "The 'Kaddish Special'" (Teddy Preuss, *Davar*, June 3, 1994)—touch on the religious aspect of the affair. Thus, most of the texts give the ceremony direct and allusive support and hint at some sympathy for it by defining it as its organizers do; namely, the media refrain from political and public attacks on the event and its organizers, even as they cover it widely, and do not structure it within the opponents' conceptual world.

A small minority of texts frame the event adversely. *Hatzofe*, following an explicit policy that needs no further elaboration, expresses sweeping objection to the event and calls it "the conference of the perverts...a provocation [meant] to defile Jewish sanctity, the prayers of the Jewish people, and the memory of the Holocaust" (May 31, 1994). Surprisingly, *Al Hamishmar* (June 3, 1994) also decries the event as a "shameful incident" and "a provocative attempt to use Yad Vashem to celebrate coming out." Similar framing occurs twice in *Yedioth Ahronoth*: "a publicity stunt...mobilizing the national symbol of Holocaust remembrance for political and communication demands" (Amos Carmel, June 2, 1994) and "part of a public relations...sales-promotion campaign" (Ilana Baum, May 31, 1994).

Seemingly, the homosexual/lesbian community, which organized the ceremony as part of its fight for equality, inclusion, and acceptance, is perceived contrarily as concocting a gratuitous provocation. The

---

77 Naming, i.e., specifying the name of the person represented in the media, expresses respect for the individual's identity and human uniqueness. Non-naming is part of symbolic annihilation that devalues an interviewee's humanity; it is typical of the representation of disadvantaged minorities.

organizers of the event emphasize again and again, in all interviews, that they had made no attempt to subvert the centrality of the Holocaust and/or Yad Vashem, or undermine them. On the contrary, they had based their ceremony on the accepted establishment protocol.[78] As evidence, Ilan Sheinfeld claims that, "We came to hold a ceremony in accordance with the official paradigm of Yad Vashem...like any other group...There's no reason in the world to paint ourselves in special colors...They're discriminating against us as though they're trying to kick us out of the Jewish people" (Kobi Medan, *Al Hamishmar,* June 1, 1994).

The ceremony comported with the dominant strategy of mainstreaming and striving for full integration into Israeli society,[79] similar to the struggle to abolish discrimination against homosexuals in the Israel Defense Forces that had evolved a year earlier. Therefore, it was meant to express the homosexual/lesbian community's aspiration to be perceived as untainted, to constitute its identity as such within the social system, and to validate it emphatically. The arguments voiced in the media—by most interviewees and also by a minority of journalists— concerning the event having been a provocation staged for "public relations" needs show that the attempt to integrate triggered existential anxiety. The fact that the ceremony took place at all was perceived as a threat to the memory of the Holocaust and an affront to and distortion of its remembrance.

In a surprising contrast to the fundamental principle of balance that typifies journalistic writing generally and that of the homosexual/lesbian context particularly—in which editors insist on balance lest they be suspected of overly favoring homosexuals and lesbians[80]—the texts clearly tend to describe the opposition in negative terms. In a few cases the opposition is described in words that lack negative connotations, such as "recurrent disruptions" (*Davar,* May 31, 1994), "riot" (*Ma'ariv,* May 31, 1994), or "melee" and "fracas" (*Jerusalem Post,* June 1, 1994). Mostly, however, it is defined in blunt and unequivocal terms: "an ugly

---

78 With the exception of one detail, to which an editorial in *Al Hamishmar* took vehement exception: inserting the words "homosexual" and "lesbian" into the *El Male Rahamim* prayer.

79 Aeyal Gross, "The Politics of LGBT Rights in Israel and Beyond: Nationality, Normativity and Queer Politics," *Columbia Human Rights Law Review,* 46 (2015), pp. 81–152.

80 Edward Alwood, *Straight News: Gays, Lesbians, and the News Media* (New York: Columbia University Press, 1996).

and violent riot, a monstrous and frightening onslaught" (Yael Dayan, *Ma'ariv*, June 2, 1994); "the most shameful spectacle ever held in the Hall of Remembrance...a frenetic scene" and "foolish fulmination" (Ilana Baum, *Yedioth Ahronoth*, May 31, 1994); "a thuggish display" (*Ha'aretz*, June 1, 1994); "rowdiness and violence...[a] violent confrontation" (Macy Gordon, *Jerusalem Post*, June 3, 1994); and "ghastly shrieking" (Voice of Israel). Ilana Baum, writing for *Yedioth Ahronoth*, describes one of the opponents as: "It looked as though he'd go out of his mind in another moment. Rage turned into madness. He seemed to be losing control" (May 31, 1994). B. Michael, in an article headlined "Who Owns This Holocaust Anyway?" (*Yedioth Ahronoth*, June 3, 1994), notes sarcastically: "Of course you need not wonder about Kach people who carried on like goons. It's only natural and warranted to find homophobia and fearmongering among their other outstanding virtues." Meir Shalev (*Yedioth Ahronoth*, June 1, 1994) seconded this view: "The Kach people yearn for the natural laws: the law of the fist and hatred of the different and the outsider."

Thus, perceptible sympathy for the participants in the ceremony is contrasted to the pejorative portrayal of the opponents and their actions, an approach that may allow readers to empathize with the former and summarily reject the latter. To sum up, some of the media side with the event and its organizers by inference, on the basis of their choice of words, by using many neutral terms in their accounts of the event and a preponderance of harsh-sounding lexemes in reference to the opposing side.

In quite a few texts (N=17), the writers take a favorable stance toward the event. This is expressed in diverse ways, sometimes explicitly in the headline ("The Homosexuals, My Brothers," Haim Hanegbi, *Ma'ariv*, June 2, 1994); in other cases in the text proper (from a *Davar* editorial: "It isn't the homosexuals and the lesbians who are endangering Israeli society but violent fanatics who don't recognize the other's right... to be different from but equal to them"; June 1, 1994); and at times by the very act of interviewing the organizers of the event or MKs who are identified with the homosexual/lesbian struggle. Most texts support the participants and the event indirectly by excoriating the opponents. An editorial in the *Jerusalem Post* (June 1, 1994) does this with particular bluntness: "Those who place their own political-religious agenda... rude people...intolerant and disturbed...irresponsible and fanatic." Notably, the *Jerusalem Post* stood alone among the newspapers in its unmitigated solidarity with and sympathy for the participants. It did publish an opinion piece by a rabbi who vigorously objected to the "sin" and "abomination" and explained why homosexuals should not be tolerated in a Jewish state, particularly in the public sphere (and *a fortiori* at Yad Vashem). Nevertheless, the paper's editorialist uses a plethora of rhetorical devices to signal that the disruption of the "dignified" event itself amounts to a "desecration"; for example, in an interview with one of the participants, one finds the expression "His anger is understandable." One may interpret the editorial position as an insinuation of regret for having published the advertisement from the "Supreme Rabbinic Court of America," which, as described above, had set the chain of events in motion.

Only nine texts express opposition to the event, and the organizers are censured bluntly (as in the headline of a news item in *Hatzofe*: "Conference of Perverts at Yad Vashem," May 31, 1994), or depicted negatively (Amos Carmel: "Mobilizing the national symbol of Holocaust remembrance for political and media exigencies is one of those games that's forbidden to all groups...This is exactly the sin of these men and women"; *Yedioth Ahronoth*, June 2, 1994). Interestingly, *Al Hamishmar* published the largest number (three) of texts that frowned on the event. Eight texts cover the event and the resistance to it in neutral terms, describing it simply as a "memorial ceremony," and the opposition to it only as "disruptions."

Most of the texts—either written by journalists or in quotations from interviews (with politicians, representatives of Yad Vashem, or organizers of the event)—are concerned with the principle of whether homosexuals and lesbians have the right to hold an event at Yad Vashem. The headline in *Yedioth Ahronoth*, "Who Owns This Holocaust Anyway?," expresses the point well. Proponents of the event, heard more clearly than the opponents, tend to invoke the principle of equality among all. MK Yael Dayan, for example, followed up on her remarks before the Knesset by asserting in *Ma'ariv* (June 2, 1994):

> It's not the Holocaust we're dealing with but the right to be different and the imperative of equality...to define a public that's equal before the law and mustn't face discrimination [as though] unworthy of remembering and lamenting their brothers and sisters who were murdered in the Holocaust under the roof that was erected for us all...Anyone who believes in our future in an egalitarian,

democratic, and humane society that accepts the different and looks out for our rights as a minority, must attach a pink badge to his chest.

Aliza Hatuel, writing for *Al Hamishmar*, reinforces this argument: "The riot...revealed islands of darkness, primitive thinking, and heedlessness to a person's basic right to live in accordance with his belief and conscience" (June 1, 1994). Haim Hanegbi (*Ma'ariv*, June 2, 1994) notes: "The *ge'im* and *ge'ot*[81] told us: here we are as we are, offspring of Adam and Eve." Other texts strengthen the view that Yad Vashem should not be monopolistic and that heterosexual Jews have no exclusive title to the right to hold memorial events there. The editorial in *Ha'aretz* (June 1, 1994) demonstrates this perspective:

> On what account are Jewish men and women who are surely free of any blemish of racism and antisemitism facing such fury?...Our opinion is that mentioning the suffering of non-Jewish minorities does not deprive the Jewish people of anything...The memory of the Holocaust is not impaired when people express pain for additional victims...Let's not blind ourselves to the suffering of those who were not descended from Abraham as well.

Avner Bernheimer wrote the following in *Ma'ariv* (June 1, 1994): "Here of all places, the act of eternalizing the memory of the Holocaust is selective and monopolistic...The ceremony...is no provocation; its point is to correct a 'mistake,' the deliberate omission of a piece of history."

Accordingly, most of the arguments, pro and con, focus on the political aspect of the matter, that is, the protracted struggle among social groups for the character of social reality and their ranks in the hierarchy of power.[82] Only a few rest their case on religion. Thus, just as the proponents of the ceremony see in it a power struggle among different groups over defining the features of social and political realities, the opponents find the organizers' "sin" in having taken a politically-tinged step at a place that should in no way be part of the political game. For instance: "Yad Vashem...is beyond the political pale...Mobilizing the national symbol of Holocaust remembrance for political and media exigencies is one of those games that's forbidden to all groups" (Amos

---

81 *Ge'im* (masculine) and *ge'ot* (feminine) mean "proud ones." These neologisms were short-lived and are no longer in use.

82 Kama and First, *Al Hahadara*.

Carmel, *Yedioth Ahronoth*, June 2, 1994). As we have argued above, the event was also depicted in pronouncedly political terms by means of far-reaching descriptions of the opponents: "Two residents of Kiryat Arba rioted at a ceremony at Yad Vashem in remembrance of homosexuals who were murdered in the Holocaust" (*Ha'aretz*, May 31, 1994). In contrast to the political debate, the religious aspect and the question of Yad Vashem's sanctity drew attention in the discussion of whether homosexuals and lesbians were "allowed" to hold the ceremony, but this was found in a relatively small group of texts. For example: "The *ge'im* and *ge'ot* centered [their case] on their Jewishness…The homosexuals who chose to recite the *Kaddish* surely didn't mean it as an act of defiance…under the banner of sanctity" (Gail Hareven, *Ma'ariv*, June 5, 1994). Teddy Preuss also employs a religious tone:

> Were the collective *Kaddish* and *El Male Rahamim* really directed at heterosexuals alone? If so, it is the homo-les[83] themselves, and not the Kahanists and the sundry saints, who exclude themselves from the Jewish people…Just as the Nazis took no interest in whether a Jew was homo-les…so, too, those who said the *Kaddish* took no interest, for the opposite reason (*Davar*, June 3, 1994).

Even *Hatzofe* (May 31, 1994) soft-pedaled the religious aspect ("to defile Jewish sanctity, the prayers of the Jewish people, and the memory of the Holocaust") but lavished words on the political aspect by describing the event as a "provocation" or a "demonstration."

Summing up, the media tended rather clearly to examine the event through political lenses by contextualizing a range of arguments as the homosexual/lesbian community's struggle for visibility and for its right to participate in the Jewish Israeli ethos as an equal. In other words, the press framed its discussion of the event in diverse ways that yielded one question: Was the homosexual/lesbian community permitted or entitled to be an integral and organic part of Israeli society? The opposition to the ceremony, too, was mainly phrased politically and only slightly in religious terms.

---

83 In Hebrew this was rendered into a homonym for "homeless" and punctuated as an abbreviation that suggested an allusion to homosexuals and lesbians. Needless to say, the word "homeless" carries an obvious negative connotation.

A Quarter of a Century On

In an interview upon his appointment as chairman of the Yad Vashem Directorate, ten months before the ceremony, Avner Shalev commented on the findings of studies on collective identity that were conducted at the time: "Remembering and empathizing with the Holocaust have become a highly conspicuous and important commonality among all components of Israeli society."[84] Every effort should be made to preserve the Holocaust as a unifying and coalescing event. Allowing various groups to carve their own niches in the official remembrance may, according to Yad Vashem's guiding policy, fray the delicate and arduously produced tapestry that creates a common denominator among all elements in Jewish Israeli society.

As the homosexual/lesbian community gained traction in the 1990s—in a process called "the gay legal revolution"[85]—it also sought recognition of its group's singular victimhood. Members of this community had been murdered foremost due to their Jewishness, but many had been primarily identified also as homosexual/lesbian and were persecuted because of it, and sometimes they were murdered because of the two facets of their identity combined. However, non-Jewish homosexuals had been murdered just as well, and public empathy and identification with them was important to the community. From the community's standpoint, it was high time to correct their non-commemoration and recognize their suffering at the hands of the Nazis. Thus, it saw the ceremony as a remedy of sorts, a corrective act, for its exclusion—in the current context, exclusion from the commemoration of members of the community in the collective memory and from participation in the state memorial ceremonies—as well as the symbolic annihilation that had been the community's lot until then.[86]

At issue here, however, is more than correction. The Holocaust and its memorialization are glue—using Benedict Anderson's metaphor[87]—that brings together and unites Israeli society in the nation-state. Therefore, since joining the circle of Holocaust remembrance, of the

---

84 [Author not named], "Be'ikvot Minuyo Shel Avner Shalev Leyoshev Rosh Hahanhala," *Bamuze'on* (Hebrew), 5 (1993), p. 3.

85 Alon Harel, "The Rise and Fall of the Israeli Gay Legal Revolution," *Columbia Human Rights Law Review*, 31 (2000), pp. 443–471.

86 Kama, "From *Terra Incognita* to *Terra Firma*."

87 Benedict R. Anderson, *Imagined Communities: Reflections on the Origin and Spread of Nationalism* (London: Verso, 2010).

victims and the memorializers, is a *sine qua non* for acceptance in Israeli society, a memorial ceremony may confer epitomic and official entrée to the social core. One may even be so bold as to claim that approval of the ceremony and recognition of the homosexuals' and lesbians' suffering in the Holocaust could promote the processes of their social acceptance.

Israel fought over the character of Holocaust remembrance in 1994, and continues to do so today. Competing and contrasting parallel narratives are not manifested in the state commemorations—at the symbolic, ritualistic, and official levels alike—and are excluded from the hegemonic narrative. Israeli society still strictly guards the boundaries of the sphere of remembrance, as Erella Shadmi explains:

> Recognizing the Holocaust of others will not subvert the uniqueness and singularity of that of the Jews; instead, it will reveal the multifacetedness of evil and the intertwining of all these facets: antisemitism, "Final Solution," ethnic cleansing, racism, colonialism, misogyny, homophobia, xenophobia, and exploitation of children. [...Yad Vashem has to choose] whether it's a venue for one story or for the story of many, a place that commemorates the Holocaust of the Jews or protests against evil.[88]

A quarter of a century has passed since the event. We have sought to track processes that ensued at possible rendezvous points between the LGBT community and Yad Vashem. The memorial ceremony, it turns out, left a grim imprint on the community and was never repeated. Perhaps the community's organizations did not fear the public's response; they were simply uninterested in holding a similar event. In 2016, however, two representatives of the Jerusalem Open House for Pride and Tolerance (an LGBT organization established in 1997) laid a wreath for the community as part of the Holocaust Remembrance Day events. This wreath-laying, to the best of our knowledge, was the only such occurrence since the one carried out by the Aguda in 1994. The wreath-laying in 2016, unlike the event twenty-two years earlier, included an overt affirmation of the identity of those in whose name the wreath was placed and the full name of the Open House as part of the ceremony.

The homosexuals' and lesbians' ceremony at Yad Vashem inadvertently challenged the symbolic boundaries of Holocaust remembrance and memorialization. Indirectly, it brought into the public

---

88 Erella Shadmi "Shel Mi Ata Yad Vashem?" (Hebrew), *Ha'aretz*, June 8, 1994, p. B4

agenda—only briefly, as it turned out—the extent of social demarcation of those entitled and authorized to carry on this memory. It tested Israeli society by challenging the society's tolerance, acceptance of the Other, and legitimization of the Other's existence. It is difficult to answer firmly if Israeli society successfully passed this test, as the picture is complex. On the one hand, it seems—at least from a review of the press at the time and remarks made in the Knesset—that the ceremony and its organizers received rather broad support. Quite a few speakers expressed sympathy and even advocated for the right of non-heterosexuals to be included in the remembrance community. For them the principle of equality surmounted any other consideration, and nothing stood in the way of adding non-heterosexual victims of the Holocaust to those commemorated; nothing about memorializing them impairs the resilience of pan-Jewish memorialization. On the other hand, the opposition—even if marked at the time as a manifestation of mere political extremism—had far-reaching effects. One may argue that the success of the resistance (inestimable at the time) remains evident to this day in that no similar ceremonies have been held since then and no further attempts to initiate such rituals have been made. Furthermore, even if the LGBT community seems to have attained momentous accomplishments in social, legal, and other contexts in recent years, its exclusion from active, express, and overt participation in ceremonies at Yad Vashem—which derive their importance from the Holocaust as a cornerstone of Israeli society and as a test of admission into it—still leaves its members Othered.

Translated from the Hebrew by Naftali Greenwood

Challenging the Illusion of Exceptionality: Czechs, Germans, and the Holocaust of Bohemian and Moravian Jews

Wolf Gruner, *The Holocaust in Bohemia and Moravia: Czech Initiatives, German Policies, Jewish Responses* (New York: Berghahn, 2019), 442 pp.

Reviewed by
Jan Láníček

Research on the Holocaust in the German-occupied Protectorate of Bohemia and Moravia has traditionally remained in the shadow of the research into the wartime history of the neighboring countries. Local historians rarely publish their studies in English, and foreign scholars are not attracted to the topic, perhaps not seeing it as interesting as research into other areas of Holocaust studies. The last comprehensive study in English is from 2005, and even this monograph was mostly based on much earlier research.[1] This is why historians should welcome the new study by the German-American scholar Wolf Gruner, which tackles some of the most pressing topics of Holocaust research in the Bohemian lands head-on, and brings the history closer to mainstream Holocaust research.

Hitler created the Protectorate of Bohemia and Moravia after the Nazi invasion in mid-March 1939, and it was one of the last territories liberated by the Allies in April and early May 1945. The Nazis considered the territory part of their *Lebensraum* (living space), though their policies against the Czech population were also influenced by the indispensable economic role the industrialized territory played in the German war efforts, and so they decided to postpone most of their Germanization plans until their anticipated victory in the war.[2]

1   Livia Rothkirchen, *The Jews of Bohemia and Moravia: Facing the Holocaust* (Lincoln and Jerusalem: University of Nebraska Press and Yad Vashem, 2005).
2   Detlef Brandes, *"Umvolkung, Umsiedlung, rassische Bestandsaufnahme": NS-*

Annexed even before the war, the Protectorate was the first non-German-majority territory incorporated into the Third Reich. Officially Hitler took the territory "under the protection" of the Reich, and promised to respect its autonomy. The Protectorate was ruled by a quasi government, headed by the aging President Emil Hácha and four successive prime ministers or government chairmen (after 1942). As Gruner outlines: "In contrast to Austria and the Sudetenland...the Protectorate administered itself, with the exception of foreign policy, military matters, transport, and communication" (p. 58). Yet the real power was in the hands of the *Reichsprotektor*, appointed directly by Hitler.

At lower levels the pre-invasion administration and bureaucracy remained largely intact, though German officials soon assumed key decision-making positions. Similarly to other territories, as Gruner demonstrates, the Germans remained dependent on the work of local non-German officials in all spheres of administration, including the police and gendarmerie: "In total, around 15,000 Germans worked in the occupation and Czech authorities as opposed to around 400,000 Czech civil servants" (p. 265). At the same time there was a duality of administration: alongside the Czech Protectorate offices, the Nazis established a network of German regional bureaus or commissioners (*Landräte* and *Oberlandräte*), all of them members of the NSDAP or associated agencies. They monitored and directed the Czech administration and served as a low-level bureaucratic body for Germans in the Protectorate, who officially became Reich citizens.

The persecution of the Jews in the Protectorate was closely linked to the progress of the persecution in the Reich and post-Anschluss Austria. The first two years, until the beginning—or, as Gruner argues, the renewal—of the mass deportations in October 1941 (p. 271), were filled with the gradual segregation and isolation of the Jews and their exclusion from economic life. The Nazi and Czech Protectorate officials supported Jewish emigration for as long as it was possible, until its official ban in October 1941. At the same time Reinhard Heydrich, the chief of the Reich Security Main Office (RSHA), occasionally stopped emigration, when he believed that the flight from the Protectorate

"Volkstumspolitik" in den böhmischen Ländern (Munich: Oldenbourg, 2012); Chad Bryant, *Prague in Black: Nazi Rule and Czech Nationalism* (Cambridge: Harvard University Press, 2007).

endangered the smooth expulsion of the Jews from the Reich. In September and October 1941, Hitler bound the fate of the Protectorate Jewry to that of their German and Austrian brethren, and ordered their quick evacuation to the East (p. 275). The deportations took almost two years, until July 1943, when the last major transport of "full Jews" left Prague for the Theresienstadt ghetto. Between January and March 1945, the Nazis also deported those living in the so-called mixed marriages. In the end only 2,803 Jews remained in Prague when the Soviet troops arrived two months later.

Over 26,000 Jews emigrated from the Protectorate between 1939 and 1941, with perhaps up to 20,000 fleeing from the rump Czechoslovak state between Munich and the German invasion.[3] According to the official registration in October 1941, 88,105 Jews lived in the Protectorate, and around 78,000 of them perished in the Holocaust—in Theresienstadt and in other places across Eastern Europe, including Lodz, Auschwitz, ghettos and death camps in eastern Poland, Belorussia, and the Baltic States. After the war less than 25,000 Jews were living in the Bohemian lands, many of them returning from exile in the uniforms of the Allied armies; there were also 8,500 Jewish repatriates from Subcarpathian Rus, the easternmost province ceded, in 1945, to the Soviet Union.[4]

Gruner's study is strongest in the parts where he builds on his previous research; for example, in the detailed analysis of the forced labor for the Protectorate Jewry,[5] or when he contextualizes anti-Jewish policies in the Protectorate with the persecution in the Reich (for instance, the deportation to the so-called Jewish reservation in the Lublin area in the autumn of 1939). In relation to the situation in the Protectorate, Gruner sets himself an ambitious goal. He analyzes the initial stages of the persecution, with the main focus on the interactions among the Nazi authorities, the "Czech" Protectorate administration at various levels, and the Jewish community structures before the conclusion of the main deportations in mid-1943. The chapters are presented in chronological order, each discussing the interactions between various agencies, as well as responses among those experiencing the persecution. In the opening chapter Gruner also discusses the prewar history of Czech-

---

3   Jan Láníček, *Arnošt Frischer and the Jewish Politics of Early 20th-Century Europe* (London: Bloomsbury, 2017), pp. 64ff.

4   Láníček, *Arnošt Frischer*, p. 145.

5   Wolf Gruner, *Jewish Forced Labor Under the Nazis: Economic Needs and Racial Aims, 1938–1944* (Cambridge: Cambridge University Press, 2006).

Jewish relations; later in the book he includes a brief discussion of the fate of the so-called *Mischlinge* in the last years of the war; and, finally, he concludes with the postwar period. However, the book does not take the readers beyond the territory of the Protectorate, for example to the Sudetenland, nor do we learn much about the situation in the Theresienstadt ghetto.

The Sacred Ground:
Do Not Lecture Us About the Holocaust

Gruner has contributed to two key topics related to the history of the Holocaust in Bohemia and Moravia: the involvement of the so-called Czech authorities in the persecution; and the role of the Jewish community structures. His book, originally published in German in 2016 (and in Czech in 2019), has already led to a critical backlash among Czech historians, sensitive to any criticism of the Czech population during the war from their colleagues in the Czech Republic or overseas. The publication of the Czech version came at the time when Czech historians—and also the general public—were undergoing several intense discussions about the wartime responses in the Czech population to the persecution of the Jews.

The predominantly negative responses to the publication of Gruner's book are in line with the Czechs' self-perception purely as victims of the Nazi rule in the Protectorate. The discussion about the role of the Czech population in the Nazi persecution of the Jews and Roma is still in its infancy, but any efforts to challenge the established official versions of the history are met with sharp rejection from nationalist sectors among historians and politicians.[6] This has been confirmed recently when two minor incidents triggered a heated debate about the image of Czechs purely as martyrs and as having resisted.

In the first instance the public Czech TV screened a program that discussed a case related to the centerpiece of the Czech wartime memory, the liquidation of the village Lidice on June 10, 1942.[7] One week before

6   See, for example, responses to the discussion about the role Czech guards played in the persecution and death of Roma prisoners in the Lety camp; https://www.institutvk.cz/clanky/1083.html Jiří Weigl, "Český" koncentrák (accessed February 8, 2018).

7   See https://www.ceskatelevize.cz/porady/1142743803-reporteri-ct/219452801240021/0/66320-v-predvecer-tragedie (accessed December 15, 2020).

the liquidation, a local resident allegedly denounced to the "Czech" Protectorate gendarmerie a Jewish woman living illegally in the village, and she was later murdered in Auschwitz. The allegation triggered the almost unprecedented effort of other historians to prove that a woman from Lidice, a symbol of Czech victimhood, could not commit such a heinous crime. In these efforts they were supported by nationalist politicians and activists.[8] The case remains open, but there is strong evidence that the woman from Lidice was involved in the denunciation. Nevertheless, nationalist pressure groups have forced the government to remove the head of the Lidice memorial, Martina Lehmannová, because she–in their opinion–did not outrightly reject the allegations.[9]

The second case occurred with the recent publication of a new history of the Jewish community in the Bohemian lands, which contains a chapter on the Holocaust by the American historian Benjamin Frommer. His findings largely support Gruner's conclusions.[10] Among other issues Frommer points to the instances during the first war years when local Czech authorities developed initiatives to segregate Jewish communities even before it was ordered by the Germans. In response, Ivo Cerman, a historian of the Enlightenment and the early modern era from the University of South Bohemia in České Budějovice, accused Frommer and Gruner of anti-Czech bias. This, according to Cerman, was part of a larger American effort to place the blame for the Holocaust on the "morally backward" East European states (partly for their unwillingness to accept Muslim refugees from the Middle East during the 2015 crisis). Alternatively, because the volume with Frommer's study was published in German, and the German embassy organized a book launch, Cerman and other historians also presented it as a German effort to relativize their guilt for the Holocaust. In what is often characterized as far-right "alternative media," Cerman confronted the editor of the book, the

---

8   Vojtěch Šustek, "Nepravdivé obvinění z udavačství lidické ženy Alžběty Doležalové," *Slánský obzor: ročenka společnosti Patria, Vlastivědného muzea ve Slaném a Státního okresního archivu v Kladně*, 25 (2017), pp. 48–75; https://www.parlamentnilisty. cz/arena/monitor/Udani-zidovky-v-Lidicich-Archivar-promluvil-Takhle-to-byt-nemohlo-Vazne-chyby-Dobova-fakta-612352 (accessed December 15, 2020).

9   Lehmannová resigned after it was made clear to her that the government would remove her from the position. See https://jewishnews.timesofisrael.com/czech-museum-director-fired (accessed December 15, 2020).

10 Benjamin Frommer, "Der Holocaust in Böhmen und Mähren," in Kateřina Čapková and Hillel J. Kieval, eds., *Zwischen Prag und Nikolsburg: Jüdisches Leben in den böhmischen Ländern* (Munich: Oldenbourg, 2020), pp. 266–318.

Czech historian Kateřina Čapková. In the final bizarre statements, Cerman commented that Čapková and other Czech historians "curry favor with influential American colleagues," and called the book a piece of "radical anti-Czech propaganda."[11]

It is a shame that, instead of an informed discussion, scholars such as Cerman engage in an unintelligent shaming, which takes quotes out of context and twists statements of the said historians. Instead of the suggestion that Czech institutions contributed to the segregation of the Jews through a multilateral process at the local regional or city level, as argued by Gruner or Frommer, their critics misquote them as blaming Czech people for the Holocaust. Instead of accepting the dynamic situation in the Protectorate, as elsewhere in Europe, the nationalist historians defend the dream of Czech exceptionalism.

The situation during the war was complex, and history is not a zero-sum game. Pointing to acts of involvement on the part of the Czech population during the Holocaust does not remove the ultimate responsibility from the Nazi officials. Berlin initiated the genocide, and the German authorities in the Protectorate oversaw the whole apparatus of persecution, but the space they created allowed others to become involved in the persecution on the ground. It is not possible to stifle the discussion of Czech behavior during the war with appeals to emotions or with defamatory attacks. We must critically evaluate Gruner's or Frommer's conclusions in order to further the field of Holocaust history in the Bohemian lands.

Czech Initiatives and German Policies

The introduction of the first anti-Jewish laws in Czechoslovakia predated the German invasion. They stemmed from the moral degradation and national frustration after the Munich dictate in late September 1938, when Czechoslovakia was forced to cede the borderlands to Germany, and later also to Hungary and Poland. Gruner is not the first historian who identifies these efforts by the post-Munich government and various professional associations to remove Jews from certain occupations (e.g., state service, law, medicine, and so on). The government also

11 See https://www.parlamentnilisty.cz/arena/rozhovory/Je-mi-uzko-co-pisou-o-Cesich-Historik-Cerman-byl-v-USA-sleduje-to-i-jinde-Jde-o-2-svetovou-613789; https://ivocerman.blog.idnes.cz/blog.aspx?c=744268 (accessed December 15, 2020).

intended to investigate the cases of individuals who had received citizenship after 1918, with the clear objective to focus on the Jews. Gruner suggests that "these anti-Jewish measures were independent developments influenced by radical Czech circles and had little to do with any direct pressure imposed by Hitler" (p. 43). He thus minimizes the importance of the oft-quoted pressure exerted by Hitler on Czechoslovak Foreign Minister František Chvalkovský during their meeting in January 1939, at which time the Führer insisted on the removal of the Jews from Czech public life.

In the main parts of the book, Gruner analyzes the involvement of the Protectorate government (unfortunately, perhaps because of the English-speaking audience, quite often it is awkwardly referred to as the Czech government) and local administrations in the radicalization of anti-Jewish policies during the German occupation.[12] The book spends much less space on responses within the Czech population, though Gruner emphasizes their lukewarm attitude to the Czech fascist groups, and also gives evidence of Czechs' public demonstrations of sympathies with the Jews during the deportations in the autumn of 1939 and later in 1941. Although Gruner mentions the activities of Czech fascists on several occasions, including their involvement in physical attacks on the Jews and their institutions, he could have also added more on their actual strength and influence. Even the German authorities in the Protectorate were aware of the marginal support the local fascists, largely a fringe group, had among the population. On the other hand, as Frommer in his studies persuasively argues, the Czech fascist press, even if not widely read, contributed to the segregation of the Jews. They published cases of those breaking anti-Jewish laws, or of non-Jews who kept fraternizing with their Jewish friends. "Czech" Protectorate police then investigated such allegations and helped enforce the "social death" of the Jews.[13]

Gruner clearly depicts the complex interactions between the central

---

12 This topic has also been discussed in the work of the Czech legal historian Helena Petrův, *Zákonné bezpráví: Židé v Protektorátu Čechy a Morava* (Prague: Auditorium, 2011).

13 Benjamin Frommer, "Verfolgung durch die Presse: Wie Prager Büroberater und die tschechische Polizei die Juden des Protektorats Böhmen und Mähren isolieren halfen," in Doris Bergen, et al., eds., *Leben und Sterben im Schatten der Deportation: Der Alltag der jüdischen Bevölkerung im Großdeutschen Reich 1941–1945* (Munich: Oldenbourg, 2013), pp. 137–150. On social death, see Marion Kaplan, *Between Dignity and Despair: Jewish Life in Nazi Germany* (Oxford: Oxford University Press, 1999).

and local authorities during the first years of the war. Local administrations, "chief county commissioners, German government commissioners, Nazi Party offices, and Czech district authorities" (p. 231) kept independently introducing anti-Jewish policies, thus creating administrative chaos in the Protectorate. Such local initiatives were ex post extended by the "Czech" interior ministry to the whole territory of the Protectorate. In this context Gruner speaks of an "'institutional quadrangle' of anti-Jewish measures, consisting of Berlin, the Reich protector, the Czech [sic!] government, and the local authorities..." (p. 98).

The system allowed local municipal and regional administrations considerable space for maneuver, and they, not the SD, Gestapo, or the Nazi Party, played "a leading role in the formulation of anti-Jewish policies" (pp. 394–395), "feeding into one another and reinforcing their mutual momentum" (p. 390). The only area in which the Germans quickly established their dominance, initially against the opposition of the Czech officials and economic elites, was the economic dispossession of the Jews and Aryanization (p. 381). Local informers of the Czechoslovak government-in-exile were certainly correct when they characterized the Aryanization as a stepping stone to the economic Germanization of the Protectorate territory.[14]

In October and November 1941, the representatives of the Security Police and the Central Office for Jewish Emigration (Zentralstelle) made it clear to the Protectorate government that henceforth the Jewish policies would be exclusively in the hands of the Nazi agencies (p. 327). However, as Gruner cogently argues, local initiatives to further restrict the remaining public space of the Jews continued even in the second half of the war. Gruner could have made a clearer distinction. While local authorities continued to issue new minor restrictive measures, the key policies, especially the ghettoization in Theresienstadt and deportation to the East, were fully in the hands of the Nazi agencies (pp. 126 and 386), even if Czech officials and policemen helped enforce the measures.

Another main contribution in Gruner's study is the identification of what he calls the first cases of "ghettoization" in the Bohemian and Moravian countryside as early as the spring of 1940, "in fact, prior to the establishment of ghettos in certain parts of occupied Poland" (p. 387). Local authorities, Gruner argues, "were quick to ghettoize Jews" as a way

---

14 Jan Láníček, *Czechs, Slovaks and the Jews, 1938–48: Beyond Idealisation and Condemnation* (Basingstoke: Palgrave, 2013), p. 30.

to confiscate their houses. These conclusions contradict previous studies that identify the main phase of the ghettoization only after the creation of Theresienstadt in late November 1941. It would help if Gruner defined what he means by "ghetto" in this context. There was a large variety of ghettos all over the occupied Eastern territories, but, as Dan Michman in his key study argues, we also need to look at the terminology used by the Nazi ideologues and bureaucrats.[15] It is unfortunately unclear from Gruner's text whether the terms "ghetto" or "Jewish houses" appear in the original documents, or if just he employs this terminology.

The documents I have consulted mention Jewish "houses" and "streets," but not "'ghettos."[16] Michman identifies Theresienstadt as the only ghetto in Bohemia and Moravia. He also points to the minutes from a key meeting in Prague in October 1941, at which Heydrich discussed the future possibilities for the ghettoization of Czech Jews, with the aim to create one or two ghettos.[17] Frommer, in his recently published study, gives three or four examples of what could be seen as "ghettoization" efforts, though he personally does not use the term.[18]

I believe that in the Bohemian and Moravian context it is more appropriate to talk about "concentration" in the countryside, as well as in some major cities, including Prague. Even in Prague, where the Nazis attempted to concentrate the Jews in three districts (though there were also Czechs and Germans living in the areas), there were Jews who continued to live in other quarters until the deportation.[19] The differences in our view of terminology notwithstanding, Gruner's insights into the progress of persecution in the Czech countryside further confirms the need to study the development of the persecution at the local level.

These sections of Gruner's book would benefit from a clearer discussion of a comparative contribution of Czech and German officials to the process of the Jews' segregation. The sources Gruner used did not lead him to such insights,[20] though he correctly describes the gradual

---

15 Dan Michman, *The Emergence of Jewish Ghettos During the Holocaust* (Cambridge: Cambridge University Press, 2011).

16 Yad Vashem Archives, O.7/56.

17 Michman, *Emergence of Jewish Ghettos*, pp. 134–137.

18 Frommer, "Der Holocaust in Böhmen und Mähren," p. 287.

19 See, for example, the story of Marie Bader in Kate Ottevanger and Jan Láníček, eds., *Life and Love in Nazi Prague: Letters from an Occupied City* (London: Bloomsbury, 2019).

20 These parts are mostly based on weekly reports submitted by the Jewish Religious

encroachment of the Germans on the local levels of the Protectorate administration:

> Ninety-five cities and towns were under German leadership in late December 1939 and 125 a year later. German mayors now headed all localities with more than 25,000 inhabitants, except Prague and Pilsen; there, however, the deputy mayors were German. The mayors and district chiefs, who later grew in number, particularly from 1940 onwards under Heydrich, came mostly from the Sudetenland (p. 156).

The number of Germans in other official positions, such as in the police, railways, labor deployment, and so on, also increased (pp. 157–158). Despite the efforts to Germanize the administration, the occupation authorities still had to rely on the cooperation of Czech bureaucrats, including members of the police and gendarmerie, in their efforts to enforce their anti-Jewish policies. Their motivation for cooperation with the Germans varied; they could range from those with antisemitic prejudices, to those who continued to work in the position for material gain, or because of career prospects (p. 396).

Each of the acts of segregation discussed by Gruner should be put in its specific context. The segregation and isolation of the Jews at the local level was a complex process. The previously quoted study by Frommer persuasively argues that even fringe groups in Czech society possessed immense power in their efforts to encourage more radical policies. They reported cases of Jews who were breaking anti-Jewish regulations, or petitioned local Czech Protectorate and German authorities to push for more radical policies. This pressure was one of the factors that led to the introduction of new local measures that restricted the "Jewish map," the public space of the Jews, and helped to segregate them from Czech non-Jews. Evidence from other archives also demonstrates that this was a multilateral process, with the involvement of local Czech Nazi sympathizers and those benefiting from the removal of the Jews as initiators of the measures.[21] The task for future historians will be to move to the microhistorical level and analyze the interactions between the Protectorate institution, the Protectorate police, local population,

---

Community in Prague to the Nazi authorities. In some places Gruner supports his conclusions with reports prepared by local German authorities deposited in the Bundesarchiv in Berlin.

21 See documents in USHMM, RG-48.016M, reels 162–164.

and German offices. We must commend Gruner for opening this crucial question for the history of the Holocaust in the Protectorate, but we need more research.

Responses in the Jewish Community

There has been a significant shift in Holocaust historiography in the last decades to focus on experiences in the victim communities. Gruner makes another contribution to this field by offering insights into responses in the Jewish community organizations in Bohemia and Moravia, as well as among those who, according to the Nazi racial laws, were identified as Jews. Gruner portrays the leadership as committed activists who attempted to cushion the impact of the Nazi and Protectorate policies, and protect for as long as possible the community from the effects of the social and economic death. First, as already suggested by other historians, the Jewish Community Office facilitated and supported the emigration of the Jews, also by offering retraining courses in the first years of the war.[22] Later it supported those who had lost their employment and petitioned the authorities in order to challenge the new measures that were constantly introduced. Leaders such as František Weidmann and Jacob Edelstein took part in official negotiations with the Nazi authorities in Prague, Vienna, or Berlin, and coordinated efforts with Jewish leaders in other places, including Palestine and Amsterdam. In October 1939, Edelstein, a committed Socialist Zionist, even traveled together with the first deportees to the so-called "Lublin reservation," which the Nazis planned to turn into a dumping ground for the Jews in the Old Reich, Austria, and the Protectorate. After his return Edelstein pledged to protect the Jews from further deportations to the East, which was one of the reasons why he initially welcomed the creation of Theresienstadt, in the hope that it would stop deportations to occupied Poland.[23]

Gruner praises the Jewish leaders, arguing that,

> Despite the strict surveillance to which it was subject in all matters relating to emigration, finances, housing, and labour deployment

---

22 On Jewish emigration from the Protectorate, see also Laura Brade, "Networks of Escape: Jewish Flight from the Bohemian Lands, 1938–1941" (PhD diss., University of North Carolina, Chapel Hill, 2017).

23 Rothkirchen, *The Jews of Bohemia and Moravia*, p. 235.

outside of Prague, the Prague Jewish Community did not allow Eichmann's Central Office to turn it into a mere organ of policy implementation (p. 397).

The book avoids more problematic chapters in the history of the Jewish communal agencies, such as their contribution to the registration of the Jews and their property, and their role in the deportations, which is a subject that continues to raise controversies among survivors and historians. But the community leadership was under immense pressure from the very beginning of the occupation. Some of the leaders were even imprisoned for a short time; others managed to escape to Palestine or elsewhere.[24] Those who remained were terrorized into submission. In October 1941, *SS-Obersturmführer* Karl Rahm, the deputy in the *Zentralstelle* in Prague, ordered the deportation of two members of the Prague Jewish Community, Hanuš Bonn and Erich Kafka, to their death in Mauthausen, allegedly because they had been sabotaging the preparation for the renewed deportation from the Protectorate. The Jewish Community was soon informed that both died in the infamous camp.[25] It is likely that the aim of such an act of terror was to ensure the cooperation of the remaining members of the Jewish Community office, and the allegedly slow execution of the deportation order was used merely as a pretext.

The pressure continued in the following years. Abraham Fixler, who worked as a liaison of the Jewish Community in the *Zentralstelle*, frequently experienced humiliation and physical attacks.[26] František Friedmann, the last wartime head of the Council of Elders in Prague until the liberation, was even temporarily imprisoned when the Nazi authorities were not satisfied with his work.[27] None of the community leaders, unless they had a non-Jewish spouse, survived the war. They were all murdered in Auschwitz during 1944.

Other reviewers of Gruner's work have raised questions concerning the source base that he used, as, in their opinion, it offers a skewed view of the work of the Jewish Community during the war.[28] It is correct that

---

24 Láníček, *Arnošt Frischer*, pp. 52–66.
25 Rothkirchen, *The Jews of Bohemia and Moravia*, p. 126.
26 See https://www.holocaust.cz/databaze-dokumentu/dokument/121433-fixler-abraham-zprava-o-lekarskem-osetreni (accessed December 15, 2020).
27 Transcript of interrogation of Erich Kraus, December 17, 1951, Archiv bezpečnostných složek ministerstva vnitra ČR, V-1649.
28 Michal Frankl, "Review of: Wolf Gruner, Die Judenverfolgung im Protektorat

his detailed research is based mostly on weekly reports prepared by the Prague Jewish Community office for the *Zentralstelle*. However, this is certainly a highly problematic source, as the Jewish Community wanted to present itself as a body that smoothly executed all orders issued by the SS. Thus, we need documents from other sources to offer a more nuanced view of the Jewish Community activists during the war.[29]

On the whole I agree with Gruner's effort to present the Jewish leadership as an activist group that did their utmost to support the Jews in the Protectorate. This applies also to Gruner's limited portrayal of members of the general Jewish public. The definition of "Jewish resistance" has often been contested among historians. Gruner understands the term in quite a wide scope and includes any acts of defiance against Nazi rule, even if the aim was not to harm the Germans politically, economically, or militarily. This stems from the belief that the Nazi goal was not only to murder the Jews, but to dehumanize them in the process and destroy any sense of community and solidarity. Yehuda Bauer famously applied the Hebrew term *Amidah* (standing up against) to characterize Jewish resistance to the Holocaust. In Bauer's opinion, Jewish resistance can be defined as "any group [or individual] action consciously taken in opposition to known or surmised laws, actions or intentions against the Jews by the Germans [and their collaborators]."[30]

Gruner asserts that, "Every time a Jew violated German or Czech ordinances, he or she did so consciously and at great personal risk" (p. 160). Such acts of resistance included, for example, shopping outside of the permitted hours, breaking the curfew, or visiting prohibited parts of towns. It is possible that some readers will disagree with this wide, all-encompassing understanding of the term, because it may relativize the importance of more organized efforts among the Jews to undermine the German rule. However, we must keep in mind the unequal relationship between the persecuted Jewish communities and the German military and political power that controlled most of Europe. Under such circumstances even individual acts of support for Jewish families and

Böhmen und Mähren. Lokale Initiativen, zentrale Entscheidungen, jüdische Antworten 1939–1945," *Bohemia*, 58:2 (2018), pp. 405–409.

29 Magda Veselská, "Sie müssen sich als Jude dessen bewusst sein, welche Opfer zu tragen sind…" in Doris Bergen et al., eds., *Alltag im Holocaust: Jüdisches Leben im Großdeutschen Reich 1941–1945* (Munich: Oldenbourg, 2013), pp. 151–166.

30 Yehuda Bauer, *Rethinking the Holocaust* (New Haven: Yale University Press, 2001), p. 119.

attempts at weakening the impact of the Nazi and Czech measures that, for example, restricted Jews' access to food, entertainment, or other social activities—all important for physical and psychological survival—were acts of resistance.

On the other hand, we will need further research to establish the scale of such resistance activities. Gruner gives examples of anti-Jewish resistance with references to reports prepared by local German administrators, who, for example, complained about "the Jews... conducting themselves in an intrusive manner in public streets" (p. 182). He also gives the example of Heydrich who, in late September 1941, ordered to close all synagogues in the Protectorate, as centers of "subversive Jewish elements and the epicentres of illegal whispering campaigns" (p. 267). But how seriously shall we take such allegations? Local German commissioners, often radical Nazis, pursued their agenda and demanded the removal of the Jews from the area, or their isolation in parts of the city or in the countryside. From their perspective even simple daily activities manifested "intrusive" or "defiant" Jewish behavior, because they did not want Jews in their areas at all. Similar elaboration would be helpful in the case of Karl Hermann Frank's comments in the summer of 1941, that, "Jews' anti-Reich activities are growing by the hour," which started a chain of events leading, in September 1941, to the official branding of the Jews with the Star of David throughout the Reich (p. 234). I would take such comments from leading Nazis with a grain of salt.

Conclusions

Despite my critical comments, Gruner's work is a crucial addition to the relatively neglected field of Holocaust studies in the Protectorate. He introduces multiple questions that still await historians' attention. Not enough is known about the attitude of the Czech population toward the Jews. Gruner correctly claims that the Nazi agencies were highly critical of the Czechs' lack of understanding for the anti-Jewish actions; however, local Czech authorities clearly contributed to the segregation of the Jews. How shall we reconcile this difference in attitudes? More crucially, if we accept that the Czech population for various reasons opposed German antisemitism and, in 1939–1941, manifested public sympathy for the Jews, how is it possible that the Protectorate had one of the lowest number of Jews who survived the war in hiding supported by the local population? This number was lower than even in Germany.[31] The aim of such future studies will not be to place blame on Czech society—as some opponents of such research argue—but to identify, analyze, and explain the factors that contributed to so few Jews surviving in the Protectorate.

Those who criticize efforts to deal with difficult questions in the history of the Bohemian lands must understand that Gruner and others are not trying to relativize the guilt of Nazi Germany.[32] The Holocaust in Bohemia and Moravia happened because of the German invasion and Nazi dominance over Central Europe. At the same time parts of the subjugated nations—for various political, ideological, economic, or social reasons—utilized the Nazi dominance and the status quo in order to pursue their own interests and contribute to the segregation, isolation, and dispossession of the Jews. Ota Ornest, a famous Czech playwright and director who managed to escape to Great Britain, called this a "brilliant plan" by the Nazis: they created a hierarchy of races, which pitted all against the Jews, the lowest of the low.[33] Although the Czechs were also terribly persecuted and humiliated, they could benefit from the removal of the Jews, and some of them decided to seize this opportunity.

31   See, for example, Benjamin Frommer, "The Saved and the Betrayed. Hidden Jews in the Nazi Protectorate of Bohemia and Moravia," in Ari Kohen and Gerald Steinacher, eds., *Unlikely Heroes: The Place of Holocaust Rescuers in Research and Teaching* (Lincoln: University of Nebraska Press, 2019), pp. 37–56

32   Vojtěch Blodig, "Recenze — Wolf Gruner, Die Judenverfolgung im Protektorat Böhmen und Mähren. Lokale Initiativen, zentrale Entscheidungen," *Terezínské listy*, 46 (2018), pp. 90–98.

33   Ota Ornest, *Hraje Váš tatínek ještě na housle? Rozhovor Marie Valtrové s Otou Ornestem* (Prague: Primus, 1993), pp. 30–32.

Icons, Trodden Sand, and the Violence of the Gaze: Looking at the Holocaust

Tal Bruttmann, Stefan Hördler, and Christoph Kreutzmüller, *Die Fotografische Inszenierung des Verbrechens. Ein Album aus Auschwitz.* (Darmstadt: WBG, 2019), 304 pp.

Christophe Cognet, *Éclats: Prises de vue clandestines des camps nazis.* (Paris: Seuil, 2019), 432 pp.

Martin Cüppers, Annett Gerhardt, Karin Graf, Steffen Hänschen, Andreas Kahrs, Anne Lepper, and Florian Ross, *Fotos aus Sobibor: Die Niemann-Sammlung zu Holocaust und Nationalsozialismus*, eds. Bildungswerk Stanisław Hantz and Forschungsstelle Ludwigsburg der Universität Stuttgart. (Berlin: Metropol, 2020), 382 pp.

Reviewed by
Jan Burzlaff

T raditionally there are two ways of engaging with Holocaust images. On the one hand, pictures taken by arriving U.S. troops, war journalists, and Soviet Jewish photographers have shaped public knowledge of the events.[1] Thirty or so icons dominate this figurative canon—including images of the crimes of the Einsatzgruppen hovering over pits, the boy in the Warsaw ghetto, and Stanisław Mucha's epoch-making shot of Auschwitz-Birkenau's gatehouse.[2] Nowadays these photos often merely confirm what the

---

1   Among others, see Dan Stone, *The Liberation of the Camps* (Oxford: Oxford University Press, 2015); David Shneer, *Through Soviet Jewish Eyes: Photography, War, and the Holocaust* (New Brunswick: Rutgers University Press, 2011).

2   See Nicholas Chare and Dominic Williams, eds., *The Auschwitz Sonderkommando: Testimonies, Histories, Representations* (Berlin: Springer, 2019); Frédéric Rousseau, *L'Enfant juif de Varsovie: histoire d'une photographie* (Paris: Seuil, 2009); Israel Gutman and Bella Gutterman, eds., *The Auschwitz Album: The Story of a Transport* (Jerusalem: Yad Vashem, 2008); Serge Klarsfeld, ed., *L'Album d'Auschwitz* (Paris: Canopé, 2014).

public already knows.[3] On the other hand, reacting to these effects of deluge and fetishization, French filmmaker Claude Lanzmann and students of visual culture have pointed out photography's limits. As this school of thought surmised, the perception of the Holocaust would not be grounded in seeing but in accepting the painful presence of absence. By the same token many scholars have emphasized the difficulties inherent in determining the provenance of certain pictures and have lambasted the emphasis on commemoration at the expense of historical research.[4]

However, pictures are able to guide us toward a fuller understanding of the Holocaust. For example, the 1995 and 2001 exhibitions of Wehrmacht images were crucial in sparking public and scholarly debates about the importance of private photography.[5] Over the past two decades, scholars have laid the foundations for a now-blossoming "pictorial history" that questions reception, context, interpretation, and spectatorship of Holocaust photography, and this has become an ever-growing trend in the context of public history and massive digitization.[6] We now know that even the most famous four photographs taken by the Sonderkommando at Birkenau remain "images in spite of all," pictures that were produced, transmitted, and received in various political and social contexts.[7] Thus, it is time to assess this ongoing "visual turn" in

3   Early milestones were Barbie Zelizer, *Visual Culture and the Holocaust* (New Brunswick: Rutgers University Press, 1998); Cornelia Brink, *Ikonen der Vernichtung: Zum öffentlichen Gebrauch von Fotografien aus nationalsozialistischen Konzentrationslager* (Berlin: Akademie Verlag, 1998). See also Sebastian Schönemann, *Symbolbilder des Holocaust. Fotografien der Vernichtung im sozialen Gedächtnis* (Frankfurt: Campus Verlag, 2019).
4   One such example is Janina Struk, *Photographing the Holocaust: Interpretations of the Evidence* (London: I.B. Tauris, 2004).
5   Judith Levin and Daniel Uziel, "Ordinary Men, Extraordinary Photos," *Yad Vashem Studies*, 26:2 (1998), pp. 265–293; early calls by Sybil Milton, "Images of the Holocaust, Part 1," *Holocaust and Genocide Studies*, 1:1 (1986), pp. 27–61, and Yitzhak Arad, ed., *The Pictorial History of the Holocaust* (New York: Macmillan and Yad Vashem, 1990).
6   For recent examples see Elizabeth Harvey et al., eds., *Private Life and Privacy in Nazi Germany* (Cambridge: Cambridge University Press, 2019); Hildegard Frübis, Clara Oberle, and Agnieszka Pufelska, eds., *Fotografien aus den Lagern des NS-Regimes. Beweissicherung und Ästhetische Praxis* (Vienna: Böhlau, 2019). Paul Betts, Jennifer Evans, and Stefan-Ludwig Hoffmann, eds., *The Ethics of Seeing: Photography and Twentieth-Century German History* (New York: Berghahn, 2018) is an important volume but does not deal with the Holocaust per se.
7   Georges Didi-Huberman, *Images in Spite of All* (Chicago: University of Chicago Press, 2008).

Holocaust studies through three books that discuss and reproduce more than 330 photographs from concentration and death camps.

The books under review represent this new path in visual histories of the Holocaust, beyond sanctification and mere illustration, first by unraveling what had been unknown material.[8] In 2015, a grandson of *SS-Untersturmführer* Johann Niemann (1913–1943), who was killed in the Sobibor uprising on October 16, 1943, handed two albums, comprised of 361 photographs and dozens of paper documents, to the Stanisław Hantz educational organization. The 2020 edition uniquely documents Niemann's murderous career in the camp system, including various concentration camps, T4 killing centers, Belzec, and Sobibor. German historians led by Martin Cüppers examine these photos in the context of the scarce documentary landscape of "Operation Reinhard," which now makes Sobibor the best-documented Reinhard camp, with sixty-two photos.

However, visual histories of the Holocaust can also shed new light on existing collections, such as the 2019 edition of the "Lili Jacob Album" ("Auschwitz Album"), named after the survivor who discovered and then donated it to Yad Vashem. Taken by SS photographers Bernhard Walter and Ernst Hoffmann upon the arrival of three deportation trains from Hungary, the pictures follow groups of victims from "selections" to moments before they were killed in the gas chambers. These famous photographs enabled the identification of victims and perpetrators in the Eichmann (1961) and Auschwitz trials (1963–1965). Still, they are ultimately misleading in their highly staged representation of the "Final Solution," as Christoph Kreutzmüller, Tal Bruttmann, and Stefan Hördler demonstrate. The three historians aptly reconstruct the album's original context and scrupulously dissect each of the 192 photographs. Rather than representing Birkenau's usual chaos and the victims' suffering, these photos intended to showcase the camp's efficiency at the height of "Aktion Höss," the murder of up to 349,000 Hungarian Jews in the summer of 1944. Adding victims' perspectives in his 2019 monograph, French film director Christophe Cognet's *Éclats* ("shards" in English) reconsiders eighty photographs taken by eight Jewish and non-Jewish

8   Ernst Klee, Willi Dreßen, and Volker Riess, eds., *"The Good Old Days:" The Holocaust as Seen by Its Perpetrators and Bystanders* (Old Saybrook: Konecky & Konecky, 1991) provides snapshots of Bełżec commandant Gottlieb Hering that have remained largely unknown to the public.

prisoners under extreme conditions in Dora-Mittelbau, Buchenwald, Ravensbrück, Dachau, and Birkenau.

Taken together, these three titles demonstrate that photography in the camps prompted not only German and non-German perpetrators to stage their roles in the genocide, but also forced Jewish victims to react to this additional layer of violence—be it as minimal as looking away.[9] These visual histories of the Holocaust trace individuals and plausible life stories as much as possible while also allowing for the necessary unknown. All the authors, by interpreting photos as autobiographical sources, scrutinize the movements the camera's lens made, examine the production of the photographs, and contextualize the images' audiences. Most of the German and French contributors are trained historians who shift the focus from the photographs' meaning, style, and montage—often emphasized in visual critics' universal reflections—to rather understanding how the photographs could have been made, why they existed, and what they represent. In a sense, in their empirical analysis of each image, the authors echo Raul Hilberg's fear of asking big questions, only to come up with small answers.[10] Here all the scholars ask each of the 334 photos small questions about the stances of the subjects, the position of sunlight, who and what is shown; in short, a history of traces and gazes gathered one by one to constitute the fullest picture possible.

What ties the Niemann and Auschwitz albums together is the widespread use of the camera for and by the perpetrator networks. The fact that the official prohibition on photos beyond the standardized *Erkennungsdienst* (police identification/records department), which provided identification photos for the SS, was breached is well-known. Indeed many "trophy photos" evince soldiers' pleasure in documenting their deeds.[11] Niemann was equally proud of documenting his career.

9   For photos as weapons, see Sybil Milton, "The Camera as Weapon: Documentary Photography and the Holocaust," *Simon Wiesenthal Center Annual*, 1:1 (1984), pp. 45–68.

10 Raul Hilberg, *The Politics of Memory* (Chicago: Ivan R. Dee Publisher, 1996), 63ff. Conversations regarding this topic/quote are also reported in Emil L. Fackenheim, "The Holocaust and Philosophy," *The Journal of Philosophy*, 82:10 (1985), pp. 505-514.

11 Stefan Hördler, "Sichtbarmachen. Möglichkeiten und Grenzen einer Analyse von NS-Täter-Fotografien," *Vierteljahrshefte für Zeitgeschichte*, 65:2 (2017), pp. 259–271; Paul Lowe, "Picturing the Perpetrator," in Geoffrey Batchen et al., eds., *Picturing Atrocity* (London: Reaktion Books, 2012), pp. 189–200.

Once in Sobibor, where he served as the acting commandant after the summer of 1942, Niemann found himself in good company with three prewar photographers—Franz Wolf, his brother Josef Wolf, and Thomas Steffel, as well as shutterbug Herbert Floss. As a result of the ample supply of photographers, many duplicates and negatives of the photographs could have existed.[12] Each of the eleven sections of the 2020 edition, akin to a criminal investigative reconstruction, follows Niemann from his native Völlen in East Frisia (Ostfriesland), through the Esterwegen and Sachsenhausen concentration camps and the T4 killing centers in Grafeneck, Brandenburg, and Bernburg to Belzec and Sobibor. After historian Martin Cüppers' cogent introduction, which expounds upon the exceptional breadth of the Niemann collection as compared to other known perpetrator albums, the ten chapters provide a detailed historical background to Niemann's career in different concentration camps, Belzec, and Sobibor. The last chapter is a much-needed reflection by survivor Semion Rozenfeld about the experiences he lived through in Sobibor.

First and foremost the album visualizes Niemann's steadily growing commitment to Nazism and reflects the notion of comradeship that Thomas Kühne has carved out in his discussion of the emotional glue among male perpetrators in Eastern Europe.[13] In Sobibor cheerful camaraderie prevailed right next to the gas chambers, and similar to the guests at the Auschwitz guards' resort Solahütte, these men enjoyed being photographed while laughing and drinking. Each chapter helps contextualize these photographs for a broad audience, including a powerful analysis of motifs and snapshots, such as Niemann's self-staged portraits with a horse, gloves, and dogs. Short biographies of survivors of Sobibor and of German perpetrators serve to round out this historically remarkable edition.

Firmly centered on the new historiography of Operation Reinhard, the authors of the Niemann edition notably probe the visualization of

---

12 Cüppers et al. (pp. 18–20) feature the explanation that one negative from the leisure trip to Berlin has the number "30" written on the back; the authors aptly explore the personal continuities with Sobibor.

13 Thomas Kühne, *The Rise and Fall of Comradeship: Hitler's Soldiers, Male Bonding and Mass Violence in the Twentieth Century* (Cambridge: Cambridge University Press, 2017). For a cogent summary of the field, see also Kühne, "Epilogue: The Holocaust and Masculinities," in Björn Krondorfer and Ovidiu Creanga, eds., *The Holocaust and Masculinities: Critical Inquiries into the Presence and Absence of Men* (Albany: SUNY Press, 2020), pp. 285–304.

personal continuities in these death camps.[14] Similar to what Niemann did, Gottfried Schwarz, Siegfried Graetschus, and other SS men transferred from the T4 "euthanasia" program to Belzec, Sobibor, and Treblinka. Here the role of the Reich Chancellery emerges more from the photographs than from surviving written records. There are those that show the organization of recreational trips for SS officers with and for their wives, as well as the financial support they received after Operation Reinhard. But the visibly flat hierarchies among the SS during leisure-time activities (demonstrated in twenty-nine photos) also seem to have allowed for more intimacy with the Trawniki guards than previously assumed. Guards, possibly including Ivan Demjanjuk and Alexander Kaiser, appear in ten of the Sobibor photos, and eighty-four in the entire collection. Besides its focus on Trawniki, one of the book's merits lies in envisioning the gendered perpetrator network at large, in the form of a fascinating biography of Henriette Niemann. We learn about her political sympathy for Nazism in rural East Frisia, her financial benefits from and conscious complicity in Sobibor's massive theft of Jewish goods, and her postwar remarriage to a former Dutch Nazi. Up to 15,700 Reichsmarks had been transferred to Niemann's various bank accounts, but they became valueless after the 1948 monetary reform in Germany.

Niemann and his comrades also undertook a leisure trip to Berlin, documented in eighty photographs (Cüppers, Gerhardt, Graf, Hänschen, Kahrs, Lepper and Ross, pp. 228–255, 336). These are similar to millions of snapshots that were taken across Nazi Germany. Thanks to visual historian Gerhard Paul's pioneering work, we know that around 10 percent of Germans possessed a camera in 1939, and that both professional and private photographers were actively engaged under the dictatorship.[15] Here, however, the authors could have explained further to what extent the Nazi visual culture influenced the ongoing genocide, especially after the onset of the 1941 mass shootings. Indeed, photography did accelerate and shape the Nazi genocide—Sobibor was embedded in the broader Nazi visual culture.

These perpetrator networks were equally active in their use of photography at Auschwitz, perhaps increasingly so as the tide of war turned against them. In the Auschwitz Album, SS perpetrators are largely

14 Stephan Lehnstaedt and Robert Traba, eds., *Die "Aktion Reinhardt:" Geschichte und Gedenken* (Berlin: Metropol, 2019).
15 Gerhard Paul, *Bilder einer Diktatur: Zur Visual History des "Dritten Reiches"* (Göttingen: Wallstein, 2020).

absent, figuring as the central object in only ten, and in the foreground or background in barely twenty. But this absence makes sense within the album's broader ideological purpose. Its aim was not to focus as much on the SS men themselves but on an ideal model of the various steps through which Hungarian Jews and their possessions were "processed" upon their arrival. After a preface by Serge Klarsfeld, Bruttmann, Hördler, and Kreutzmüller present an excellent up-to-date history of Auschwitz in the first section (pp. 19–54), before tracing the album's origins and Lily Jacob's personal story (pp. 54–73). The second section reproduces the album in its entirety (pp. 74–131), while the third section deconstructs and reconstructs each of the photographs according to topics and places (pp. 133–267). The three authors convincingly argue that Commandant Rudolf Höss sought to stylize Auschwitz as the superior death camp and elevate himself as the quintessential expert of the "Final Solution." In a sense Auschwitz's postwar embodiment of the Holocaust realized one of the long-term goals of what was initially visual propaganda for a small circle of Nazi leaders.[16] In all likelihood Höss planned the album in coordination with his superiors Oswald Pohl and Richard Glücks, and perhaps even Heinrich Himmler—but the accompanying report would never be written.

As Bruttmann, Hördler, and Kreutzmüller reveal, 90 percent of a series of 197 photos (192 of which have survived) were taken between

Bruttmann et al., p. 94. Birkenau, Poland.
Women and children on the selection ramp, May 1944.
Yad Vashem Archives (YVA), 14BO3.

16 An argument already advanced by Cornelia Brink, "Das Auschwitz-Album vor Gericht," in Irmtrud Wojak, ed., *Auschwitz-Prozess 4KS 2/63* (Frankfurt am Main and Cologne: Snoeck, 2004), pp. 148–159.

May 19 and May 30, 1944, by the chief of the *Erkennungsdienst* Bernhard Walter and his subordinate, Ernst Hofmann, upon the arrival of Jews from Ungvár, Beregszász, and Técső, Hungary. For instance, the arrival from Beregszász on the morning of May 26, represented an ideal opportunity for photographic documentation as the camp's SS leaders inspected the so-called "new ramp." Furthermore, the three authors analyze a series of pictures that tackle questions of antisemitism, violence—inside and outside—noises, stench, thirst, and witnesses, and they ably identify individual Jews, SS men, and wagon numbers and their labels.

The book's most significant insight is certainly the staged "order" of the arrivals, most clearly seen in photos 22, 23, and 59. These images are often used in public to illustrate Auschwitz's cruel selections without relaying the album's intention. Indeed, the arrival and selection processes, shown in two-thirds of the photos, certainly do not reflect Birkenau's prevailing conditions. Instead, the sequence of pictures reducing Jewish victims to other material flowing through the death camp is indicative of the inhumane SS gaze at the Final Solution. The illusion of sanitized operations also applies to images of the deportees' goods stacked up after the selections (176–180) and in the "Kanada" warehouses for looted property (181–197). Ultimately—so went the rationale presiding over the photographs—the Nazi "order" could only be achieved once

Bruttmann et al., p. 130. Birkenau, Poland.
Sorting personal belongings next to the "Kanada" barracks, May 1944.
YVA, 12AO1.

"children, mothers, the elderly, the sick, and disabled were 'sorted out'" (Bruttmann, Hördler, and Kreutzmüller, p. 274).

As a result, violence resides not so much in the images themselves, but in the gaze Walter and Hofmann share with their contemporaries and impose on their modern viewers. Still, what bare violence *is* shown in the Auschwitz Album and deliberately omitted in the Sobibor photos must be integral to any visual analysis. What mattered to the killers were the ongoing efforts to build this racial community of peers and the movements on the ramps rather than the inner workings of mass murder. Across 107 photographs no image conveys the full extent of the "new ramp," inaugurated for Aktion Höss. Furthermore, the photographers never accompany the same Jews from the ramp to their final moments. As art historians have made clear over the past decade, photography is a social relationship between photographers and viewers, an endless process of representations of the self, "we," and others.[17] For the SS perpetrators and their intended viewers, violence was not only natural, but the knowledge of the gas chambers was mere common sense—so why explicitly photograph them? Only when the war effort became increasingly doomed in the eyes of even the most ardent SS believers, in the spring of 1945, did these identity-creating pictures leave the official realm and were turned into a private recollection. The only surviving copy of the Auschwitz Album probably belonged to the photographer Walter, the lowest-ranking perpetrator among all fifteen or so intended recipients.

Examining Holocaust photography just for incriminating evidence does not exhaust the productive tension between visibility and invisibility that allows for a more precise understanding of daily life and death in the Nazi camps. For example, in the Auschwitz Album, women are underrepresented, and the painful registration process and the inside of the wagons are hidden. Only twenty-three pictures show the concentration camp proper.

Yet the violence inflicted by the camera's shutter comes to light upon closer inspection. Deportation trains bound for the death camps were never a priority for Nazi-controlled railways across Europe, leaving survivors with angst-producing memories of hours or days waiting on the tracks. However, all other activities seemed to freeze for the benefit

---

17 See John Roberts, *Photography and Its Violations* (New York: Columbia University Press, 2014).

Bruttmann et al., p. 113. Birkenau, Poland. Jewish women and children deemed unfit for work on the way to Gas Chamber 3, 27/05/1944. YVA, 12FO8.

of the Final Solution after a train arrived at the ramp. In photo sixty-nine, tools are spread unattended on the ground as if inmates working on *Strasse A* had to suspend their work in haste. Birkenau's Crematoria III and IV are at times visible on the horizon (photos 3, 4, 16, 19, 20, and 27) and in the background (photos 118 and 134). Hofmann also photographed a disabled man, who meets his gaze, a boy dressed in nationalist clothing (Lily Jacob's brother, photo fifty-four), which is the only portrait of a child, and an older woman dragged to Crematorium V (photo 134). The last picture is the only one in which the size of the crematorium's chimney is distinguishable. Hofmann and Walter also forced an older man to take off his hat, a humiliating breach of religious commandment, and a group of women and children to turn around and face the camera on their way to the crematorium.

Traces of the extermination process in Sobibor are even more difficult to detect. One of the Niemann album's most considerable merits is the confirmation of the topography that archaeologists have established from recent excavations, notably of *Lager I* and the front camp. Niemann's photos do not show the gas chambers and their surroundings, but a picture of *Lager III*, the actual killing center, displaying the corpse excavator. At most, trodden sand in one picture suggests that victims had just finished undressing in front of a wooden fence and were chased naked to the gas chambers (Cüppers et al, pp. 137–155, 181).

Bildungswerk Hantz et al., p. 181. Sobibor, Camp II, summer 1943.
Box 1/Folder 11, Photograph 78, Sobibor perpetrator collection (2020.8.1), United
States Holocaust Memorial Museum Archives, Washington, DC.

Nonetheless, there are ways to break through the thick gaze of the perpetrators. To begin with, Semion Rozenfeld (1922–2019) commented on Niemann in general and validated the camp's topography in particular. In the Auschwitz Album, designer Andrea Lei recreates the missing perspective of victims facing the SS photographer on the ramp, based on photos 22, 23, and 59 (Bruttmann et al, p. 145). The book is dedicated to the young women and a child who, in four shots, stick their tongues out at the photographer, which was a risky gesture under those extreme circumstances. Women often attempted to look away from the camera or even hide their faces (photo 164). Despite the existing ban, an inmate of the *Kanada-Kommando* is seen speaking with a woman.

Here Christophe Cognet's *Éclats* shows particularly well the difference between photographs taken by victims and those the perpetrators staged. In his book from 2019, prefaced by historian Annette Wieviorka, Cognet offers a fine-grained analysis of some eighty photographs in ninety-five short chapters; all are scrutinized at length, and then put back into their contexts. He argues that those pictures shot by inmates convey equality between photographer and subject and capture the immediacy of the moment. Consisting of images taken between early 1943 and the autumn of 1944, this selection excludes many well-known photographs, such as Francisco Boix's pictures of Mauthausen's liberation; yet the advantage in this display is being able to see and analyze the series together to the greatest possible extent. Some fifty photos stem from Rudolf Cisar and Jean Brichaux in Dachau; seven from three Czech deportees in Mittelbau-Dora; eleven from Georges Angéli in Buchenwald; five from Joanna Szydlowska in Ravensbrück; and four from Alberto Errera in Auschwitz-Birkenau.

In French discourse the term "*les camps*" often designates both death and concentration camps. Thus Cognet is careful to emphasize the "radically different nature of Auschwitz" (Cognet, p. 38). But in examining the very act of photography, he distills something akin to a shared sense of resistance—not so much in the spirit of the *amidah* that has dominated much of recent historiography, but rather as an effort to document the camps' inner workings and to warn the outside world. Three sections—the concentration-camp universe (pp. 42–221), the medical experimentations (pp. 225–284), and the killing center (pp. 287–398)—trace the fate of the photographers and describe their risky preparations in a typically French combination of interdisciplinary texts and testimonies. After finding a camera either in the camp's *Erkennungsdienst* or in clothing from the Kanada warehouses, prisoners had to assemble its parts, choose an appropriate time to take the pictures, decide whether to do so with or without the subjects' complicity, and, finally, hide the negatives or transmit them to the underground. In illuminating passages Cognet surveys images that depict the camp's interiors, the crematorium's smoking chimney, the fence, the military hospital, mattresses, self-portraits, prisoners known among the inmates as "female rabbits," who exhibited their wounds that were inflicted by the barbaric "doctors" in Ravensbrück, and scars on the back of a child's head.

As a result, we must understand *Éclats* ("shards") in a double sense— as both the small pieces of human ashes that Cognet found while visiting the Birkenau site, and the many snapshots whose blurred movements translate fear and haste. The primary goal of these photographs, Cognet convincingly argues, lies in restoring the individuality of each photographer. Unlike the Niemann and Auschwitz albums, which aim to forge the collective identity of elite SS men, in the context of the camp, the notion of "victim" alone does not convey these images' complexity. The latter holds particularly true for our impressions of Alberto Errera's

Cognet, p. 370. Auschwitz, Poland,
cremation of bodies by the Sonderkommando.
YVA, 20AO8.

four photographs, especially the best known, taken on the threshold of
a gas chamber. Cognet rightly warns us about theoretical abstractions
that have served as a barrier to the images' violence. Shifting focus back
onto a collective project that the Dragon brothers and Errera elaborated
within the Sonderkommando, Cognet concludes that two of the four
pictures were likely taken from inside the gas chamber, but not shot one
after another as previously supposed. Gideon Greif's essential interviews
with all Sonderkommando survivors in Israel, which bent the harsh
postwar judgments on the dilemmas, tensions, and anxieties faced by
those Jewish prisoners to participate in the cremation of corpses, also
finds a visual echo in *Éclats*. In one picture, while one person seemingly
walks through a sea of corpses, he takes care not to step on them, in an
ultimate act of postmortem delicacy (Cognet, p. 370).[18]

It is this blend of perspectives and gazes that opens new avenues
for research on the Holocaust. To be sure, we are still far from mapping
its visual landscape. Future studies need to expand findings from other
places and times in order to avoid earlier Auschwitz-centered narratives.

---

18 See Gideon Greif, *We Wept Without Tears: Testimonies of the Jewish Sonderkommando
from Auschwitz* (New Haven: Yale University Press, 2005); Nathan Cohen, "Diaries
of the Sonderkommandos in Auschwitz: Coping with Fate and Reality," *Yad Vashem
Studies,* 20:4 (1990), pp. 273–312.

Are there major differences in motives, density, and locations from previous stages of the Holocaust? Most of the photographs reproduced in the three books were taken between the winter of 1942 and the autumn of 1944, after the photographic peak between late 1941 and the summer of 1942, during which the entire force of 15,000 military photographers (PK) swarmed to all war fronts.[19] What visual system(s) prevailed during the "Holocaust by bullets" and the wave of "intimate violence" in the summer of 1941?[20] The well-known pictures of the Lwów pogrom (early July 1941), for instance, require scholars to tackle the thorny question of ostentatiously sexualized violence.[21] Shot by a dozen photographers, these photos hint at questions about communal violence, non-German perpetrators, and their nation-building projects and complex visions in the most literal sense. A focus on secrecy, visibility, and local communities also invites comparative perspectives on roundups, deportations, and smaller ghettos, the first hints of which can be found in Bruttmann et al. (p. 41). Furthermore, the Niemann album raises questions about Sobibor's and other Reinhard camps' environments: why are the camp's non-Jewish neighbors invisible in the album?

Images do not only passively reflect history; they also shape and sometimes generate it. We now know that pictures are independent objects of violence. When we set out to examine the ethics of seeing, as visual culture studies enjoin us to do, an urgent need appears for systematic research into the history of photography and overlapping visual cultures between 1933 and 1945. In this vein Gerhard Paul has revealed first insights into the diversity and modernity of Nazi

---

19 Milton, "Camera as Weapon," p. 50. See also Daniel Uziel, *The Propaganda Warriors: The Wehrmacht and the Consolidation of the German Home Front* (New York: Peter Lang, 2008), pp. 105–183.

20 Patrick Desbois, *La Shoah par Balles* (Paris: Plon, 2019); Jeffrey S. Kopstein and Jason Wittenberg, *Intimate Violence: Anti-Jewish Pogroms on the Eve of the Holocaust* (Ithaca: Cornell University Press, 2018).

21 Gerhard Paul, "'Bloodlands' '41: Gewalt in Bildern—Bilder als Gewalt—Gewalt an Bildern," in Paul, ed., *BilderMACHT: Studien zur Visual History des 20. und 21. Jahrhunderts* (Göttingen: Wallstein, 2013), pp. 155–198, in which he rightly analyzes the case as a multidimensional, multimedia event. For a call for visual studies of the 1941 pogrom wave, see Jeffrey S. Kopstein, "The Victims' View: The Pogroms of June–July 1941 on the Eastern Front," *Yad Vashem Studies*, 43:1 (2015), pp. 241–247. On sexual violence see, for instance, Elissa Mailänder, "Making Sense of a Rape Photograph: Sexual Violence as Social Performance on the Eastern Front, 1939–1944," *Journal of the History of Sexuality*, 26:3 (2017), pp. 489–520.

Germany's visual appearance in his book published in 2020.[22] With many German soldiers carrying small cameras across Europe, it is now clear the regime's efforts to dominate what was to be seen from the Holocaust quickly got out of control—which makes it disturbingly similar to our own overladen visual culture.

Perpetrator images are not homogenous, and future studies should further investigate the notion of comradeship as reflected in the photos. The SS representation of Auschwitz contrasts with the two snapshots taken by German soldiers, bribing their way into the gas chamber's anterooms, or those kept by Karl Otto Koch and Kurt Franz, which expose more directly than did Niemann the unabashed gazes of mass murder.[23] One could also imagine, as Wendy Lower and the late David Shneer describe, tracing the many lives and reappropriations of one specific photograph from its wartime purposes to our days.[24] And given the recent discovery of another Auschwitz album, that of the SS military hospital (*Truppenlazarett*), which had been held by heirs of chief physician Eduard Wirths until 2015, it is more than likely that other collections are gathering dust in basements and attics. This is mentioned in all three books: Cüppers et al. (p. 19); Bruttmann et al. (p. 72); and Cognet (p. 148).[25] But we do not have to wait for spectacular discoveries on the level of the Niemann album. The USHMM houses more than 100,000 photos, YIVO some 250,000, and Yad Vashem over 396,500, which is the most extensive database in the world. The vast collection of the Nazi propaganda companies, to say nothing of many other films

---

22 Paul, *Bilder einer Diktatur*. For the diversity of survivor photographs, see Tim Cole, "Photographing Survival: Survivor Photographs of, and at, Auschwitz," in Victoria Aarons and Phyllis Lassner, eds., *The Palgrave Handbook of Holocaust Literature and Culture* (London: Palgrave Macmillan, 2020), pp. 632–649.

23 Bildagentur Bpk, Stiftung Preußischer Kulturbesitz, no. 30011681 and 30011683; Ute Wrocklage, "Die Fotoalben des KZ-Kommandanten Karl Otto Koch—Private und öffentliche Gebrauchsweisen," in Frübis, Oberle, and Pufelska, *Fotografien aus den Lagern*, pp. 179–207. Martin Cüppers is preparing the first edition of Franz's album.

24 David Shneer, *Grief: The Biography of a Holocaust Photograph* (Oxford: Oxford University Press, 2020), tackles the history of an image taken by Soviet photographer Dmitri Baltermants after the Nazi mass atrocity at an anti-tank trench near Kerch in January 1942. For the excellent analysis of a photograph taken near a shooting pit as a hidden act of resistance, see Wendy Lower, *The Ravine: A Family, a Photograph, a Holocaust Massacre Revealed* (Boston: Houghton Mifflin Harcourt, 2021).

25 See also Christophe Busch, Robert Jan van Pelt, and Stefan Hördler, eds., *Das Höcker-Album. Auschwitz durch die Linse der SS* (Darmstadt: WBG, 2016).

and 30,000 surviving artworks, awaits scholars.[26] The three books under review, which should be translated promptly, are important milestones for more systematic visual histories, a challenging domain for Holocaust scholars. We will not emerge unscathed from such analyses, but they are essential to ending the continuing commodification of Holocaust icons.[27]

26 Janet Blatter and Sybil Milton, *Art of the Holocaust* (London: Routledge, 1982). For a similar call, see Carol Zemel, "Holocaust Photography and the Challenge of the Visual," in Simone Gigliotti and Hilary Earl, eds., *A Companion to the Holocaust* (Hoboken: Wiley, 2020), pp. 503–519.

27 For a powerful analysis, see Tim Cole, *Selling the Holocaust from Auschwitz to Schindler: How History is Bought, Packaged, and Sold* (New York: Routledge, 1999).

An Ordinary Town: The Kielce Pogrom Reexamined

Joanna Tokarska-Bakir, *Pod klątwą. Społeczny portret pogromu kieleckiego*, 2 vols. Warsaw (Wydawnictwo Czarna Owca, 2018), 1,576 pp.

Reviewed by
Marta Marzańska-Mishani

I travel through the thriving land,
and I feel less and less comfortable as I do.[1]

Jean Amery

On July 4, 1946, the local Polish inhabitants of Kielce murdered forty-two Jewish men, women, and children who, for the most part, resided at 7 Planty Street. The Kielce pogrom was one of the most notorious such events in postwar Poland, although not the only one. In the first trial immediately following the pogrom (on July 9–11, 1946), nine people were sentenced to death and three to imprisonment. The executions took place the following day. Eight subsequent trials followed, and twenty-six additional perpetrators received short prison sentences. Yet the question of the perpetrators' motives remained an unclear and volatile historical and political issue. The Communist authorities blamed the events on the Polish underground—the Home Army (Armia Krajowa, AK), Freedom and Independence (Wolność i Niezawisłość, WiN), and National Armed Forces (NSZ). On the other hand, WiN, in a report from July 1946, blamed the Communist authorities' security services.[2] Representatives of PSL (Polskie Stronnictwo Ludowe, the opposition to the Communist authorities, led by Stanisław Mikołajczyk) and of

---

1   Jean Amery, *At the Mind's Limits. Contemplations by a Survivor on Auschwitz and Its Realities* (Bloomington and Indianapolis: Indiana University Press, 1980), p. 80
2   Studium Polski Podziemnej w Londynie Archive, "Wypadki kieleckie. Raport WiN," Collection 195, file 37, pp. 1–2.

the Polish government-in-exile (e.g. Adam Pragier) claimed that the pogrom was the provocation of the Communist security forces and the Soviet authorities.[3] There were also voices suggesting that the Jews— Communists or Zionists—were behind the pogrom, in an attempt to encourage emigration to Palestine.[4]

After 1989, some of the archival documents from the investigations were declassified, and, in the first historical book on the pogrom published in Poland, *Pogrom Żydów w Kielcach 4 lipca 1946*, Bożena Szaynok reconstructed the events of the day, based on the newly available archival evidence and on interviews with witnesses, and presented them in light of the political situation during and after the war.[5]

In the same year, 1992, Judge Andrzej Jankowski, director of the District Commission for Investigation of Crimes Against the Polish People in Kielce, launched a five-year investigation into the Kielce pogrom. He

---

3 See interview with Adam Pragier, *Dziennik Polski i Dziennik Żołnierza*, 163 (1946). See also Michał Chęciński, *Poland: Communism, Nationalism, Anti-Semitism* (New York: Karz-Cohl Publishers, 1982); Jakub Perkal, *Życie polityczne w Polsce 1944–1948* (Warsaw: Niezależna Oficyna Wydawnicza Nowa, 1983), p. 25; Tadeusz Piotrkowski, *Poland's Holocaust: Ethnic Strife, Collaboration with Occupying Forces and Genocide in the Second Republic, 1918–1947* (Jefferson: McFarland & Company, 1998), pp. 134–142, for an attempt to present this side of the argument; Adam Penkalla, "Władze o obecności Żydow na terenie Kielecczyzny w okresie od wkroczenia Armii Czerwonej do pogromu kieleckiego," *Kwartalnik Historii Żydów*, 4:208 (2003), pp. 557–578; Mieczysław Adamczyk, "Pogrom Żydów kieleckich w świetle polskiej prasy emigracyjnej," *Annales Universitatis Mariae Curie-Skłodowska*, 6 (1999), pp. 289–300.

4 Józef Orlicki, *Szkice z dziejów stosunków polsko-żydowskich 1918–1949* (Szczecin: Krajowa Agencja Wydawnicza, 1983). See, for example, Bishop Czesław Kaczmarek's report, written shortly after the pogrom for the American ambassador in Warsaw, Arthur Bliss, in Łukasz Kamiński and Jan Żaryn, eds., *Wokół pogromu kieleckiego*, Vol. I (Warsaw: IPN, 2006), pp. 185–201: "Certain Jewish communist elements, working in agreement with the Security Services, which they have taken over, took advantage of this [hatred toward the Jews and instances of disappearance of children in Kielce], and initiated a pogrom, which they could later pronounce as a proof of the need for the Jewish emigration to their own country, as a proof that the Polish society is possessed by antisemitism and fascism and finally as proof of the reactionary nature of the Church, whose members participated in the pogrom." For a summary of the controversies surrounding the pogrom, see Krystyna Kersten, "The Pogrom of Jews in Kielce on July 4, 1946," *Acta Poloniae Historica*, 76 (1997), pp. 197–212; Bożena Szaynok, "The Jewish Pogrom in Kielce, July 1946 - New Evidence," *Intermarium*, 1:3 at http://ece.columbia.edu/files/ece/images/kielce.html; and Joanna Michlic, *Poland's Threatening Other: The Image of the Jew from 1880 to the Present* (Lincoln: University of Nebraska Press, 2008), pp. 221–229.

5 Bożena Szaynok, *Pogrom Żydów w Kielcach 4 lipca 1946* (Warsaw: Bellona, 1992).

concluded that the security services did not cause the pogrom. In 2001, the proceedings were reopened on behalf of the Institute of National Remembrance, but were discontinued in 2004. Some of the findings and the trial records were published by Stanisław Meducki and Zenon Wrona in 1992, and in 1994,[6] and some twelve years later in a two-volume edition prepared by Jan Żaryn and Łukasz Kamiński for the Institute of National Remembrance.[7] While the second volume included archival material, the first contained articles by Bożena Szaynok, Jan Żaryn, and Ryszard Śmietanka-Kruszelnicki. Szaynok pointed to the ways in which Jewish-Polish relations, or Jewishness, became an important part of the political manipulations in postwar Poland. Kruszelnicki argued for the involvement of the Communist authorities in framing the Polish underground for the pogrom. Żaryn's article, titled "The Leadership of the Catholic Church in Poland and Polish-Jewish Relations Between 1945–1947," partly placed the responsibility for antisemitic sentiments in Poland on the Jews' involvement in Communist politics; he argued that the Polish clergy showed empathy toward the Jews before and after the pogrom, and took a stand against the folk belief in the "blood libel."[8] According to Żaryn, the pogrom in Kielce was a result of a premeditated

6   Stanisław Meducki and Zenon Wrona, eds., *Antyżydowskie wydarzenia kieleckie 4 lipca 1946 roku. Dokumenty i materiały*, Vol. I (Kielce: Kieleckie Towarzystwo Naukowe, 1992); Stanisław Meducki, ed., *Antyżydowskie wydarzenia kieleckie 4 lipca1946 roku. Dokumenty i materiały*, Vol. II (Kielce: Kieleckie Towarzystwo Naukowe, 1994).

7   Jan Żaryn and Łukasz Kamiński, eds., *Wokół pogromu kieleckiego*, Vol. I (Kielce and Warsaw: Instytut Pamięci Narodowej, 2006); Leszek Bukowski, Andrzej Jankowski, and Jan Żaryn, *Wokół pogromu kieleckiego*, Vol. II (Kielce and Warsaw: Instytut Pamięci Narodowej, 2008).

8   Jan Żaryn's text reflected to an extent the discourse prevalent in recent years among some historians of the Institute of National Remembrance regarding the "historical politics" of Jewish-Polish relations. In this context the Institute's priority has been to promote the "good" image of Poles. See the Institute of National Remembrance's research efforts focusing on Poles saving Jews and locating and commemorating Polish families who helped Jews during the Holocaust; for example, *Polacy ratujący Żydów w latach II Wojny Światowej* (Warsaw: Teki Edukacyjne IPN, 2008); Sebastian Piątkowski, ed., *Relacje o pomocy udzielanej Żydom przez Polaków w latach 1939–1945*. Vol. 1: *Dystrykt Warszawski Generalnego Gubernatorstwa* (Lublin and Warsaw: IPN, 2018); Martyna Grądzka-Rejak and Aleksandra Namysło, eds., *Represje za pomoc Żydom na okupowanych ziemiach polskich w czasie II wojny światowej* (Warsaw: IPN, 2019); Agnieszka Dziarmaga, Dorota Koczwańska-Kalita, and Edyta Majcher-Ociesa, eds., *Nasi sąsiedzi Żydzi. Z dziejów relacji polsko-żydowskich na kielecczyźnie w XX wieku* (Kielce: IPN, 2018); Elżbieta Rączy and Igor Witowicz, eds., *Polacy ratujący Żydów na Rzeszowszczyźnie w latach 1939–1945* (Rzeszów:

Communist plot to discredit the Polish nation—namely, the Polish Catholic Church and the Polish underground—in the eyes of the Anglo-Saxon world.[9]

Other noteworthy studies of the Kielce pogrom include those of Krystyna Kersten, the author of the first historical article on the Kielce pogrom and other texts on the event, who postulated a wide, panoramic approach to the singular historical event.[10] Jan Tomasz Gross presented the Kielce pogrom as the result of the overwhelmingly dominant antisemitism in *Fear: Anti-Semitism in Poland after Auschwitz: An Essay in Historical Interpretation*.[11] The findings of these works, as well as the reactions and public debates they caused, testify to the centrality of the murder in Kielce within the historical and political narratives that relate and explain the story of Jewish-Polish relations.

Joanna Tokarska-Bakir's *Pod klątwą. Społeczny portret pogrom kieleckiego* ("Cursed. A Social Portrait of the Kielce Pogrom"), a two-

IPN, 2011); Mateusz Szpytma, *Sprawiedliwi i ich świat. Markowa w fotografii Józefa Ulmy* (Kraków: IPN, 2015), among others.

9   See also an interview with Jan Żaryn from July 4, 2016, *Dzieje.pl Portal Historyczny*, https://dzieje.pl/aktualnosci/prof-jan-zaryn-komunisci-wykorzystali-pogrom-kielecki-do-ataku-na-podziemie-i-kosciol (accessed January 17, 2021). Jan Grabowski regarded Żaryn and Śmietanka-Kruszelnicki's texts as "an affront to the memory of the victims of the Kielce pogrom" and a work that merely showed that historical truth was a prisoner in the Polish "battle for memory." Jan Grabowski, "Rewriting the History of Polish-Jewish Relations from a Nationalist Perspective: The Recent Publications of the Institute of National Remembrance," *Yad Vashem Studies*, 36:1 (2008), pp. 253–269.

10   Krystyna Kersten, "Kielce, 4 lipca 1946" in *Tygodnik Solidarność*, December 4, 1981; Krystyna Kersten, "Pogrom kielecki — znaki zapytania, " in *Polacy, Żydzi, komunizm — anatomia półprawd 1939-68* (Warsaw: Niezależna Oficyna Wydawnicza, 1992).

11   Jan Tomasz Gross, *Fear: Anti-Semitism in Poland after Auschwitz: An Essay in Historical Interpretation* (Princeton and Oxford: Princeton University Press, 2006). Other treatments of the subject include Joanna Michlic-Coren, "Polish Jews during and after the Kielce Pogrom. Reports from Communist Archives, *Polin*, 13 (2000), pp. 253-267; David Engel, "Patterns of Anti-Jewish Violence in Poland 1944–1946" (*Yad Vashem Studies*, 26 (1998), pp. 43–85), who showed that the pogrom in Kielce was not an isolated incident; Łukasz Krzyżanowski, "Nieznane dokumenty do historii pogromu kieleckiego: Protokoły przesłuchań Henryka Błaszczyka i Gerszona Lewkowicza z lipca 1946 roku," *Kwartalnik Historii Żydów*, 2 (2014), pp. 388–395; and also in his book, *Dom, którego nie było. Powroty ocalałych do powojennego miasta* (Wołowiec: Czarne, 2016); Stanisław Meducki, "The Pogrom in Kielce on July 4, 1946," *Polin*, 9 (1996), pp. 158–169; Krzysztof Urbański, *Kieleccy Żydzi* (Kraków: Małopolska Oficyna Wydawnicza, 1993); Michał Chęciński, "The Kielce Pogrom: Some unanswered questions," *Soviet Jewish Affairs*, 5 (1975), pp. 57–72.

volume monograph, is the result of a decade's worth of ethnographical, anthropological, social, and historical research. She has extensively examined "blood libel," Polish Holocaust memory, postwar pogroms in other areas in Poland and elsewhere, and the Kielce pogrom in particular. Some of her reflections on Polish-Jewish relations were published in her book *Rzeczy mgliste: eseje i studia*. From 2005, she led a research team that collected oral histories on the Holocaust and the "blood libel" in southeastern and eastern Poland. Her book *Legendy o Krwi: Antropologia Przesądu* ("Blood Libel Legends: Anthropology of Prejudice") is an interdisciplinary examination of the longevity and prevalence of the "blood libel" legend. One may see in that impressive work a kind of 800-page introduction to the current volume, an attempt to understand deeply the immediate cause of the Kielce pogrom. Her article in *Yad Vashem Studies*, "Communitas of Violence: The Kielce Pogrom as a Social Drama" is also worth mentioning here; in it Tokarska-Bakir presents an anthropological interpretation of the event based on Victor Turner's theory of social drama. Among her other publications is an article on the attitudes and perceptions of the Jews among the postwar anti-Communist underground organization, "Wolność i Niezawisłość," an analysis of the state of mind of the participants in the postwar pogroms in Rzeszów, Kraków, and Kielce, as well as a 2012 study of the figure of the Jew as a bloodsucker in religious, national, and left-wing Polish discourse.[12]

Tokarska-Bakir's monograph is a fresh attempt to shed light on the events that took place in Kielce.[13] It is new in the sources she presents

12 Joanna Tokarska-Bakir, *Rzeczy mgliste: eseje i studia* (Sejny: Pogranicze, 2004); *Legendy o krwi, Antropologia przesądu* (Warsaw: WAB, 2008); "Cries of the Mob in the Pogroms in Rzeszów (June 1945), Cracow (August 1945), and Kielce (July 1946) as a Source to the History of Mentality," *East European Politics and Societies*, 25: 3 (2011), pp. 553–574; "'Present Causes of Past Effects': The Background Beliefs of the Kielce Pogrom," in Jonathan Adams and Cordelia Heß, eds., *The Medieval Roots of Antisemitism. Continuities and Discontinuities from the Middle Ages to the Present Day* (New York: Routledge, 2018); "Communitas of Violence: the Kielce Pogrom as a Social Drama," *Yad Vashem Studies*, 41:1 (2013), pp. 23–62; "The Figure of the Bloodsucker in Polish Religious, National and Left Wing Discourse, 1945–1946: A Study in Historical Anthropology," *Dapim: Studies on the Holocaust*, 27:2 (2013), pp. 75–106; "The Unrighteous Righteous and Righteous Unrighteous," *Dapim: Studies on the Holocaust*, 24 (2010), pp. 11–64; "The Polish underground organization Wolność i Niezawisłość and anti-Jewish pogroms, 1945–6," *Patterns of Prejudice*, 51:2 (2017), pp. 111–136.

13 The book was enthusiastically received by Marcin Zaremba, who called it an

and in the way she uses them. Between the 1950s and the 1980s, the documentation of the first trial that took place almost immediately after the pogrom was scattered, hidden, lost, or destroyed. Tokarska-Bakir began her archival research in 2013. Both volumes of her work contain a vast amount of archival material, some of it previously unseen. The first volume contains Tokarska-Bakir's analysis of these documents, and the last 200 pages of the first book contain 2,766 detailed footnotes.

In the Appendix to the first volume, among other things, there is a list of all the victims of the Kielce pogrom and any information about them that could be retraced; a comparison of the lists published by the American Jewish Joint Distribution Committee, the Kielce *Landsmanshaft*, the funeral notice of Ichud (Zionist Democrats' Union party), and the list of the victims published in "Dos Noje Lebn"; and the protocol of the judicial postmortem examination. It also contains a list of the survivors of the pogrom and some of the names of the key witnesses, including their wartime experiences and addresses. There is a record of the murders of Jews in the Kielce area from January 1945 until July 1946, other than the pogrom in Kielce. Finally, there are short biographies of the persons linked to the pogrom—both victims and perpetrators.

The second volume contains some 800 pages of archival material from the investigations into the pogrom. These contain testimonies of most of the survivors, witnesses, and perpetrators, as well as the transcript of the first day of the 1946 trial. Notably among them are also reports and testimonies of local priests from the Kielce church archives. The largest part of the sources comes from the archive of the Institute of National Remembrance, the archive of the Military Historical Bureau, the Jewish Historical Institute, and the private archives of Michał Chęciński, as well as from the Ghetto Fighters' House Archive. Some of

---

"extraordinary work," "a unique biography of evil, of a marriage between anti-Semitism and incompetence"; see Marcin Zaremba, "CV pogromu," *Zagłada Żydów*, 27 (2018), pp. 651–661. It was also critically reviewed by Bożena Szaynok, "Wokół nowej książki o pogromie Żydów w Kielcach," *Zagłada Żydów*, 28 (2018), pp. 662–667; by Marta Duch-Dyngosz, "Wspólnota przemocy", *Znak*, 762, November 2018, pp. 100–105, and by Ryszard Śmietanka-Kruszelnicki, "Between Thesis, Hypothesis and Literary Fiction: The Tale of the Pogrom of Jews in Kielce. A Review of Joanna Tokarska-Bakir's Book *Pod Klątwą. Społeczny Portret Pogromu Kieleckiego* [Under the Spell. The Social Portrait of the Kielce Pogrom] (Warsaw: Wydawnictwo Czarna Owca, 2018), vol. 1, vol. 2: Dokumenty [Documents]", *Polish-Jewish Studies*, 1 (2020), pp. 315–385 (Pol), 744–816 (Eng.).

these documents had been published in Bożena Szaynok's book; many were made available in Stanisław Meducki's and Zenon Wrona's two volumes and in Jan Żaryn and Łukasz Kamiński's volumes. Others have already been discussed by, for example, Łukasz Krzyżanowski.[14]

Still, Tokarska-Bakir presents the voices and perspectives of all those involved; they are quoted and meticulously arranged to create what she calls a "social portrait of the pogrom." This begins with the testimonies of the Jewish victims. A few of these statements regarding the entry of the militiamen and the soldiers into the house on 7 Planty Street were presented already in 1992, by Bożena Szaynok. Tokarska-Bakir found more than thirty such testimonies, and added others, collected in Israel from the second investigation into the pogrom. Some survivors' testimonies she collected personally; she also used those deposited in the Institute of National Remembrance. She succeeded in locating the personal files of most of the pogrom's perpetrators and showed that they held on to their social functions in the militia or in administration even after their dubious personal histories. Another aspect of the author's contribution to the research of the Kielce pogrom is her meticulous analysis of the sources on the involvement and the career tracks of the officers of the Polish army who were present in Kielce at the time of the pogrom and took part in it.

The novelty of this work lies also in the interdisciplinary methodological approach. Tokarska-Bakir, incorporating social and anthropological tools, describes the pogrom in Kielce in the context of social and historical continuity. She presents the event in the framework of the history of everyday life. *Pod klątwą* is a difficult book to read; not only because of its subject or the details of the violence, but because of the multiplicity of testimonies, documents, and material that is presented repeatedly, each time in a new light. It can be difficult to follow for a reader unfamiliar with the details of the pogrom and especially with the history of the controversy surrounding it. Sometimes the structure of the chapters can be confusing. But the description of the networks of relations, events, and documents that comprise this work and that together create an in-depth, nuanced portrait of the Kielce community, which helps understand what exactly happened on July 4, 1946, reaches

---

14 See Łukasz Krzyżanowski, "Nieznane dokumenty do historii pogromu kieleckiego: Protokoły przesłuchań Henryka Błaszczyka i Gerszona Lewkowicza z lipca 1946 roku," *Kwartalnik Historii Żydów*, 2 (2014), pp. 388–395; and also in his book, *Dom, którego nie było. Powroty ocalałych do powojennego miasta* (Wołowiec: Czarne, 2016).

an almost impossible degree of meticulousness. It is a new kind of attention to detail, which achieves an altogether unique effect. The microhistorical methodology used here for a "large" historical event is particularly interesting. Each chapter describes a different aspect of the intimate interactions within public, private, and national space. One way to demystify these interactions is to show how the meaning of these spaces can be shifted from the private to the national (as in the final chapter, where the private, middle-class expressions of antisemitism acquire a sinister tone when seen within the larger context), or from the public to the private (when reexamining the involvement of the secret services, for example).

On the other hand, Tokarska-Bakir's effort also shows that even with deep knowledge and understanding of centuries' worth of a problem, it is still impossible to reconstruct completely and accurately a historical moment, even if it had been most scrupulously documented. It is difficult to imagine a more precise reconstruction of an event. Still, one experiences the limits of historical research. In the end this is an investigation with twofold results: revealing the real culprit of the crime and the demystification of all aspects of the Kielce pogrom.

Tokarska-Bakir does not present an unequivocal "solution" as to who exactly committed the pogrom in Kielce—there is no one single perpetrator. The polyphony of voices in this work creates a very complex picture that, in the end, points to the entire community and its social structures.

The book begins with an impressively detailed reconstruction of the morning hours of July 4, 1946, in Kielce. In the first chapter we follow a chronological order in which the events unfolded for the Jews, who, like Anczel Pinkusiewicz, arrived in Kielce in the early morning of that day, or, like Niusia Borensztajn and Szmulek Nester, simply began their day in the city, or Jakub Aleksandrowicz, who went to the city for a business visit. The craftsmanship of the description is admirable. It is constructed mainly out of first person testimonies (of Ignacy Herman, Jakub Aleksandrowicz, Dina Szaroni, Szmulek Nester, Rafael Blumenfeld, Jechiel Alpert, Marysia Machtynger, Baruch Dorfman, Borys Wajnryb, Józef Fajngold, Jakow Średni, Dora Dajbog, Estera Mappen, and Niusia Borensztajn), with the author's narration binding them together. Tokarska-Bakir depicts the rising tension hour after hour. Shortly after the rumor of the kidnapping of eight-year-old Henio Błaszczyk had spread, and Jakub Aleksandrowicz was told by a marching crowd, "The Jews have to be beaten, they murder our children, they killed one or two" (p. 24), there was already talk of ten murdered Polish children, with their heads cut off, and whose blood had reportedly been used for transfusions to strengthen the Jews, who had been weakened during the war. The Jewish victims' testimonies speak of the beatings, the shootings, of a young woman being thrown off a balcony; they describe the violence of the crowd and the conviction that Polish children had been buried in the (nonexistent) basement of the building. There were shopkeepers, housewives, firemen, boy scouts, clergy, and militiamen in the crowd that gathered in front of the building and demanded that the Jews be handed over and began beating the people who were forced out of the building. The victims also relate their mistreatment at the hospital, where they were taken in the afternoon. Each voice has its history and its context; many testimonies are accompanied by the speakers' photographs. An attempt is made to reconstruct the exact circumstances of the death of each of the victims of the pogrom. The detailed description of each person there, as well as the familiar setting and topography that was transformed in the course of that day into a site of terror, produces a truly "uncanny" (*Unheimliche*) effect, in the Freudian sense of the word.

The second chapter focuses on the physical evidence of the pogrom. First the photographs that Julia Pirotte took that day in Kielce of the scene of the pogrom and of its victims. These were some of the most important pieces of evidence in the investigation that followed. Then, using the autopsy reports, Tokarska-Bakir describes in minute detail the injuries and wounds of the Jewish victims of the pogrom—both of those who survived it and those who did not. Eighteen of the victims remained unidentified. She attempted to reconstruct the exact circumstances of the death of each of the victims of the pogrom using the autopsy reports. Among other evidence is the testimony of Helena Majtlis, a Jewish nurse, who volunteered to come to Kielce from Częstochowa to help the pogrom victims, and spoke of severe mistreatment of the patients even by the local medical staff at the hospital.

By using the photographs and the testimonies of the participants in the events, Tokarska-Bakir also describes the funeral, which was attended by the survivors of the pogrom, military representatives, Minister of Security Stanisław Radkiewicz, Minister of Reconstruction Michał Kaczorowski, Marek Edelman, Chief Rabbi David Kahane, as well as the local population of Kielce and the local factory workers, who had played an active role in the pogrom. The chapter's unpredictable movement in time is sometimes confusing, and occasionally the rationale for the inclusion of certain testimonies is unclear, although, in the end, together they create an overwhelmingly disturbing impression of the events during and after the pogrom.

In the next chapter Tokarska-Bakir goes on to relate and examine the perpetrators' and eyewitnesses' testimonies. She focuses on the story of Henio Błaszczyk, the eight-year-old whose disappearance sparked the rumors of the "blood libel" in Kielce on that day and immediately preceded the pogrom. Tokarska-Bakir attempts to retrace Henio Błaszczyk's movements. According to the official version of the events presented during the trial, Antoni Pasowski, the administrator of Henio's building, had held the boy for three days and suggested to him that the Jews had kidnapped him. According to Tokarska-Bakir, this version, presenting Pasowski as the mastermind of the pogrom, is unconvincing. In fact Henio Błaszczyk changed his original story of being kidnapped by the Jews many times and produced different accounts of the events both when he was a child and later as a grown man. He simply said what, it seemed to him, the others wanted to hear.

She also shows that Henio Błaszczyk's case should be seen in the wider context of the disappearances of other children in town.[15] It turns out that the phenomenon of children escaping from their homes was both common and seasonal (occurring mainly in the summer) among the poor families in Kielce. In this context Tokarska-Bakir suggests a psychological explanation to the pogrom; namely, that those most susceptible to the panic were the parents who had neglected their children and simply projected aspects of their own behavior on the Jews. This is potentially a valuable insight, and as such would deserve more grounding—which, by now, is probably an impossible task. Without that, it remains slightly offhand.

The local "authorities" or authority figures are the focus of the fourth chapter. These include the provincial governor, the chief of

---

15 Compare Marcin Zaremba, *Wielka trwoga: Polska 1944–1947: Ludowa reakcja na kryzys* (Kraków: Społeczny Instytut Wydawniczy "Znak", and Warsaw: Instytut Studiów Politycznych Polskiej Akademii Nauk, 2012); Łukasz Krzyżanowski and Marcin Zaremba, "'Bić ich za nasze dzieci!' Panika moralna i przemoc zbiorowa wobec Żydów w Polsce w latach 1945–1946," in August Grabski, ed., *Pogromy Żydów na ziemiach polskich w XIX–XX wieku*, Vol. 4: *Holokaust i powojnie (1939–1946)* (Warsaw: IH PAN, 2018), pp. 489–510.

the local Public Security Office, and the town bishop. Tokarska-Bakir examines their personal histories and the history of anti-Jewish violence in the city. For example, Eugeniusz Wiślicz-Iwańczyk, previously an AK soldier, a collaborator with the Gestapo during the war (later a founder of the first partisan unit of the Armia Ludowa in the Kielce area) (p. 109), and the provincial governor afterward, and Major Władysław Sobczyński-Spychaj, the chief of the Voivodeship Security Office, were both known to have given orders to a unit of Armia Ludowa in the summer of 1944, to execute Jews on the Kotyska River. Both became particularly dominant in the social and political constellation of the city.

Anti-Jewish ideology had been prevalent in Kielce since 1912, and the first pogrom in Kielce took place in 1918, during which four Jews were killed and a hundred were wounded. The real authority in the city was Bishop Czesław Kaczmarek, who struggled against the Communist political leadership in the city and, as Tokarska-Bakir shows, often openly expressed antisemitic sentiments. After the pogrom he produced a report in which he concluded that Jewish Communists, together with the Security Office, had decided to exploit the cases of the missing children in order to initiate a pogrom. According to Tokarska-Bakir, the church representatives in Kielce never officially castigated the "blood libel" myth or antisemitism.[16]

Antisemitism also dominated the Polish underground, the organization Wolność i Niezawisłość, which, though it had ceased functioning in March 1946, was still prominent in the following months in the underground movement. Tokarska-Bakir brings many examples of antisemitic ideology on the part of the leaders of the Polish underground from correspondence, underground publications, and diaries. They blamed the Jews for the poverty of the Polish people, exploitation of the workers, murder, violence, alcoholism, and attempting world domination (pp. 125–127). In their reports they created a clear-cut dichotomy between "Poles" and "Jews" (pp. 129–130). Finally the author shows that a real belief in the "blood libel" was common among the clergy and underground members. Not only did the priests and the underground believe in it but they also propagated the idea (pp. 131–133). The author quotes cases of other "blood libel" accusations that led

---

16 Some critics have argued that Tokarska-Bakir's treatment of the church could perhaps have been more nuanced: Bożena Szaynok, "Wokół nowej książki o pogromie Żydów w Kielcach," *Zagłada Żydów*, 28 (2018), p. 667; Marcin Zaremba, "CV pogromu," *Zagłada Żydów*, 27 (2018), p. 655.

to other pogroms, such as the first postwar pogrom in Rzeszów, which took place on June 11–12, 1945.

Antisemitism was not officially condemned by the Communist authorities either.

In chapter five Tokarska-Bakir addresses the common explanation that Jews were attacked not entirely because of their Jewishness, but rather because of their political Communist affiliation (pp. 155–157).

One of the discoveries documented in this book is the documents in a militia file that Tokarska-Bakir describes in this chapter. The file, titled "The Zionists," contains testimonies about violence against and murder of Jews that took place in the Kielce area—in Klimontów, Połaniec, Ostrowiec, Starachowice, Radom, Busko Zdrój, Antoniów, Gniewoszów, and Kozienice—between April 1945 and January 1946.

According to that report, from the end of 1945 and the beginning of 1946, 1 percent of the Jewish population in Poland survived the war. In August 1946, the report stated that 2,043 Jews had been killed since the end of the war. Tokarska-Bakir shows that the statistical figures that were hitherto accepted are not accurate. While up until now historians referred to the data that, between July 1945 and February 1946, 135 people were killed, including five Jews, according to Tokarska-Bakir's calculations, some seventy Jews were killed in the Kielce area alone between March and September 1945, and twenty between September and July 1946. In all, according to her estimate, every fourteenth Jew was killed in the Kielce area in the months after the war. She thus illustrates, providing ample evidence, that immediately after the war extreme violence became a common, even legitimate way of solving problems.

In short, the author shows that the commonly held assumption that postwar pogroms and murders were politically motivated by the victims' Communist affiliation is false. The importance of Tokarska-Bakir's book lies, among other things, in the fact that she documents and demonstrates precisely that such an assumption was a cover-up of an inability to admit to and deal with the prevalent, institutionalized antisemitism.

In chapter six Tokarska-Bakir offers a fascinating interpretation of the historiography of the Kielce pogrom, which runs through the rest of the book—the so-called "Rashomon effect," a term originating from Akira Kurosawa's film (1950), relating to notorious unreliability of eyewitnesses. This is one possible explanation as to the impossibility of reconstructing fully the Kielce pogrom, despite the many sources and the detailed documentation. According to Tokarska-Bakir, even the well-documented testimonies, when examined thoroughly, blur the coherent narrative:

> The representatives of all the uniformed services on Planty—the Militia, the Secret Services, the Internal Security Corps, and the 2nd Warsaw Infantry Division—each presented a perspective favorable to them. Their testimonies contradict one another and make it impossible to unify them into one coherent narrative. Though its frames have been established, when we go in deeper, these, too, fade (p. 186).

Moreover, the incompetence of the militia and of the security services, coupled with the fact that the participants in the pogrom changed their names and places of residence, contributed to the inefficiency of the investigations. In time, and during the subsequent trials, all the participants learned to deny their involvement in the events. Eventually they also began to be presented as freedom fighters in their struggle against Stalinism.

Tokarska-Bakir suggests a psychological solution to the mystery of the Kielce pogrom:

> In Kurosawa's "Rashomon" everyone lies out of shame...This book defends the thesis that shame is at the root of the mystery of the Kielce pogrom. During the investigation in 1946 the Communist authorities quickly understood that there was no "external enemy" behind the pogrom...But it was unthinkable to reveal the fact that wartime and postwar Jew-killers were employed in all the uniformed Communist formations, and with the approval of the party authorities. It would mean loss of face and further estrangement of the Communists from the society. Therefore, it was decided to first present the "reactionary" version, then, for the sake of making an example, drastically punish a few pogrom participants, threaten the rest, while gradually easing the punishments, and ignore the mass emigration of Jews from Poland. And when things go quiet, classify the pogrom for more than half a century (p. 192).

In an attempt to reconstruct the day—again—she divides the pogrom into three stages and fourteen segments and examines them meticulously in light of new archival evidence. One of the particularly interesting finds is the previously unseen record of militia interrogation from the day of the pogrom, July 4, 1946, of Kalman Zinger, the Jewish man identified by the eight-year-old Henio Błaszczyk as his kidnapper. Another previously unseen testimony brought to light here is that of Rachmil Tajtelbaum, who accompanied Zinger to the station and heard the militiamen say he had to be killed and who later warned the Jews at Planty of the coming danger. Tokarska-Bakir guides the reader through the events, again and again, this time presenting the testimonies of the perpetrators and the hitherto unknown witnesses. These voices, too, have their histories and their contexts.

This division, the re-examination of each group of segments, and the meticulous analysis of the sides involved in the pogrom resemble Roland Barthes's reading of Balzac's "Sarrasine" in *S/Z*; the same kind of desire to demystify the link between the signifier and the signified, between the event (or its reconstructable fragments) and its interpretations, is the main driving force of this book.

What emerges is the plurality of this event in the sense that it is retold again and again, that it consisted of many horrific incidents, that it was not unique but also happened in other places at the same time, that it received many political and historical interpretations, that this act of murder held so many different meanings—and its inevitability, given its historical and social setting.

In the following chapters Tokarska-Bakir continues to reveal, or to draw, a network of social relations in Kielce; how family ties extended among rival organizations, such as the security services and the militia, the Polish Workers' Party and the opposition, and how the various social groups came together to play a role on July 4, 1946.

In chapter seven the focus falls on the involvement of the workers in the local Ludwików factory. One of the conclusions is that the evidence, while detailed with regard to the beginning of the pogrom, becomes blurry from 1:00 P.M. onward. This was the point when the factory workers joined in the violence—it was their involvement, and not the behavior of the militia, army, or security services, that should be considered as the real enigma of the pogrom. Regrettably, there is not enough evidence to really understand their role. Naturally they were not the only perpetrators. Tokarska-Bakir traces the social networks that were in play on the day of the pogrom, and which included restaurateurs, shopkeepers, and militiamen. She stresses that participation in the violence cannot in this case be limited (and thus dismissed) to any "riffraff" from the social margins, or to the lower classes, but rather was spread over the whole cross section of society, and included teachers, housewives, firemen, and boy scouts, along with the doorkeepers, shopkeepers, factory workers, militia, and soldiers. Some of them were economically motivated, which Tokarska-Bakir again proves meticulously.

In chapter eight Tokarska Bakir draws on extensive literature—the known theories of Mary Douglas, Sigmund Freud, Victor Turner, Shulamit Volkov, Eric Hobsbawm, and Roberta Senechal de la Roche, among others—and analyzes the mechanisms in play during an event like the pogrom. Again the aim is to demystify the common conceptions of the pogrom. She shows the details of involvement of women and children in the extreme violence, documented and quoted from eyewitness testimonies. Tokarska-Bakir finds here some previously unexplored lines of inquiry into specific murders during the pogrom. She also shows how the rare stories of help extended to the Jews during the pogrom, which appear in a few testimonies, have been used for the purposes of construction of the Polish "Righteous" identity in this paradoxical context.

In chapter nine Tokarska-Bakir addresses the issue of the economic motives of the pogrom and how the common places and behaviors of the local community were suddenly transformed. Any property that had belonged to the Jews was considered legitimate spoils, preferably merchandise, characteristically called by Poles "post-Jewish" (*pożydowskie*) (p. 285). Those who had taken over Jewish properties—janitors, bakery owners, shop owners—therefore had a special interest in participating in the pogrom. On the day of the pogrom, shops and restaurants turned into hubs of planning for further attacks (p. 281), such as the murder of Rywka Fisz and her four-week-old baby. Restaurants, shops, and bakeries functioned as portals of social networks from which alcohol, murder, and robbery flowed. Testimonies show that many perpetrators were drunk; some even took breaks from the violence to visit the local restaurant and drink, only to return to 7 Planty Street. In order to build this network, one needed a shop, a restaurant, and a militiaman—the shopkeeper knew who had money and where they lived, and he showed where the victims were for a share in the loot. The militiamen accompanied willing volunteers and covered their tracks. This, argues Tokarska-Bakir, was the common mechanism at work in postwar Poland. For example, in Skarżysko, in the autumn of 1945,

Jewish owners of a restaurant were attacked by a local shopkeeper, a militiaman, and Polish restaurateurs, who preferred to settle their debt to the Jewish family by having them killed.

Another important contribution of this book is the reconstruction of the prewar Jewish presence in Kielce, both with regard to their cultural contribution to the life of the city and their immovable property. Out of 8,000 buildings in Kielce in 1938, 1,660 belonged to Jewish residents, including a theater, hotel, bookshop, printing shop, lawyers' office, photography shop, dentist clinics, and so on. The dispossession of their property happened gradually, from 1939 onward. Some doorkeepers of the buildings in which apartments belonged to Jewish owners either took an active part in the pogrom or encouraged the violence and then took over the property, later concealing it during the investigations into the pogrom. The author calls them the "facilitators," to use Raul Hilberg's term (p. 292).[17] A picture of collaboration between the militia and the mob emerges from the testimonies. The mob, though not directed by any one person, behaved in a synchronized way in various parts of the city. This group consisted of a whole range of "respected citizens": mothers, fathers, teachers, firefighters, clerks, artisans, as well as the local factory workers. Antisemitism and the belief in "blood libel" was the ideology that united them, regardless of their social class. This belief also united the underground officers, militiamen, soldiers, and priests, along with their community.

Chapter ten deals with the so-called "third stage of the Kielce pogrom"; i.e., the violence and the murder of the Jews traveling by trains near the city. Again Tokarska-Bakir extensively quotes eyewitness testimonies of perpetrators and victims, relating how passengers spontaneously murdered Jews traveling with them and how militiamen pulled Jews out of the trains. It was mainly the railway workers who initiated the lynchings.

In chapter eleven the author deals with the volatile subject of the involvement of the security services. What emerges from her analysis is the degree of incompetence and helplessness, rather than a calculated plan of action. There was also the fear of being associated with the Jews or identified as their protectors. It seems that, from the morning of that day, the security forces' involvement during the pogrom was pushed

---

17 Raul Hilberg, *Perpetrators, Victims, Bystanders: Jewish Catastrophe 1933–1945* (New York: Harper Collins, 1993).

to the margins. Instead the militia and the army took center stage, to the applause of the "mob." According to the evidence she presents, the Russian military forces refused to take an active part in stopping the violence, and, without their help, the security forces were helpless.

In Kielce the Voivodeship Security Committee (Wojewódzki Komitet Bezpieczeństwa) was the body that took control in case of unexpected dangers. It was headed by Lieutenant Stanisław Kupsza, a Red Army soldier; Major Sobczyński was his deputy. Tokarska-Bakir disagrees with the view that Sobczyński, tried in court and acquitted in 1946, was the main culprit of the pogrom. Sobczyński waited for Kupsza's orders and attempted to convince him to act more decisively in defense of the Jews. Yet Kupsza had immunity and was not concerned that his career would be hurt by the consequences of the pogrom. Sobczyński was never punished for giving the order to shoot Jews on the Kotyska River in August 1944, killing Ukrainians, theft, or sexual abuse of co-workers. According to Tokarska-Bakir, Sobczyński's priority on July 4, 1946, was to emerge unscathed from what seemed like an uprising and to minimize its damage. During his attempts to mobilize the Russian forces, he was told that the pogrom was an internal Polish matter and that there were not enough uniformed men to intervene. Yet Sobczyński watched the pogrom from a balcony in his headquarters, while his superiors, Russian officers in civilian dress, arrived at the scene and attempted to stop the soldiers. From the reports written on that day, it appears that all the officers working under Sobczyński could not understand his inaction.

Tokarska-Bakir also examines the actions of the Jewish officers on that day. Mieczysław Kwaśniewski refused Sobczyński's order to go to the site of the pogrom with a group of men and, after the pogrom, filed a request to be dismissed from the ranks of the security services, because as a Jew he would not "contribute to the rebuilding and strengthening of democracy but, despite his best intentions, only interrupt the process by the hatred he provokes" (p. 327). Albert Grynbaum arrived at the scene of the pogrom early on and attempted to stop the militiamen and the soldiers from entering the building, but he was escorted out by five of his fellow officers at noon. He was murdered a month and a half later by the Polish underground.

Tokarska-Bakir takes this opportunity to examine the attitude of the Communist party toward the Jews and the tendency prevalent in the late 1940s to encourage the Jewish comrades not to be "overly sensitive" about the issue of nationality, yet camouflaging all the Jewish party members behind new Polish surnames. Still, as the author admits, the sources pertaining to the abetment of the security services and that of the army are contradictory and incomplete, yet she maintains ruling out the conspiracy theory that they pre-planned the pogrom. In contrast, Bożena Szaynok insists that the sources remain inconclusive and do not exclude the possibility of Communist and Soviet engagement in the pogrom.[18] A similar reservation applies to chapter twelve, which deals with the militiamen of Kielce and those among them who could have been personally involved in the pogrom. This chapter incorporates their biographies, which include the murder of Jews during the war, cases of collaboration with the Nazis, and political affiliations in the aftermath of the pogrom. This is undoubtedly an important contribution, but examining their participation is complicated by the fact that most of the documents regarding their cases have been lost or destroyed.

Chapter thirteen is a description of the political atmosphere in Kielce after the war and focuses on the provincial governor, his political agility, and those of others in his circle. Tokarska-Bakir attempts to trace his career first within the history of the Polish partisan group "Świt," a unit of the People's Army (AL) known for hunting the Jews who had escaped from the labor camps in the Kielce area. Later its members were given senior administrative positions in the region. At the time of the murder of the Jewish escapees, Eugeniusz Wiślicz and Mieczysław Moczar were in charge of the group. After the war Wiślicz held the position of the Kielce county commissioner. He had authority over the two main forces of influence in Kielce, the security forces and the militia. During the pogrom Wiślicz sent his car to bring his tailor, Szlama Koński, to his apartment, along with the eldest of the Jewish community, Pinchas Ajzenberg. When it was decided that all Jews should be moved to Łódź, Wiślicz confiscated the building on Planty Street and gave it to the "Świt" group. At the time of the pogrom Wiślicz turned to the church representatives in Kielce with a request to calm the masses and, a day later, to write a joint proclamation with the same aim, but, unsurprisingly, the two sides could not reach a consensus. In the end, emphasizes Tokarska-Bakir, neither side used their influence to clarify the untruthfulness of the "blood libel" myth.

18 Bożena Szaynok, "Wokół nowej książki o pogromie Żydów w Kielcach," *Zagłada Żydów*, 28 (2018), pp. 665–666.

Chapter fourteen deals with the presence of the army in Kielce on the day of the pogrom, including their exact movements and the effect of their presence on the events. Tokarska-Bakir shows the inconsistencies in the pogrom reports written by the army; for example, the changing versions about the fact that the army troops who entered the building on Planty Street demanded that the Jews give up their weapons. Majors Konieczny and Markiewicz, the high-ranking officers in charge, whose indecisiveness had an adverse effect on the events of the day, never ordered their men to stop people from entering the building. The soldiers removed the Jews and handed them over to the mob outside. Reports of the security services mention the fact that soldiers personally took part in the murder of Jews. The mob applauded. Tokarska-Bakir attempts to reconstruct the exact circumstances of the death and the exact identities of the murderers of Seweryn Kahane, the chairman of the community, who was shot by the Polish officers as he attempted to alert the authorities on the telephone. The Polish officers venomously elected Jewish officers to attempt to disperse the mob. Finally Artur Pollak, a prewar officer, and some fifty men, managed to disperse the crowd and remove the survivors from the site.

In the end, writes Tokarska-Bakir, the cause of the extent of the pogrom was a combination of "antisemitic militia, the demoralized army, and delegitimized Security Services—institutions, that while drifting around, not just failed in controlling the outburst of anti-Jewish panic, but they amplified it" (p. 405).

Chapter fifteen is a concluding, though not the final, chapter. Here the author addresses the previous theories and research regarding the Kielce pogrom—those published immediately after the event and since then. For example, Tokarska-Bakir dismisses the theory that fear itself or "social strain" was the motivating factor of the pogrom (p. 415). Instead she suggests a reversal of the martyr fantasy: the perpetrators were those, who—identifying themselves as martyrs—turned violently against their imagined oppressors (p. 417).

Neither was "provocation," a concept often used in the context of the Kielce pogrom, a necessary explanation (pp. 406–407). Social changes that were transpiring in Polish society in the postwar years were enough to cause it. For the newly emerging middle class—some of whom enjoyed improved social status thanks to the appropriation of "post-Jewish" property and the new institutional and social bastions of native Communism—hostility toward the Jews was an easily activated social resource (pp. 409–417). The second crucial cause of the pogrom, according to Tokarska-Bakir, was the common belief in the "blood libel," supported by the church and the Polish underground (p. 409). The third factor was the fear of the Poles who had taken over the Jewish property (p. 409). And the last but most important factor was the common belief—and the alarm—that the Jews were "running rampant" and acquiring more political, economic, and social power (p. 409).

In the final chapter Tokarska-Bakir quotes (this time with no word of commentary) interviews conducted with the Polish witnesses to the pogrom some forty years after the event, collected for Marcel Łoziński's film *Świadkowie* (English title: *Witnesses*, 1987). It is impossible to miss the paradox of the prevalent antisemitism and its simultaneous denial among the Polish population—again, across the entire society. "They [the Jews] knew how to irritate us—as Poles, as Catholics, as Christians. Not that there was any antagonism. I never felt any hatred flowing from the hearts of Poles. Only the commerce that was in their hands irritated us. Sure, there were instances of rabidness, both among the Poles and among the Jews. In my opinion—there were too many Jews in Poland before the war. This irritated us and caused reactions: sometimes military, sometimes cruel, sometimes malicious" (p. 437), is just one example, in this case spoken by a math teacher in Kielce. The author once more refutes the commonly accepted view that associates (and thus downplays) Polish antisemitism with the uneducated. The effect of relating this firsthand discourse is chilling.

The driving force of this work is the demystification of all the myths, taboos, and some political interpretations attached to the Kielce pogrom. In order to accomplish this, Tokarska-Bakir had to show how the familiar setting, with the homely restaurants, streets, and backyards, were transformed into sites of violence and premeditated murder, how relations between social authorities worked to amplify the antisemitism, how people arranged themselves into networks aimed to harm and kill, and that, with very few exceptions, this transformation had been cultivated and nurtured by all the social structures. We are the mob. We all are Kielce. Of course this does not imply that Tokarska-Bakir removes the responsibility from the physical perpetrators of the crime. She merely succeeds in laying out its complexity. What I value most about her book is this successful setting of the pogrom within the context of everyday life in postwar Kielce. Tokarska-Bakir pulls the event of violence into the realm of "eventless history." This is a fascinating feat, partly because it also allows her to present a "total history" (in the sense of the *Annales* school)[19] of a singular event.[20] She succeeds in drawing a map of the place, tracing the paths taken each day by the inhabitants of the city, their thought patterns, and the structures that govern them. Some critics would have preferred a more political interpretation of the Kielce events and postulated considering the effect the war had had on the local Polish population. Yet by rejecting the exclusive emphasis on political interpretations and the traumatic effect of war, and instead considering equally all participants in the events, their economic and personal motives, the long-term social (both local and national) processes and historical structures, the religious and cultural imprints on the national subconscious, Tokarska-Bakir is able to give us a glimpse of the infinite complexity of that one day. It is equally a fascinating idea and a frightening threat to interpret a pogrom in a Polish town through the prism of eventlessness, or, as the author warns us in the preface, "not through the perspective of singularity and rupture but continuity and duration, in the hope to understand how that which is everyday—violence—became normative" (p. 13). For me, this is a liberating approach.

19 See, for example, Lucien Febvre, *A Geographical Introduction to History* (London: Kegan Paul, 1932); Lucien Febvre and Lucien Paul Victor, *A New Kind of History: From the Writings of Lucien Febvre* (London: Routledge and Kegan Paul, 1973).

20 Compare Michel De Certeau, Fredric Jameson, and Carl Lovitt, "On the Oppositional Practices of Everyday Life," *Social Text*, 3 (1980), pp. 3–43; Michel De Certeau, *The Practice of Everyday Life* (Oakland: University of California Press, 2011); Alf Ludtke, ed., *The History of Everyday Life: Reconstructing Historical Experiences and Ways of Life* (Princeton: Princeton University Press, 1995).

To Whom Does Vengeance Belong?
Revenge and Responsibility After the Holocaust

Dina Porat, *Li Nakam Veshilem: HaYishuv, Hashoah, Vekvutzat Hanokmim Shel Abba Kovner* (Vengeance and Restitution Are Mine: The Yishuv, the Holocaust, and Abba Kovner's Avengers Group) (Hebrew). Haifa: Pardes Publishing and Haifa University Press, 2019, 422 pp.

Reviewed by
Avinoam Patt

Dina Porat published *The Fall of the Sparrow*, the first and definitive biography in English of the "partisan, poet, and patriot Abba Kovner (1918–1987)" to great critical acclaim (the book was winner of the 2009 National Jewish Book Award). Kovner, as the book's description notes, was an "unsung and largely unknown hero of the Second World War and Israel's War of Independence," who had escaped from the Vilna ghetto, where there had been no revolt; returning after liberation to a "Vilna empty of Jews, he immigrated to Israel, where he devised a fruitless plot to take revenge on the Germans."[1]

As Porat notes in the introduction to *Vengeance and Restitution Are Mine*, her new history of the *Nokmim* (Avengers) emerged from a promise she made to Yitzhak Avidov (Pasha Reichman), one of the leaders of the Avengers group. He had criticized her for devoting only one page of the Kovner biography to a full year of the group's work in Europe (without Kovner) from the summer of 1945 until 1946. Kovner's path in the Yishuv (the Hebrew name for the Jewish population of pre-statehood Israel) deviated from the path of the Avengers, especially after his arrest at sea by British forces on December 18, 1945, on his way back to Europe with enough poison to kill six million Germans.

---

1 Dina Porat, *The Fall of a Sparrow: The Life and Times of Abba Kovner* (Stanford: Stanford University Press, 2000).

Thus the work of the Avengers in Europe after Kovner's arrest barely figured in the biography. Porat's promise to rectify this perceived slight has led to a fascinating, meticulously-researched, and thoughtful account of the Nakam (Revenge) group, the plot for revenge, and the attitude of the Yishuv to such revenge in the overall encounter with the Holocaust.

This is not the first book to tell the story of the Avengers—unsurprisingly, the "fruitless plot" has been a topic of fascination for more than fifty years, beginning with a journalistic account by Michael Bar-Zohar in 1969,[2] and more accounts appearing after the members of the group began sharing their story shortly before the death of Kovner in 1987, and subsequently. Rich Cohen's *The Avengers* included details of the Vilna Jewish partisans' postwar exploits, building on the story of Abba Kovner, Vitka Kempner, and Ruzhka Korzcak and their wartime experiences.[3] Tom Segev recounted the failed quest for vengeance in *The Seventh Million*, concluding the plan to murder six million Germans failed because the goals of the Avengers and the state-builders diverged in the period after the war.[4]

While the history of the postwar quest for vengeance has often been presented as a "tremendous story" that captivates the imagination, sometimes bordering on sensationalism, Porat examines the significance of the plot from the broader perspective of the history of the Holocaust and the State of Israel by means of serious archival research. After writing on the Yishuv and the Holocaust in *An Entangled Leadership: the Yishuv & the Holocaust, 1942–1945* (Tel Aviv: Am Oved, 1986) (Hebrew) and the biography of Kovner, Porat is well-equipped to engage the topic under review.

What was Kovner's plan? In a nutshell, after liberation, when he discovered the levels of destruction not only in the killing fields of Vilna and Ponar, but in the extermination camps of Poland, Kovner's desire for revenge became all-consuming. Arriving in Lublin in January 1945, Kovner founded a secret organization of likeminded people called Nakam. As he articulated in a series of principles developed for the group in Bucharest in April or May 1945:

2   Michael Bar-Zohar, *The Avengers* (New York: Hawthorn Books, 1969).
3   Rich Cohen, *The Avengers* (New York: Knopf, 2000).
4   Tom Segev, *The Seventh Million: The Israelis and the Holocaust* (New York: Hill and Wang, 1993).

...We have taken it upon ourselves not to let the world forget by performing the necessary act: Retribution. It will be more than revenge; it must be the law of the murdered Jewish people! Its name will therefore be DIN [the acronym of *Dam Israel Noter*, meaning the "blood of Israel is vengeful"—and "*din*" itself means "judgment"] so that posterity may know that in this merciless, uncompassionate world there is both a judge and judgment (p. 101).[5]

The group hatched a grandiose plan to poison the water system in several major German cities after the war, aiming to kill six million Germans in retaliation for the murder of six million Jews. While Plan A for mass revenge never came to fruition, on April 13, 1946, members of the Nakam group carried out Plan B, poisoning bread meant to feed SS-unit prisoners in Stalag 13 Langwasser Camp in Nuremberg, which was under American authority at the time. The Nakam group infiltrated the kitchens of the POW camp and brushed 3,000 loaves of bread with arsenic, causing many of the prisoners to fall ill. While much of Porat's book seeks to understand why Plan A (poisoning the water supply) was foiled, she also details the exploits of the group that remained in Germany and managed to poison the bread at the Langwasser camp near Nuremberg.

The book sets out to solve several historical mysteries. With the drive to avenge, the means to avenge, the targets identified, and the tools to do so: "Why didn't they manage to take vengeance? Who betrayed them and why?" (p. 12). And how was it possible that this seemingly warm, humane, ethical group of individuals was equipped to carry out such a barbaric plan? This is where Porat's expertise regarding the Yishuv and its relationship to the Holocaust helps to inform the power dynamics at play after the war. Kovner and the Avengers sought to add their own "three lines in history." They were driven by a raw, all-consuming obligation to exact revenge. But did they? Or was it too late? Why the silence in the decades after the war? Theirs was not a story that could be used by the Yishuv in the struggle to create the state. On the contrary, it could have possibly prevented the creation of the state. Did Kovner and his friends' quest for revenge also get them written out

---

5   Please note: all translations from Hebrew to English are those of the author (Patt) unless otherwise noted.

of history? And what is the historical significance of a plan that never happened?

More fundamentally the book examines the relationship between the Holocaust and the creation of the State of Israel. It is clear that the years 1945–1948 were crucial: the decisions taken by the leaders of the Yishuv and the survivors in postwar Europe at this time made a difference in diplomatic decisions that ultimately led to the creation of the state. More than the destruction of European Jewry during the war, it was the fate of the postwar population of Jewish displaced persons that would play a critical role in the support of partition by the United Nations and international observers. As I have shown in my own work, the Zionist enthusiasm of the surviving population, coupled with the work of the Yishuv leaders and emissaries to facilitate migration and make use of the survivors in the diplomatic arena, proved critical after the war.[6]

Beyond an examination of the broader encounter between the Yishuv and the Holocaust, however, Porat's study analyzes the meetings between specific leaders and representatives of the Yishuv and individual survivors of the Holocaust. Thus, the book examines what might be considered a sort of power struggle after the war, which boils down to a question of agency: if during the war the Yishuv was largely powerless to rescue Jews and respond to the Nazi threat, who would decide what was best for the Jewish people in the aftermath of the Holocaust? Who would set the post-Holocaust agenda for the Jewish people? And yet Porat seems to ask: if revenge seemed to be such a natural response to this catastrophe, and the drive for revenge was literally on the lips of all survivors, why did it not happen? To what extent did the creation of the State of Israel become a valve for displaced rage? Porat's conclusion suggests that the Yishuv emissaries were justified in limiting Kovner's and his accomplices' plans for revenge, because the need to create the state trumped the survivors' desire in this respect. However, did they have the right to make such a determination?

Porat also raises a philosophical question: How do we make sense of revenge after the Holocaust? Was revenge not only justified but necessary after the Holocaust? And who would carry out the obligation to exact vengeance on behalf of the Jewish people? Kovner and the Avengers

6   See Avinoam Patt, *Finding Home and Homeland: Jewish Youth and Zionism in the Aftermath of the Holocaust* (Detroit: Wayne State University Press, 2009).

resolved to take revenge as a national response of a nation that was murdered against a nation of murderers, a form of revenge that would be known throughout the world, that would harm millions, revenge against Germans that would function as a general warning to all the nations of the world: Jewish blood is not cheap [*Hefker*; literally, abandoned property] as it had been throughout history, and certainly during the Holocaust (pp. 17–18).

Only through this kind of revenge could justice be achieved. Revenge, in this sense, was not only a Jewish obligation, but a mission for humanity, in order to restore balance to the world. For Kovner and the members of his group, revenge would need to take place outside the justice system, because international justice could not be trusted. Judges who had not experienced the devastation of the Holocaust would be unable to render justice (and, indeed, the absence of Jewish voices at the Nuremberg trials would only reinforce the sense that true justice would need to be extrajudicial. For many this would not materialize until the Eichmann Trial).

Furthermore, Porat asks us to consider the relationship between revenge, justice, and historical memory. Does revenge erase the past? In the absence of law and justice is revenge necessary? Does the absence of revenge elevate the importance of memory? In other words, would acts of revenge change the meaning of the Holocaust? Change the obligation of memory? Would the obligation of memory come to be a stand-in for the obligation to take revenge?

With the passage of time, the drive for vengeance declined, anger softened, and memory prevailed. In his article on the relationship between revenge and Holocaust memory, Berel Lang argues that because revenge is often silent (out of necessity), it has been an undervalued and underexamined facet of Holocaust history.

> …filtered through the displacement effect, revenge would have been silent, deliberately not announcing itself. And indeed…when we take this possibility into account, revenge turns out to have had a more substantial influence in shaping collective memory of the Shoah than has so far been recognized…[7]

At the same time, Lang argues, revenge "motivates memory - and from

7   Berel Lang, "Holocaust Memory and Revenge: The Presence of the Past," *Jewish Social Studies*, 2:2 (1996), p. 3.

the memorable starting point of pain (either directly or, in the pain of emotional loss, as reflected) - suggests a more common and important role for revenge in the construction of memory than is usually assumed."[8]

But what happens if the drive for revenge is displaced or stunted? Was there a fear that by displacing the rage of the survivors from physical revenge into the creation of the state that the sharp edges of the pain of loss would be dulled? If revenge is silenced or performed individually does it never enter collective memory?

In the case of the Nakam group then, we must ask: Has this event indeed been forgotten? Or has historical memory of the event been suppressed? Did the act of suppression take place before the dastardly deed could take place, thus writing memory of revenge out of history, because it never took place? And if this is the case, did the revenge have meaning if no one knew about it and it never happened? Who was the intended audience for the message of vengeance? Nazis, Germans, Jews, the world? Did the State of Israel work in some way to suppress both acts of revenge and the memory of acts of revenge? And, as related to resistance, how did the image of the ghetto fighters who killed Nazis during the war serve to build a usable past, while survivors driven to vengeance after the war could not? The answers to these questions reveal a great deal about the Yishuv's relationship to the Holocaust and to the writing of the history of the Holocaust.

Yet before we can answer these questions, we must understand where the idea for mass revenge originated, who supported it, and why it failed. First, Porat argues, we cannot understand the depth of feelings of the protagonists in this period without understanding the horrific scenes they witnessed and their complete powerlessness to stop it (p. 20). Kovner and his group were not alone in their passion for revenge; on the contrary, they manifested a desire that was shared by many. However, for most it remained marginal, only occasionally translated into action, and then forgotten with the passage of time (p. 24). What distinguished Kovner and the Avengers was a sense that they were on a mission to take revenge not only on behalf of themselves, but on behalf of the entire Jewish people, a sense that emerged from their prewar education and upbringing in the Zionist movement.

As Porat demonstrates, the context for this plan mattered both in terms of the Avengers' experiences—how what they had witnessed

8   Ibid., p. 16.

during the war drove them to seek vengeance—and the perspectives of the Yishuv and its leaders. Furthermore, the rapidly shifting demographic and geopolitical situation in postwar Germany affected the possibilities of the revenge plans in 1945–1946. Porat demonstrates that during the war, as news of the "Final Solution" spread in the Yishuv, there were calls for collective revenge, as well as various discussions about Jewish sources and justification for revenge; whether the entire German nation was guilty for the collective sin of mass murder, and whether punishment would be applied to all those who collaborated or just the Germans (p. 42). Prominent Yishuv writers and poets joined calls for revenge, as did soldiers who had enlisted in the Jewish Brigade for reasons of seeking revenge. Nonetheless, Porat concludes, "it is difficult to say that in the Yishuv there was a consensus regarding the obligation to exact revenge and how such revenge should be carried out" (p. 50). While public sentiment seemed to call for revenge, these discussions were vague enough to indicate that this was a generalized desire without a specific plan. Perhaps, Porat asserts, "the leadership decided from the beginning that the top priority of the Yishuv was full-scale immigration of the surviving remnant and the establishment of a sovereign Jewish state—goals which revenge would almost certainly prevent" (p. 51).

In examining the encounter between the Yishuv and the Holocaust, between the survivors and those who had preceded them in their arrival to *Eretz Israel*, Porat analyzes the postwar situation in Europe, the efforts to organize the revenge group, the encounter with the first emissaries from the Jewish Brigade, and Kovner's fateful journey to Mandatory Palestine, which affected the development of the plan. As survivors began to gather together in Lublin in January 1945, Kovner was consumed by a drive for revenge that could not be channeled into any other goal. As one who was seen as a "prophet, a leader, a commander" with great rhetorical abilities, he was especially suitable to organize a group of like-minded Avengers after the war. Pasha Avidov, his right-hand man in the revenge group, described the feeling of first meeting him after the war: "We all felt that before us stood a man who could navigate our ship to the distance, someone who possessed the depth of understanding that we had never seen" (p. 56).

What united the fifty or so members who came to join the Avengers? Was it a shared profile of a generation, of personality, or of biographical experiences? All the members of the group had participated in resistance, either in ghettos or fighting with partisans in the forests.

Kovner explained that experience in fighting groups had provided them with useful skills for this postwar mission.

Their prewar experiences in leftist groups, raised on the values of humanism, transnational solidarity, and a universal drive to struggle for justice in the world actually made them unlikely candidates for such a brutal mission. However, as Porat emphasizes, among the multiple reasons to take revenge, including of course the horror of the Holocaust, were the sense that revenge was the only way to ensure continued Jewish existence and the need to fulfill the last testament of their parents and brethren whose final words as they faced death were: "take revenge" (p. 62).

As Abba Kovner argued, they could not imagine that they had the right to return to "normal" life after the war, to move to *Eretz Israel*, to create families, without first taking revenge. The drive for vengeance also meant maintaining a connection to those who had been lost, ensuring that they would not be forgotten. Porat suggests that while multiple reasons stood at the foundation of Kovner's and his friends' actions, the basis was the deep-seated anxiety that the Holocaust would persist in the form of continued antisemitism after the war in its murderous manifestations. Porat suggests that this gave rise to three courses of action after the war: (1) organizing the *Brichah* ("illegal immigration" to *Eretz Israel*); (2) organizing a group of survivors across party affiliations and backgrounds united by revenge; and (3) forming the Avengers. There is of course a contradiction here that Porat does not address: if the loss of family and loved ones is a motivating factor, making the quest for revenge ultimately personal and individual, then who indeed can assume the right to take revenge on behalf of the Jewish people?

In Part I of the book, Porat sets the scene in terms of the context of postwar Europe, the Yishuv's attitude toward survivors and the Holocaust, and the drive of the Avengers to carry out the revenge operation. Part II focuses on the attempt to execute the operation, and the reasons why both Plans A and B never materialized in the way Kovner and his band of Avengers imagined they would. Again the timing of Kovner's arrival in Palestine was critical in the crystallization of the Yishuv leadership's position around the idea of revenge in these months (August-December 1945). Kovner's operation did not function in a vacuum; the context at the time of both the unified terror campaign against the British and the Anglo-American Committee of Inquiry rendered important considerations (p. 149). As Porat suggests, these would also influence the Yishuv leadership's attitude to Kovner's wild plan. The prospect that international observers might support a diplomatic solution to the problem of Jewish statelessness after the war altered strategic calculations. While Jews in the Yishuv could not fully understand the personal drive for vengeance expressed by Kovner, they also controlled certain levers of power necessary for "national" revenge.

Regarding Kovner's time in the Yishuv, from August to December 1945, where he hoped to secure the resources he needed to carry out his plan, Porat argues that we can draw clear conclusions that while the leaders in Palestine came to learn about Plan A, none of them agreed to it in any form. On the contrary, they all made clear that only Plan B could be carried out. Kovner managed to meet with David Ben-Gurion at some point in the last ten days of November 1945, but revenge was clearly seen by him as an obstacle to the number one priority—with which all of the leadership and most of the Brigade soldiers and emissaries agreed—and that was to focus on the immigration of the survivors to *Eretz Israel* and use them to attain the goal of establishing the state. The Yishuv leadership was suspicious of the survivors who reached *Eretz Israel* and felt they needed to be organized in a way that would channel their rage in a constructive manner. And, they concluded, the survivors needed to be closely supervised.

Such institutional opposition notwithstanding, we know that when Kovner left the Yishuv in December 1945, he had the poison and the gold he needed for his plan. How did Kovner obtain the poison for Plan A? While Kovner suggested it was Chaim Weizmann who connected him with chemists to work on the plan, Porat completely debunks this theory, arguing it would have been impossible in the autumn of 1945, as Weizmann was not in Palestine at that time. Porat argues that in fact Ephraim Katzir (fourth president of Israel, 1973–1978) and his brother, Aharon, who were lab assistants in chemical laboratories at the Hebrew University of Jerusalem and members of the Haganah, helped Kovner in obtaining the necessary chemicals. By December 1945, Kovner had been in Palestine for four months, a very long time in the eyes of his partners, who were waiting for him in Europe while scattered into small groups. Even so, with the assistance of false papers arranged by the Haganah, and armed with enough poison to kill millions of Germans and gold coins to fund the operation, Kovner left Palestine for Egypt at the beginning of December 1945, with a fake passport. He set sail on December 14, from Alexandria, on a boat with 4,500–5,000 British soldiers setting out on leave. On the ship were twenty-seven Jewish Brigade soldiers and a small group of underground agents being sent to Europe with fake papers, including Kovner. He had with him the poison hidden in twelve boxes of milk powder and gold coins hidden in toothpaste tubes. Just before the boat was supposed to land in Toulon, France, the names of Kovner and three of the other agents with fake papers were called over the loudspeaker. The poison was immediately dumped into the ocean. Nevertheless, Kovner was arrested and imprisoned for two months in Egypt before being transferred back to jail in Jerusalem. Eventually Golda Meir helped secure his release.

As Porat suggests, it is doubtful that anyone from the Haganah or the Jewish Agency would have informed on Kovner. They were the ones who had arranged for him to travel with false papers; they had provided him with the gold; he was a recognized hero; and more than likely they would have been implicated (p. 177). Furthermore, as Porat notes, the trip itself was sanctioned by the leadership; Kovner was shepherded by a guide from the Jewish Brigade; there were agents waiting for them in Marseilles; and after they were imprisoned, the group of underground agents was in contact with emissaries from the Yishuv while still in a camp in France. Furthermore, Kovner was caught under a false identity and not as Kovner (p. 180). Maybe, Porat seems to conclude, the information that led to their arrest had nothing to do with the revenge plan?

By examining all the available material, Porat arrives at the most reasonable conclusion: it seems the British had discovered the ways in which the Haganah tried to smuggle agents back into Europe under the cover of the Jewish Brigade and British ships. As Porat notes in detail, there were all sorts of reasons for the plan to fail, which had nothing to do with British knowledge of Plan A (p. 181). From the prison in France, before he was transferred to Egypt, Kovner managed to convey a message to Pasha and Vitka to get in touch with Ruzhka in *Eretz Israel* to try to get more "medicine" and establish contact in case he remained imprisoned for years (p. 184). After his release from prison in Jerusalem in mid-March 1946, he wrote a twelve-page letter in Yiddish that was deeply emotional and conveyed the depth of his anguish.

As Porat suggests, it is possible that after months in prison he decided to "choose life" and give up on Plan A. One can only speculate as to the reasons for this turn of events. Kovner's motivations notwithstanding, Porat argues that the leadership in the Yishuv tried to strike a delicate balance. They did not want to dismiss Kovner entirely, but, at the same time, they wanted to make sure that Plan A would neither materialize nor get out of control (p. 187). They also put various mechanisms in place to ensure that they could maintain supervision over the Avengers. Porat highlights a meeting between Pasha Avidov and David Ben-Gurion at the November 1945 conference of Jewish Fighters in Paris, where, in a very brief encounter, it became clear that the future prime minister of Israel did not support Avidov's revenge ideas. "I cannot promise you what will happen if you do not cancel your plan. Now is the time to build a country and now is not the time to deal with less important things," Porat writes, paraphrasing Ben-Gurion. As Porat notes, Ben-Gurion made clear, "if revenge could not bring back six million Jews, he was not interested in it" (p. 197).

Even after Kovner's arrest and imprisonment, the Avengers based in Europe remained determined to carry out the plan for vengeance. In a sense this is the point where Kovner's biography and the collective biography of the Avengers diverged. And it is the point at which Porat again asserts that the involvement of the Yishuv, and especially the Haganah commander in Europe, Nahum Shadmi, may help to explain why Plan A still failed. Porat returns the narrative to Paris, where both the Haganah headquarters in Europe and the headquarters of the Avengers were based. After Kovner's arrest, the group decided to try to create a poison on their own. Yitzhak Ratner, a survivor from Vilna involved both with the Aliyah Bet and Zionist activities after the war, also had chemical experience and played a key role in developing enough poison to kill hundreds of thousands of Germans. He ended up settling on two different poisons for Plans A and B: atropine, which could dissolve in water, for Plan A; and arsenic, to spread onto loaves of bread for Plan B.

In the absence of Kovner, Pasha Avidov became commander of the operation on the European front and worked at establishing connections with members of the French resistance, especially Jews who could help them in their mission. Ratner managed to contact a leather factory in France that would deliver 20 kilograms of arsenic to him (arsenic was used in the production of leather). Pasha was the commander; Betzalel Kak, second-in-command; and Dorka (Goldreich) Avidov, Pasha's wife, and Vitka Kempner Kovner served as couriers for the organization. Pasha also sought out ties with representatives from the Yishuv: Shaul (Meiroff) Avigur, founder of the intelligence wing of the

Haganah responsible for Mossad Le-Aliyah Bet operations, promised to help Pasha carry out his plan; Nahum Shadmi, who organized Haganah operations in Europe, also worked with Pasha, but explained that "the main goal and priority was the establishment of the State of Israel... Someone had to be responsible and to decide which activities were permitted and which were forbidden. 'You are not the deciders here, I am the one who decides,'" he told them. "'The one in charge is the Jewish people and the Jewish Agency represents the Jewish people'" (pp. 198–199).

As Porat suggests, this encounter between the Avengers bent on revenge and the Yishuv emissaries in Europe again revealed a central point of conflict between these two groups. Who actually represented the Jewish people, and who spoke in its name after the Holocaust? (p. 199). When viewed within the context of Yishuv emissaries who often regarded the survivors and the surviving population in a very instrumental light (questioning whether such "human material" could serve the needs of the state), Shadmi's assertion betrays a consistent perspective that merits further investigation: who really had the authority to decide which forms of revenge were justified?

Even so, Porat analyzes reports sent back to Palestine by Shadmi in which he made clear: although he continued to oppose Plan A, he supported Plan B, meaning an attack that would harm identifiable SS and Nazi criminals (p. 200). He also expressed concern that any revenge operation should not harm the interests of the survivors; that is, the growing population of Jewish survivors in Germany should not be hurt nor should they be seen to be those who organized the attack. Shadmi questioned whether the survivors themselves were capable of carrying out revenge on behalf of the Jewish people, both operationally and as their legitimate representatives. Porat suggests that this may have indicated some doubts regarding the ability of the survivors to make decisions for themselves and a general propensity on the part of the leadership in Palestine to believe that they were the ones best equipped to decide on their future (p. 201). Shadmi held a series of meetings with members of the group in which they negotiated who should be responsible for carrying out which portions of the plan. He of course wanted to maintain full authority.

A great deal of historical literature has pushed back against a tendency on the part of the Yishuv to present survivors as passive, powerless, and unable to act in their own best interests. But this conflict again reinforced the degree to which Yishuv emissaries maintained this view of the survivors. Nonetheless, as Porat correctly indicates, the postwar situation in Germany was incredibly complex. Shadmi's fears that a brutal revenge operation carried out by Jews in the American zone would harm the diplomatic interests of the survivors and the Yishuv were entirely justified.

Even after Shadmi pulled the plug on Plan A, the targeted attack on SS, Gestapo, and German POWs was still "a go." Shadmi authorized the operation for two locations: Langwasser near Nuremberg, a camp where 35,000 German prisoners of war were held by the Americans (p. 231); and an SS POW camp near Dachau. They decided to carry out the operation at both locations on the same night, April 13–14, 1946, a full-moon-lit Saturday night, when fewer guards would be on duty. Two Brigade soldiers delivered the arsenic prepared by Ratner. Members of the Avengers had infiltrated the bakeries in both camps, and the plan, as devised by Leibke Distel, was to spread the arsenic on the bottom of the bread (p. 234). In Langwasser a group of three Avengers managed to spread the poison onto 3,000 loaves of bread before guards came to check on a break-in at the bakery. Meanwhile, at the SS camp in Dachau, Simcha Rotem (Kazik), working together with Irena Gelblum (another ZOB member from Warsaw), was ready to carry out the same operation, but the plan was canceled at the last minute. Most likely, as Porat suggests, Shadmi worried that their cover had been blown and that the Americans were going to catch them (p. 245).

Two or three days later the poisoning at Langwasser was reported in the press with many different estimates of the number of injured. Some reported 1,800, others 3,700, while others estimated 8,000 injured and 860 killed. But, as Porat notes, nowhere was it reported that Jews had carried out the poisoning. In her research in American archives, Porat discovered that American investigators never determined who the prime suspects were; she also found that the internal American documentation suggested that no one was killed by the poison (p. 240). Even so, the investigation seemed to find that Ratner's arsenic was deadly enough to kill tens of thousands of people. To be properly delivered, however, the poison needed to be boiled in hot water in order to create a deadly paste. According to the recollections of the three involved with poisoning the bread at Langwasser, when they were stirring the poison it kept dropping to the bottom of the bottle. Thus Porat speculates that it was quite possible that the solution was not deadly enough when spread on the bread. Perhaps the interaction between the glue and the poison diminished its effectiveness. While it is also possible that the Americans minimized the number hurt or killed so as not to create an incident, Vitka Kempner would always claim that it did not matter how many were killed or injured, but that the most important thing was that the deed was done.

Noting that in his reports Shadmi was disappointed by the outcome of the operation, Porat concludes that the Jewish Brigade and the Haganah were also very disappointed, but they greatly appreciated the work of the revenge group. Shadmi believed that the leadership in *Eretz Israel* should have taken the operation much more seriously (p. 238) as the Yishuv did decide to fully support targeted revenge operations against Germans who were clearly guilty of killing Jews directly and gave the plan operational support. Porat notes that even after the original group of Avengers made it to *Eretz Israel*, Shimon Avidan returned to Germany to assist Shadmi in organizing Haganah operations in the DP camps, as well as to undertake revenge operations against identified targets (former SS in particular). He said that this led to the killing of thousands, although Porat speculates that these numbers may have been exaggerated (pp. 267–268).

The third part of the book includes an epilogue and appendices with short biographical profiles of all the group's members. As Porat notes, one of the challenges in writing the history of the group was that they had maintained their code of secrecy for forty years, until just before the death of Kovner in 1987 (p. 281). Many feared their testimony might be used by the enemies of Israel; others suggested that speaking about the plans might harm the image of survivors in Israel and the world. Nonetheless, after Kovner developed cancer of the larynx, the group met and recorded a group interview in the spring of 1987, in order to archive their testimonies (p. 282). As Porat notes, one of her central concerns in the book is to explain how it was possible that a group of individuals, raised with humanism and empathy in interwar Europe, could attempt to carry out such a plan of mass revenge, which, if successful, would have led to the deaths of millions, including Germans who had played no role in the killing operations (p. 300). Moreover, many lived with constant regret that the plan was never carried out, that by not killing millions of Germans after the war, they had somehow failed their dead parents, brothers, and sisters by not avenging their deaths. Why did the members of the group feel justified in attempting to carry out the revenge operations, in particular Plan A? In the unforgettable words of Yitzhak Pasha Avidov:

> If Jesus had gone through the Holocaust, he would have joined the organizers of the revenge group. And if Kovner had not sailed to Israel, they would have carried out Plan A. No doubt. The group did, with clean hands, dirty black work. They tried to do what God, if there was a God, should have done (interview with Porat, September 1995; p. 285).

If we take Berel Lang's conclusion to heart, that revenge after the Holocaust was far more widespread than has been understood or discussed, then the only thing that should surprise us is not that it happened, but that it has been kept quiet for so long.

Nonetheless, from the perspective of the Haganah, we get an opposite sense of events. If large-scale revenge had taken place, it is quite possible that the Jewish people would have missed their opportunity to create the Jewish state (p. 292), which was the ultimate revenge against Hitler and his disciples. As Porat concludes, the Yishuv sought to calibrate its response and that of survivors bent on vengeance:

> ...it can be said therefore that the desire to take revenge on the Germans in the drive to punish the German nation with a heavy punishment that would be remembered for generations was supported by the Yishuv and its leadership. However, they did not cross the Rubicon that divided belief and action (between "*nishma*" and "*na'aseh*"[9]): the leadership of the Yishuv with Ben-Gurion at the head, along with the heads of the Haganah, reached a decision that this was not the way, even if they did not discuss it in a formal manner, and a demonstration of national responsibility of the first degree can be seen in their decision. The issue, they decided, was first and foremost to deal with the surviving remnant—because there was no one else who would take care of them—and they needed to bring the stateless refugees to *Eretz Israel*. They decided that acts of revenge would interfere with the desire of the relief agencies to support the displaced persons and the *Brichah*; that the

---

9 A reference to Exodus 24:7. After Moses writes and reads aloud the words of the Torah, the people utter the phrase "*na'aseh v'nishma*" ("we will do and we will hear"). Here Porat suggests that belief in the need for revenge would not be translated into irreversible action.

British and the Americans would not be able to accept injuries to the prisoners they were responsible for; that the struggle for the creation of the state would face complications; that revenge, in the words of Ben-Gurion to Pasha, would not bring anyone back to life (p. 294).

Without the political will and full support of the Yishuv, Porat concludes, the full operation could not succeed. And yet what are we to make of this historical episode, of the fact that Kovner and his Avengers would never be able to forget the revenge they did not take? Or the conclusion that the Yishuv leadership exercised "national responsibility" in allowing limited revenge, while suppressing massive revenge? Porat is aware of the methodological challenges inherent in writing this history: Which sources are most reliable in such a complex tale? Letters written contemporaneously by the key actors, including members of the Nakam group and Yishuv emissaries? Or testimonies recorded more than forty years later, tinged by retrospective judgment and the passage of time? In concluding that the Yishuv exercised "national responsibility," Porat seems to give more credence to the choices made by Shadmi and others: limited revenge was justified because the State of Israel was ultimately created. But who could have or indeed had the right to make such a judgment in 1946, two years before the state came into existence?

Porat notes that even if they did not manage to carry out their mission, members of the group found some comfort in the belief that they had left behind a legend, a type of mythology, about a group that had attempted and struggled. They regarded this as a type of achievement. They were able to end the perception of the Jewish people as abandoned and powerless to stop anyone who wanted to abuse it. As Vitka suggested: both in the case of the ghetto fighters and in the case of the revenge group, it was not the outcome that mattered most, but the attempt, the ability to organize, and finding a means to carry it out. During the war, cut off from the leadership in the Yishuv, ghetto fighters and partisans took vengeance in any way they could. After the war, even if the Yishuv and its leadership believed in the need to take revenge on the Germans, this idea was set aside in favor of the very real need to rescue the survivors and bring them to *Eretz Israel* and the need to establish the state, which would then be the ultimate response. Thus the building of the state became the approved form of collective, national revenge.

Despite resentment and alienation that had developed during the war, Zionist groups worked to reestablish control over their members' activities by sending emissaries to help organize youth movements, political parties, and migration operations after the war. And yet the encounter between the agents of the state and the survivors of the Holocaust forced the Yishuv to confront the enormity of the catastrophe. In this sense Porat's book continues to build on a historiographical trend that demonstrates no matter how much Ben-Gurion and the leaders of the Yishuv wished to argue that the elements of the state in the making existed before 1939, the aftermath of the Holocaust and the creation of the state were inextricably linked. We cannot understand the state without understanding its relationship to the Holocaust and its survivors. The drive for vengeance could be sublimated and redirected into the establishment of the state, but that "fateful historical reaction" would shape the state in ways that we continue to scrape away more than seventy years after its creation.[10] Acting on behalf of the Jewish people, the leadership determined that the creation of the state (not the murder of six million Germans) would be the only appropriate response to the Holocaust. Perhaps this determination would ensure the continued perception that Diaspora Jewry remained passive in its response to persecution; only Jews in the Yishuv would be capable of taking action in history.

---

10 From remarks by Israeli MK Elimelech Rimalt, as quoted by Yechiam Weitz, "Shaping the Memory of the Holocaust in Israeli Society," in Israel Gutman, ed, *Major Changes within the Jewish People in the Wake of the Holocaust* (Jerusalem: Yad Vashem, 1993), p. 500.

Contributors

❧ ⌁

Omer Bartov, John P. Birkelund Distinguished Professor of European History, Department of History, Brown University, U.S.

Christopher R. Browning, Frank Porter Graham Professor of History Emeritus, University of North Carolina at Chapel Hill, U.S.

Jan Burzlaff, William A. Ackman Fellow, Harvard University, U.S.

Beth B. Cohen, California State University, Northridge, U.S.

James A. Diamond, Joseph & Wolf Lebovic Chair of Jewish Studies, University of Waterloo, Canada.

Amit Kama, Senior Lecturer of Communication, Max Stern Yezreel Valley College, Israel.

Jan Láníček, Senior Lecturer in Modern European and Jewish History, University of New South Wales, Sydney, Australia.

Sharon Livne, Bucerius Institute for Research of Contemporary German History and Society, University of Haifa, Israel.

Marta Marzańska-Mishani, researcher, Yad Vashem, Jerusalem, Israel.

Avinoam Patt, Doris and Simon Konover Chair of Judaic Studies and director, Center for Judaic Studies and Contemporary Jewish Life, University of Connecticut, U.S.

Zohar Segev, Lecturer in Jewish History, Haifa University, Israel.

Edel Sheridan-Quantz, researcher, ZeitZentrum Zivilcourage/ Städtische Erinnerungskultur, Zentrale Angelegenheiten Kultur, Landeshauptstadt Hannover, Germany.

Instructions for Contributors

Yad Vashem Studies publishes original scholarly articles and review essays relating to all aspects of the Holocaust.

1. Articles submitted to *Yad Vashem Studies* should be original contributions and should **not** be under simultaneous consideration for any other publication. If any other version of the article is under consideration by another publication, or has been or will be published elsewhere, authors should clearly indicate this.

2. Manuscripts may be submitted to yv.studies@yadvashem.org.il. All pages should be numbered consecutively.

3. Articles may be submitted in English or in Hebrew, and should not exceed 10,000 words (including notes). A submission must include an abstract of approximately 150 words (100 for review essays) that relates the main arguments and conclusions of the article. Details of the author's institutional affiliation, full address, and other contact information should also be included. Interested contributors are welcome to contact *Yad Vashem Studies*, in order to receive our full instructions for contributors.

4. It is the author's responsibility to obtain permission of the copyright holder for use of any copyright materials to be included within the article.

5. To be accepted for publication, articles must pass peer review both within and without the editorial board. Acceptance of an article may be accompanied by a request for revisions prior to publication. Authors will receive a PDF version of their articles and a complimentary copy of *Yad Vashem Studies*. The PDF is meant for personal use only and not for widespread distribution. No other use of the PDF is permitted without explicit permission from *Yad Vashem Studies*.

6. Copyright on articles published in *Yad Vashem Studies* rests with Yad Vashem.

Sharon Kangisser Cohen, Editor, *Yad Vashem Studies*
Yad Vashem, Post Office Box 3477
Jerusalem 9103401, Israel
Tel. 972-2-6443515, Fax 972-2-6443509
e-mail: sharon.kangisser@yadvashem.org.il

ORDERING YAD VASHEM STUDIES

Yad Vashem Studies can be purchased at:
https://store.yadvashem.org/

Prices in Israel:

Current Issue:	NIS 78
Volumes 31–48 (1–2):	NIS 78 per volume
Available Back Issues:	
Volumes 11–14, 16–18, 23–25, 27–30:	NIS 52 per volume

Entire Series:
40% discount (45 available volumes): ~~NIS 3,146~~ NIS 1,888

3-year Subscription (2021–2023):
Volumes 49 (1) – 51 (2)
30% discount (6 volumes): ~~NIS 468~~ NIS 328

Prices Outside Israel:

Current Issue:	$24 (plus $4 airmail fee)
Volumes 31–48 (1–2):	$24 (plus $4 airmail fee) per volume
Available Back Issues:	
Volumes 11–14, 16–18, 23–25, 27–30:	$16 (plus $2 airmail fee) per volume

Entire Series:
40% discount (45 available volumes): ~~$968~~ $581 (airmail fee included)

3-year Subscription (2021–2023):
Volumes 49 (1) – 51 (2)
30% discount (6 volumes): ~~$144~~ $101 (airmail fee included)